Introduction

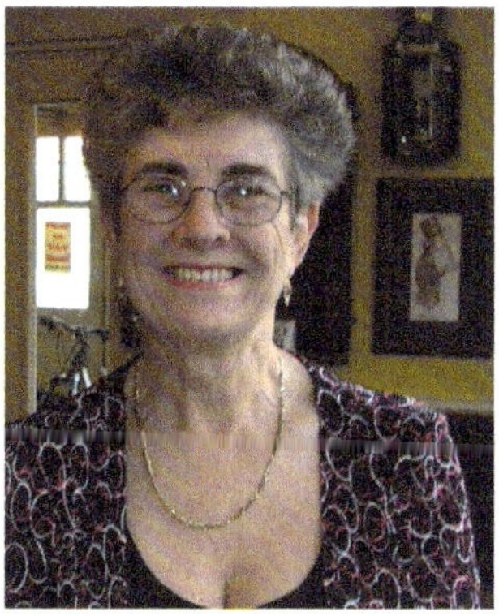

While researching my family history, I found it fascinating discovering where my ancestors came from, where they lived and their occupations over the centuries. It was from this research that the idea for this book came to me. I felt the need to share what I had learned as my family members are also ancestors of many other Folkestonians.

I am starting *Folkestone Through The Ages* in the late 1700s when a large rockfall in Lower Sandgate Road instigated Lord Radnor to have a road built. He also had the area around landscaped for the pleasure of the people. At the Sandgate end of the road a gatekeeper's house and toll gate was installed. As a child I can remember the gate across the road.

In the year 2000 the council built a Pirate Park near the Toll House, landscaped around it and now it is a lovely place for children to have fun and there is seating for parents to watch over them. The wooden groynes have been removed, with rock imported and placed on the beach into the sea at angles to stop the beach eroding. This looks attractive and gives the beach a new modern look.

So many changes have taken place from this area towards the fish market and beyond, with very few buildings left of our heritage in the town. It is no wonder locals complain when buildings are demolished – supposedly to make way for improvements to update Folkestone. This also happened with the coming of the railway to Folkestone in the early 1800s. I guess the locals felt the same then when 500 houses were demolished to make way for the railway line that was built all the way down to the harbour. These things take place, often against our wishes, and we are told we must move on and not dwell on the past.

I will try to recall memories of some of the people of Folkestone from way back and up to the present day. In the past fifteen years, Folkestone has gone through a period of modernisation, or as some would say, moved with the times.

Over the past 200 years the Folkestone seafront has seen many changes from being a place of entertainment, with outdoor and indoor swimming pools, a boating pool, to fairground rides and stalls, the usual souvenir shops and cafés, to what have we today. Nothing. I have had holidaymakers ask where the amusements and the large Sunday market Folkestone was famous for are. I have seen the disappearance of the steam trains running trips to the harbour even the cross-channel ferries no longer leave from Folkestone.

After the bomb damage from the Second World War North Street and Harbour Way was rebuilt with flats and a few houses. The bottom of Tram Road used to contain so many shops, alleyways and public houses that those of us that were born from 1935 onwards could not have imagined just how all those buildings fitted in. In actual fact, I was told the bombing probably did the area a favour as some the buildings were in need of demolition. That area now contains a car park and run-through fountain.

Folkestone played a big part getting many tens of thousands of service men and women over to France during the First World War, of which many did not return. Over the last year Folkestone has had many events, remembering various anniversaries in memory of the men and women who gave their lives so gallantly for their country, never to see their loved ones again.

As a tribute to these brave men and women, I am dedicating a section of this book to some of the Folkestone men and women who fought in the First World War and the Second World War. Some who came back and, sadly, some who did not.

My grateful thanks go to everyone who has helped me by supplying photographs and information to help make my book more interesting. I'd like to especially thank professional photographers Freddie Lee Thompson and Richard Taylor, Jules Gomez from Battle of Britain Memorial Trust, Capel Le Ferne, Bryan Williams from Dover Museum, Aisha and Andrew at the Heritage Room Folkestone Library, Vic Seymour for the Folkestone Normandy Veterans Association, Rosemary Richter, Christchurch School, Folkestone, Carol Ann Duffy, poet laureate, Maxwell Dunlop, poet, Peter Bettley, Janet Clarke, Margaret Davies, Peter Davies, Pat and Phil Goodman, Ernie Gray, Stevie Hall, John Harris, Janie Conway-Heron, Janet Johnson, Alex Kalorkoti, Trevor Minter, Robert Mouland, James O'Clee, Pat and Terry Rivers, Jane Seymour, Joan Simpkins, Derek Sutton, Dave Walker and Shook.

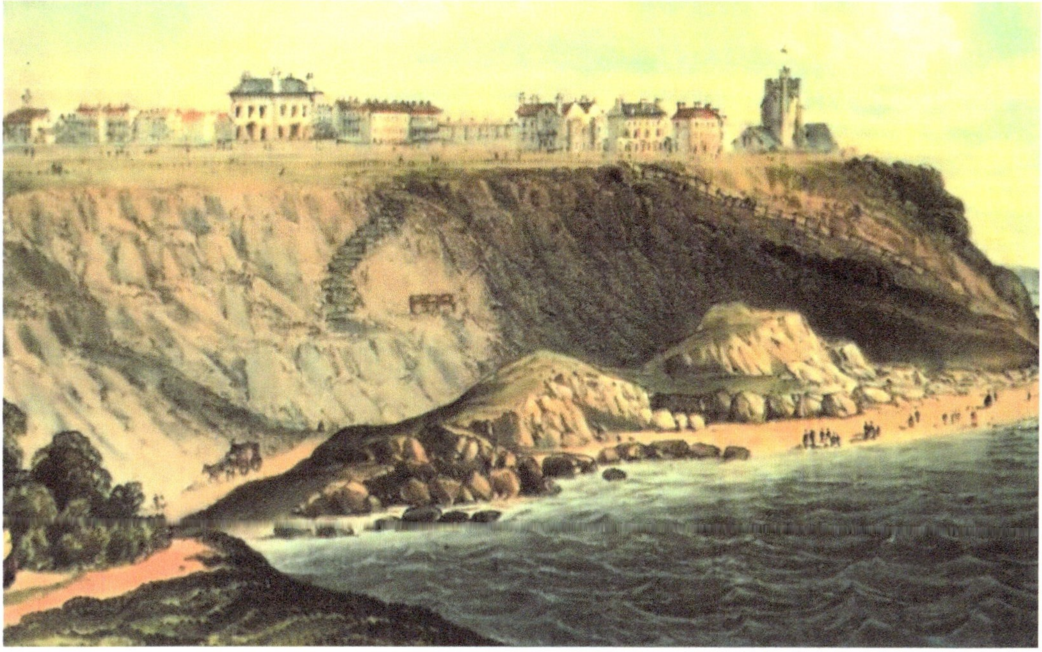

Lower Sandgate Road, Folkestone

Above: Lower Sandgate Road after a landslip in the 1790s. In the middle of the picture you will notice steps leading down from the clifftop. Today the steps are in the same place but we are unable to see them as too much foliage is in the way.

Below: The picture depicts the same area in the 1950s with the outdoor swimming pool and various amusements. Over the past ten years this area has been cleared and is now a large empty space for car parks.

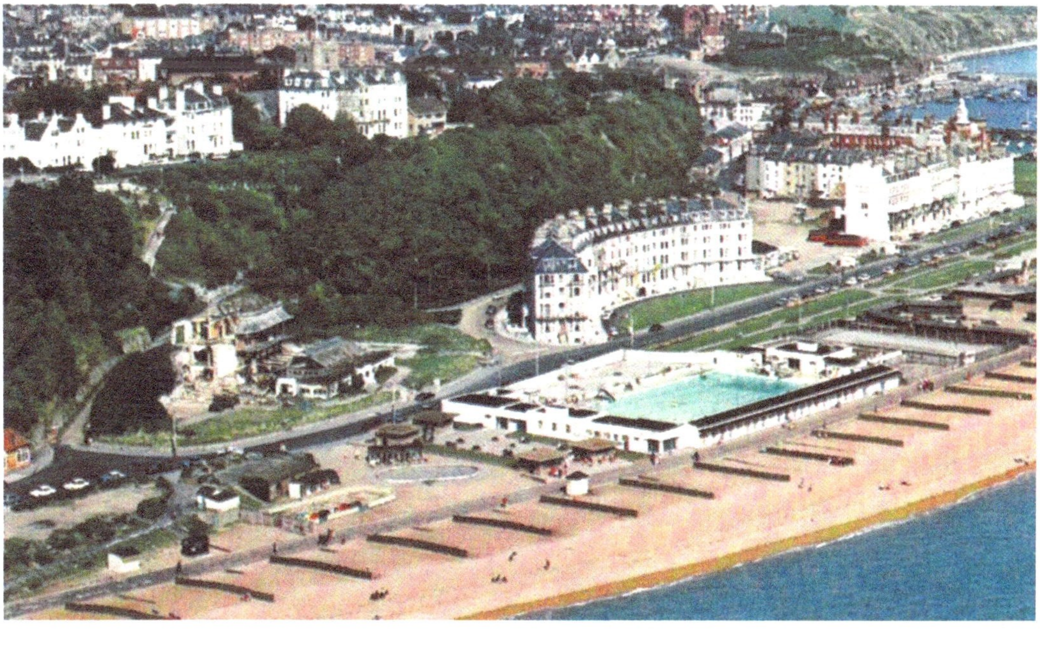

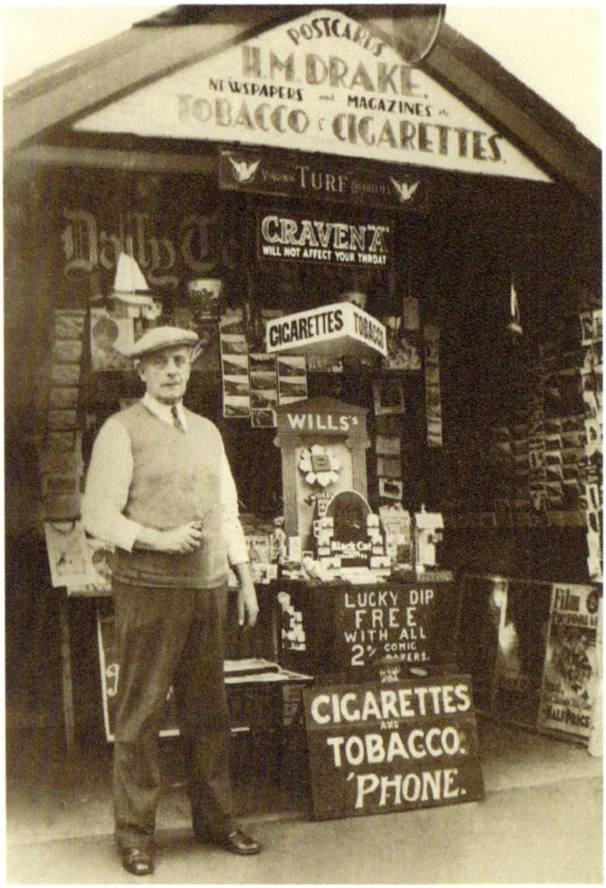

Come Buy My Wares

Left: In the 1930s Mr William Haines lived at No. 2 Bolton Road serving summer customers from Mr Drake's lock-up shop, which was situated opposite the indoor swimming pool on Lower Sandgate Road. This little shop sat alongside five others, tempting the visitors with their wares, which are just about visible in the picture below.

Below: This postcard is from the 1930s. You can see the steps from The Leas down the cliff. To the left of the postcard, in front of the bathing establishments, is the Lifeboat House, which is no longer there. The Leas lift is just out of sight to the left of the postcard. The only other buildings left now are the Marine Crescent houses to the right of the postcard.

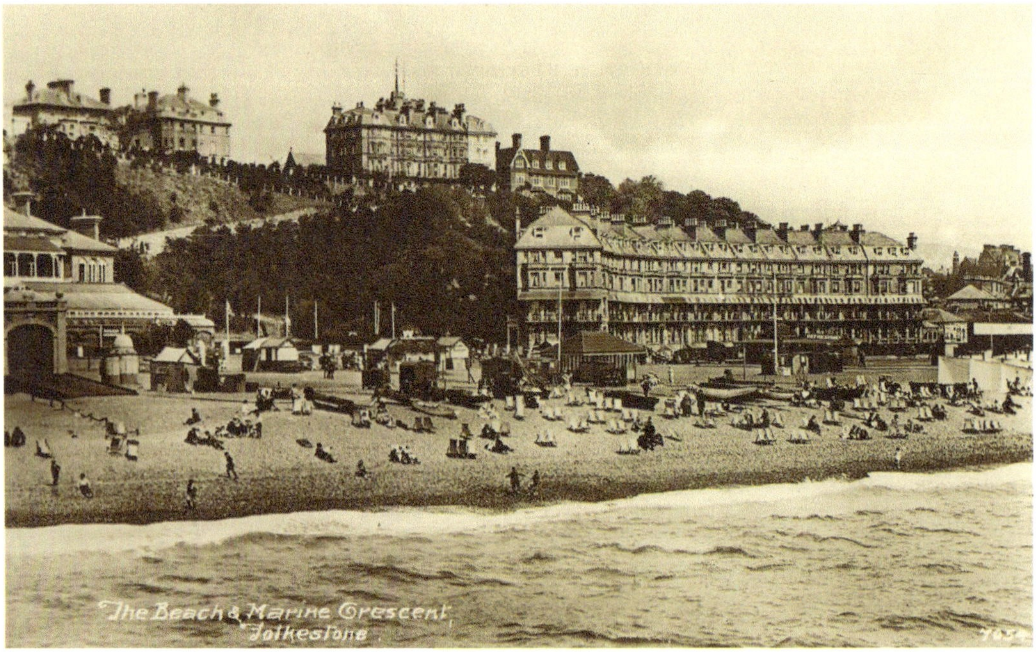

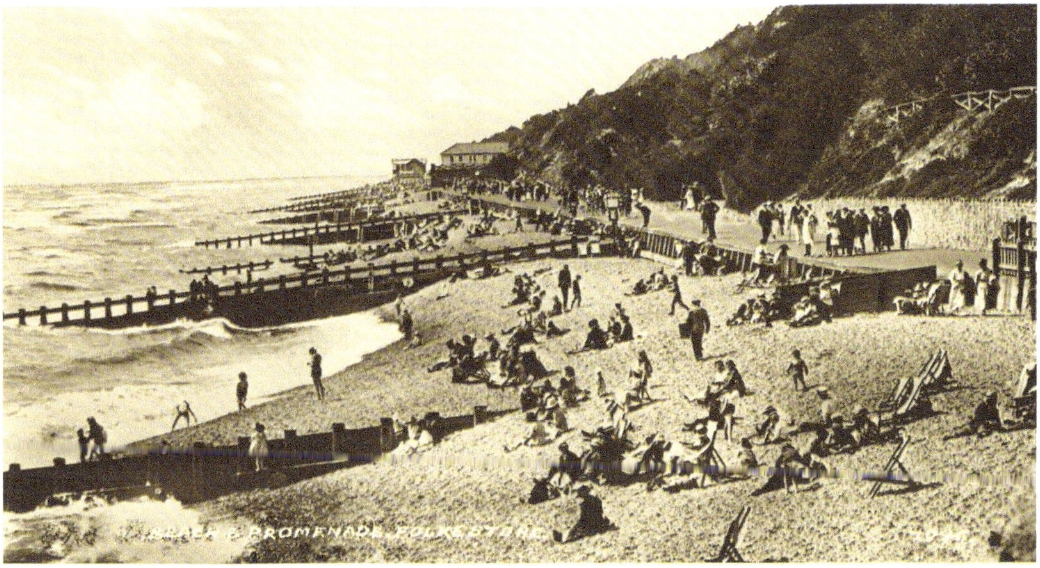

Beach Design Moving into the Twenty-First Century

Above: The photograph above, taken in the 1920s, depicts the groynes and how steep the beach had been for many years. Despite the steepness of the beach it was still enjoyed by holidaymakers.

Below: In this photograph taken in 2012 you can see the groynes have been removed. Rocks were imported, transported here and laid out. The beach now looks very modern and pleasing to the eye. It really was quite fascinating to watch the cranes take the rocks off the barge and place them just so on the beach; it was just as if the crane was doing a big jigsaw puzzle.

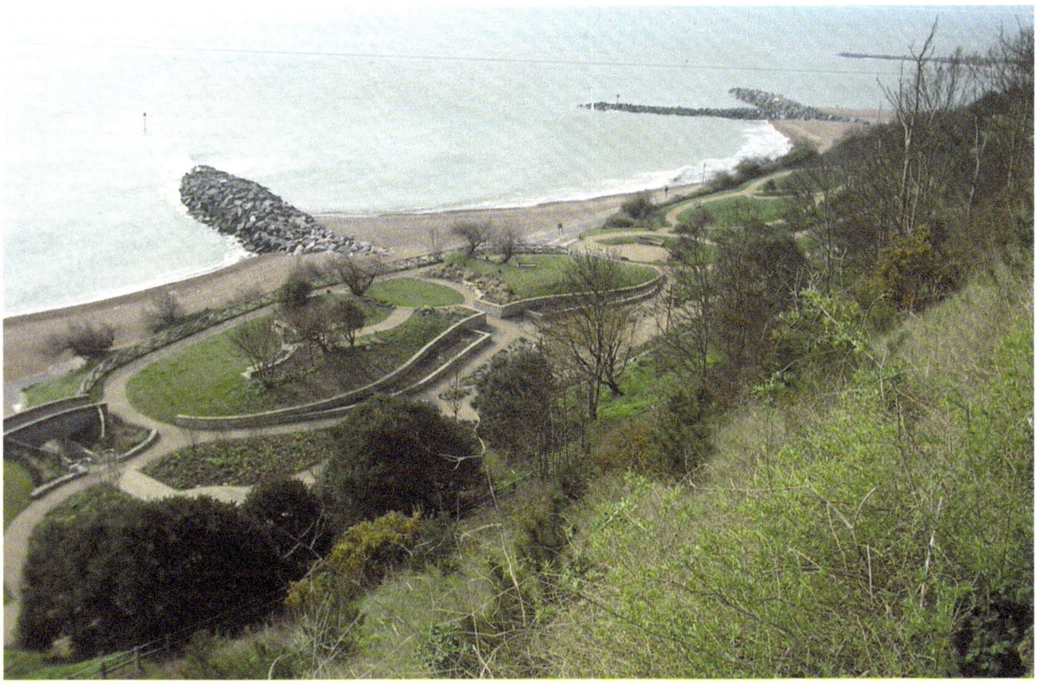

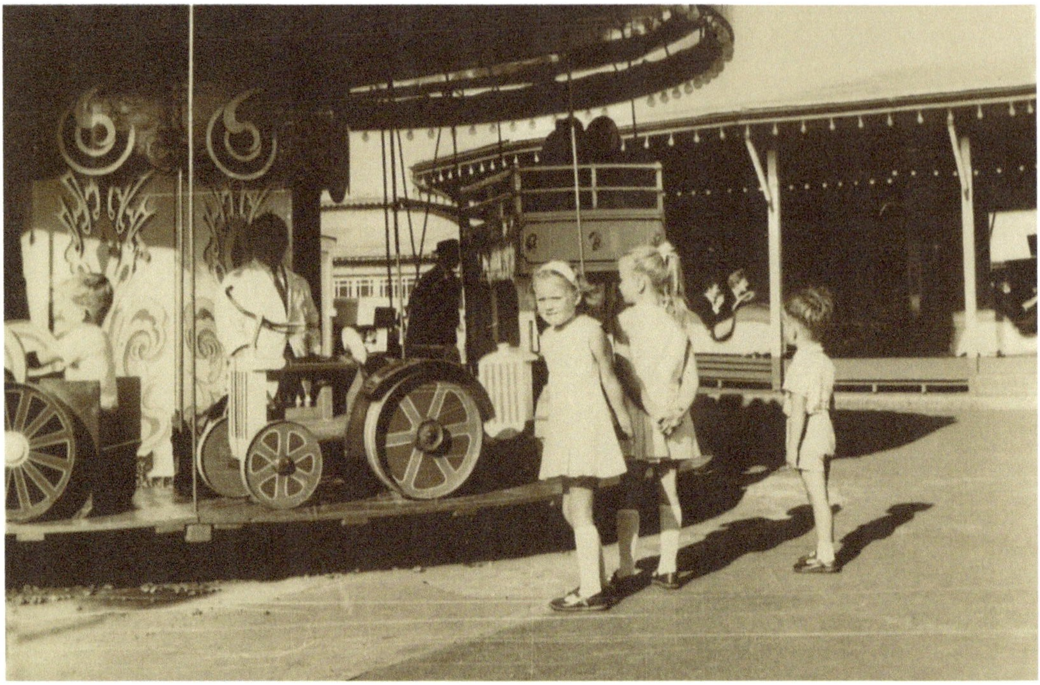

Amusements of the 1960s on Folkestone Seafront

Above: A children's ride at Jimmy Godden's amusements in the 1960s. In the background are the dodgem cars. These were two of the many rides at Jimmy Godden's amusement park at Folkestone seafront in the mid-1960s.

Below left: The boating pool at Jimmy Godden's amusements along the Marine Parade taken in the 1950s. You can see boat No. 19 with Philip Goodman pictured aged around eleven.

Below right: What a coincidence – the boat No. 20 taken in the 1970s with Philip Goodman and his two children, some twenty years apart.

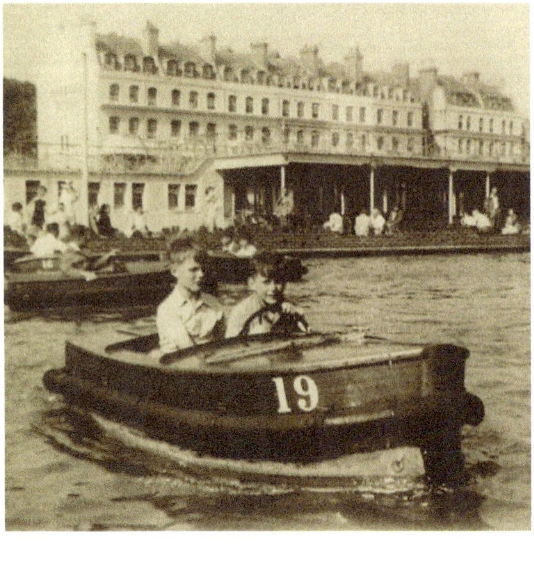

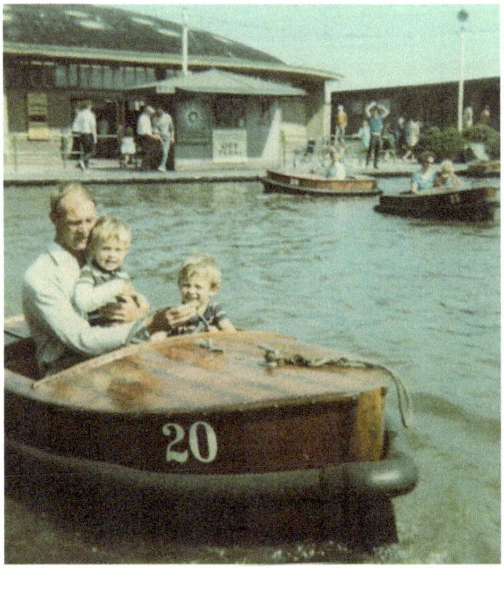

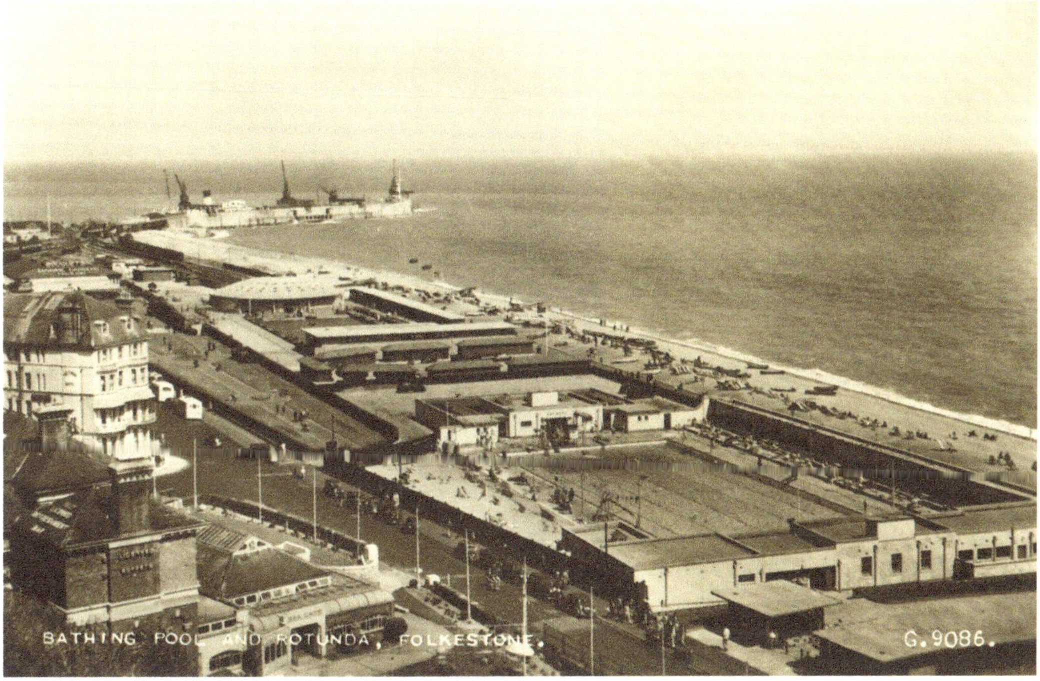

Heydays After the War in the 1950s

Above: Folkestone seafront came alive after the war, with the Rotunda, ghost train, dodgems, swimming and boating pool and Pitch and Putt Golf. Within thirty years all this changed with the swimming pool filled in and the buildings around it demolished apart from the Rotunda and restaurant. The Dome amusements and rides were built where the old pool became a car park and a place where the large Sunday market occured.

Below left: Last remains of the roller coaster, the Rotunda building and the Dome on the seafront.

Below right: I just couldn't resist this picture as it reminded me of a Tyrannosaurus Rex eating the last remains of the Dome structure in July 2003, for his dinner.

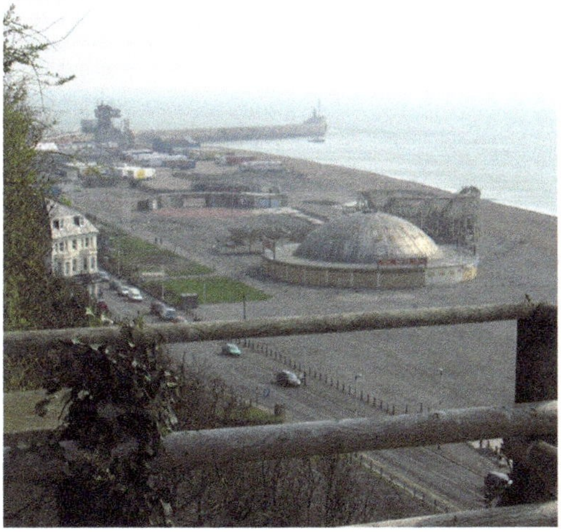

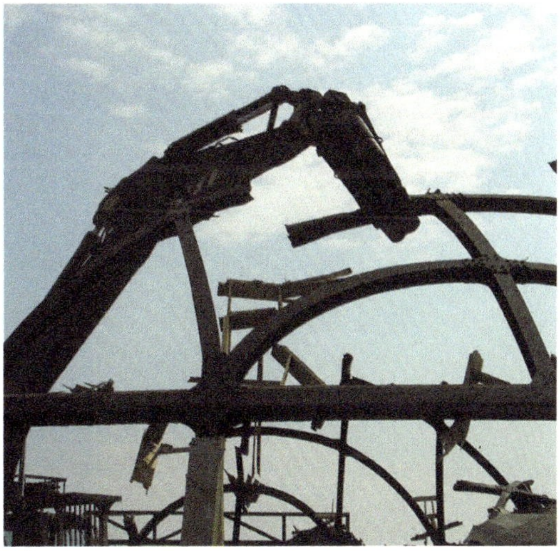

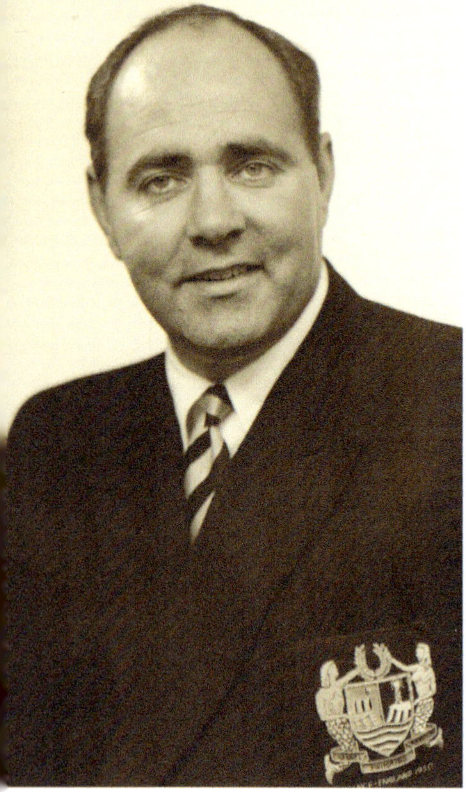

Walter Samuel Rockett

Walter Samuel 'Sam' Rockett was born in Milborne St Andrew in Dorset on 24 April 1919 and died in Folkestone on 9 November 1989.

Left: Sam Rockett was a notable man in the swimming world, which is why I wish to honour his memory by writing a few lines about his time spent in Folkestone. From personal memory I can see this kind, gentle, patient man trying to teach us schoolgirls how to swim in the early 1950s – both in the outdoor pool and indoor rock pool at Folkestone. The pools were situated along Marine Parade, which was a short distance from the Leas lift. Sam was one of nine finishers out of twenty-four in the first *Daily Mail* International Swim on the 22 August 1950. Sam was also the first Briton home from Cap Gris Nez. Whilst living in Folkestone Sam owned the Frogmore Tearooms in Sandgate Road.

Below: The building with the scaffolding around it is Nos 8–9 Marine Parade, once The Devonshire Hotel, now being converted into flats. The house on the right of The Devonshire Hotel is No. 7 Marine Parade, where Sam Rockett lived. How nice it must have been for him to live so close to the swimming pool, literally a two-minute walk along the road.

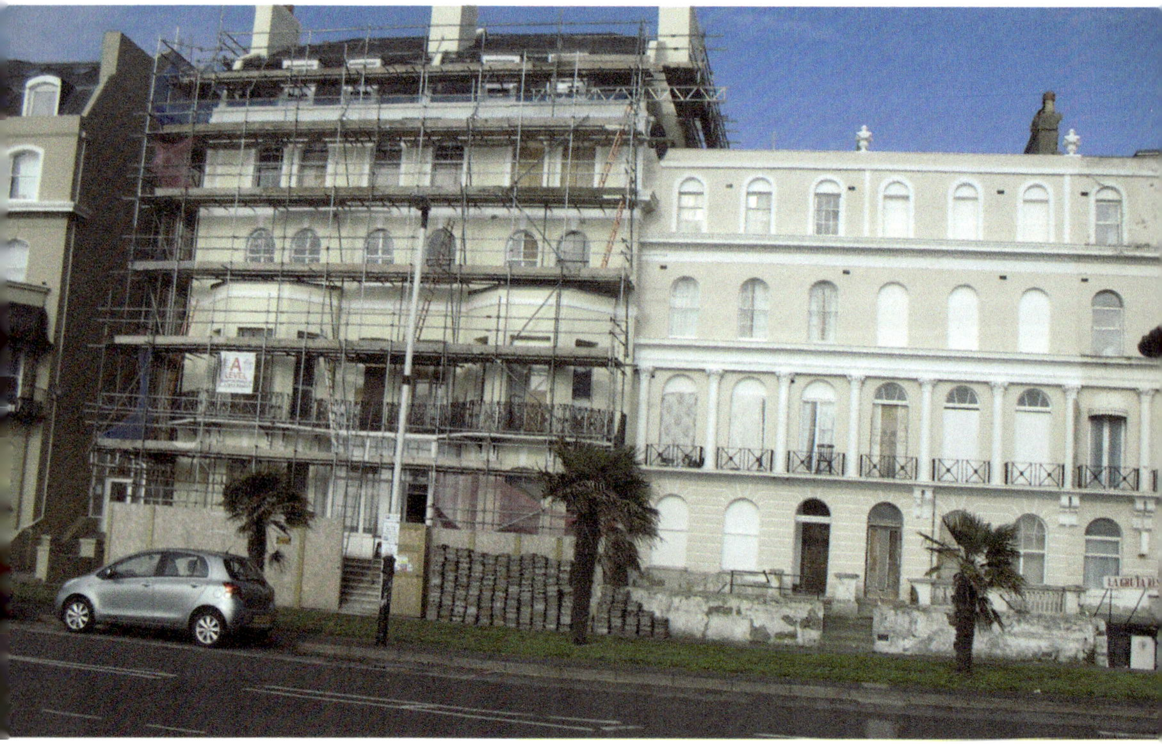

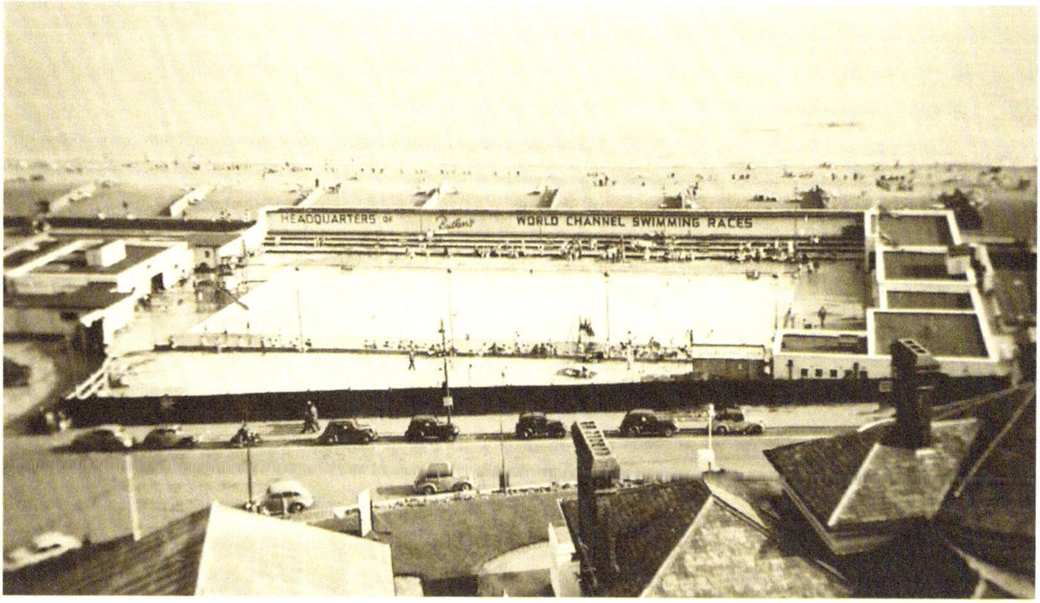

Sam resigned from being a factory foreman at ICI Plastics in Mitcham in Surrey where he was a well-known water-polo player. He moved to Folkestone where he took up the position of training supervisor in the *Daily Mail* race of 1952 and assistant manager of the Folkestone outdoor pool. Although the pool closed in early 1960s, Sam continued as a trainer for the channel swimmers until around 1964. As a trainer he had a few successes, including Antonio Albertondo who in 1961 was the first man to swim non-stop both ways.

Above: Taken in the 1950s, a picture of the outdoor swimming pool, which has the wording 'Headquarters of Butlins World Channel Swimming Races', of which he was known to be associated with. Dover Museum has been very lucky to have Sam's papers and many photos donated from his family. Now they remain available for the public to view.

Below left: The indoor swimming pool named the Rock Pool. The water always smelt heavily of chlorine and made your eyes sting; the changing rooms you can see on the left and the nearby rock where we used to jump off. If you caught yourself against any of the rocks in the area you would end up with a nasty graze. It's a wonder this photo looked so clear as it was always very steamy there.

Below right: The Rock Pool opened on Christmas Day 1953. The group below paid Sam to open the pool as they were friends and paid the overheads – he clearly didn't mind. The swimmers in the picture are Vince Bullman, Ted Blackwell, Frank Darrington, Sheila Walker, and Dave Walker.

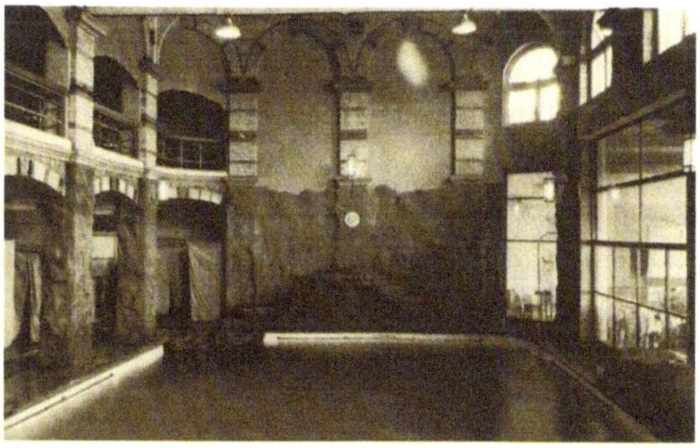

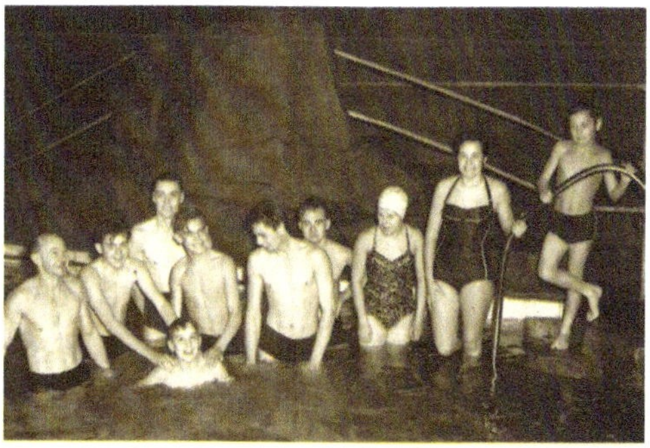

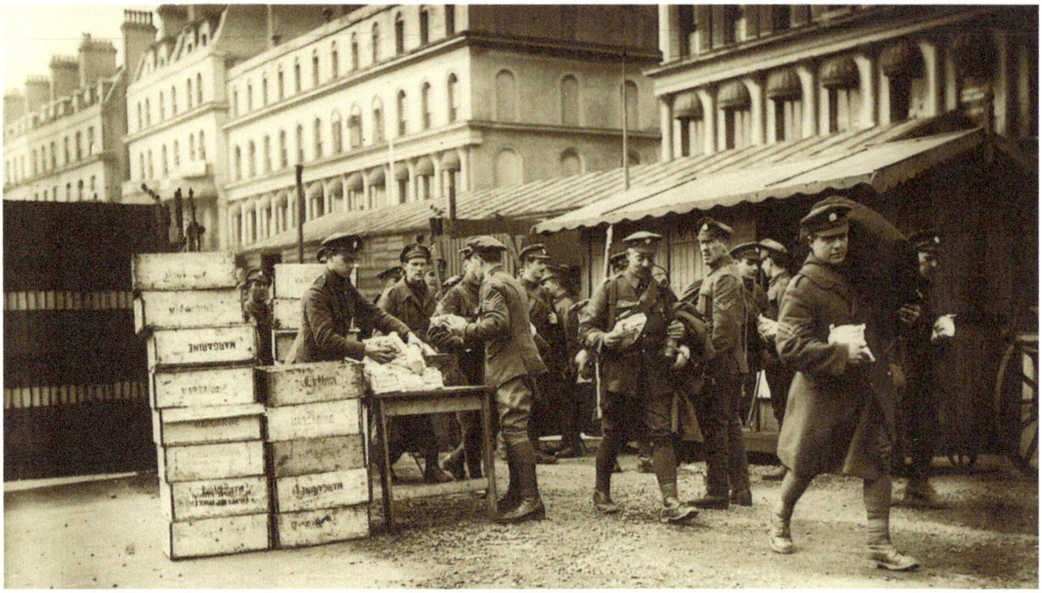

English Spy Operations in Marine Parade

Above: During the First World War many troops were stationed along the Marine Parade. These soldiers, demobilised in 1918, are receiving their last issue of rations.

Below: Taken in 2014 is the same area as the picture above. The scaffolding is around Nos 4 and 5 Marine Parade, once hotels now converted into flats. This area at one time was all guesthouses or hotels and houses of multiple occupants, according to the Kelly's street directories. Another tale to tell is that at Nos 8 and 9: The Devonshire Hotel was a base for an organisation that became MI6 after the First World War. Maj. Cameron trained recruits with sophisticated spy techniques of the day, including writing in code and hiding information in everyday objects such as fruit and jewellery. The work was very dangerous and the majority of the spies gave their lives for details they supplied to the Major who reported that it helped win the war and saved many lives in the process (Nos 8 and 9 are to the left of the scaffold).

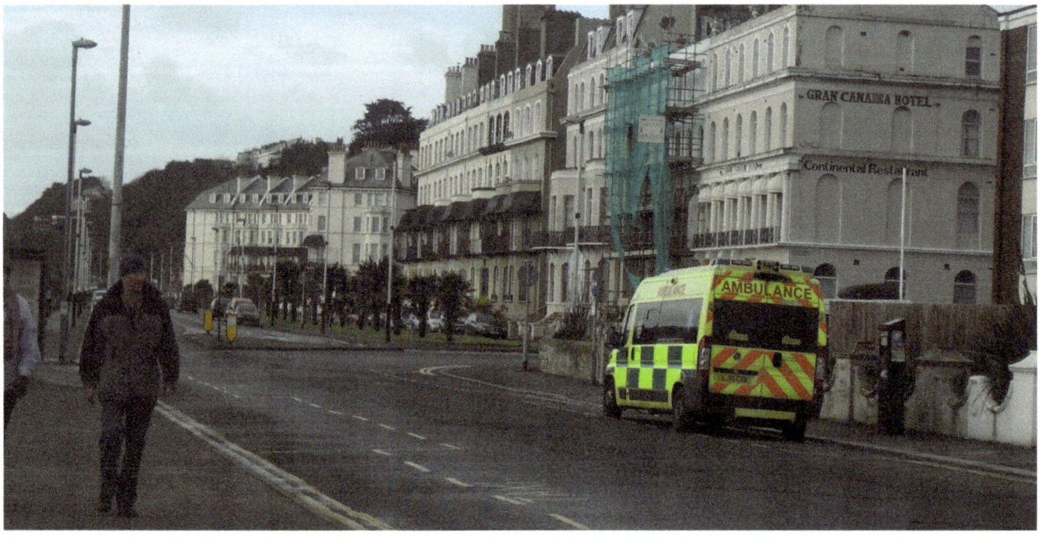

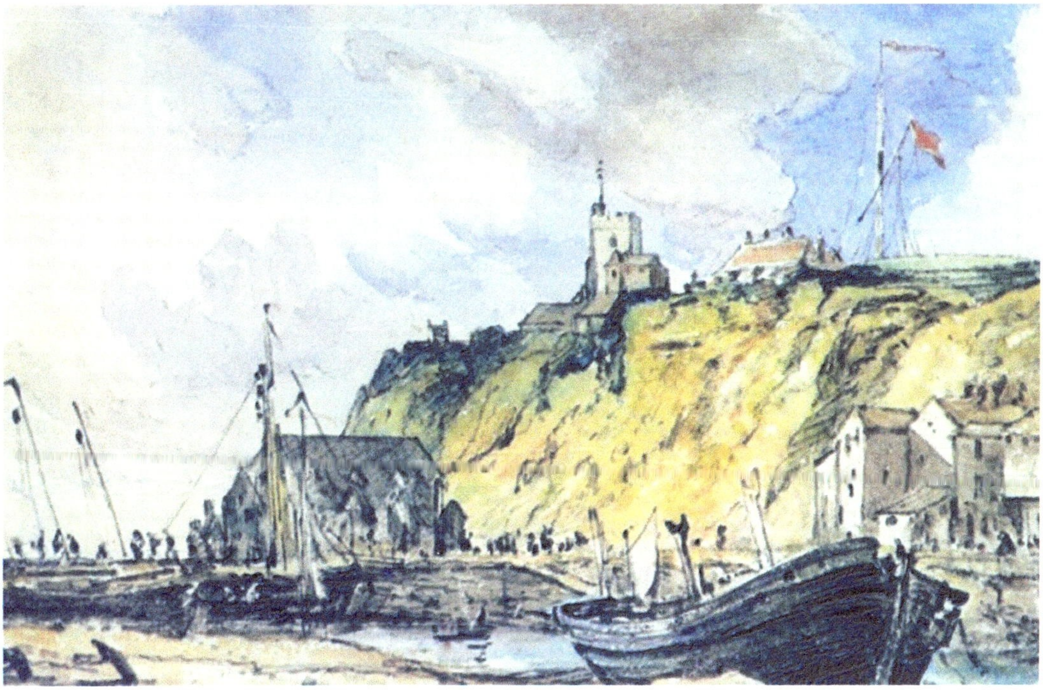

From Old Wooden Huts to a Hotel

The old wooden buildings were the carpentry workshops of Joseph Jacob's shipwrights in the early 1700s. In a report from S. J. Mackie, in his Folkestone Handbook for visitors of 1840s, he mentioned these wooden buildings as being 'most uncomfortable and unsightly sheds'. It appears that before the Royal Pavilion Hotel was built in 1843, these buildings were used to put up people who had come over on the cross-channel ships of the time. A large tarpaulin was draped over the front of the building to help visitors take cover from the elements and receive refreshments. The Jacobs also owned the nearby Saracens Head public house, possibly one of the buildings on the right of the picture. After being in the Jacob's hands from around 1767 to 1794, it was no longer licensed after that time, so possibly that too was demolished.

Joseph came to Folkestone from Dover and was an apprentice to John Ladd and his wife in 1711. When Joseph married in 1722 his apprenticeship would have finished. In his will, he left his carpenters yard, workshops and other buildings and ground to his wife and children, explaining where it was situated under Bail Cliffe and near Gulston Street (now named South Street). His son Phineas appears to have continued working there as a shipwright as there is mention of him being an apprentice for Thomas Farley to build two boats for £35 each in 1763. In 1767 Phineas died. His son, also called Phineas, followed his father's footsteps to become a shipwright. From sketchy information it appeared that he built ships from Sandgate and his uncle Thomas continues on the site of Joseph's yards.

In the 1790s the rough seas (without the protection of harbours or sea defences) often caused great damage to the beach areas. After the wars with France started in 1799, it was probably advised to move the shipbuilding. It is reported that it shifted to the Medway and Thames area by 1800; it seemed that building of big ships in these yards had finished. A report of 1812 said with heavy seas and winds, the sheds were blown down in 1809.

Thomas Telford brought the Folkestone Harbour Co. and cleared the area so that the Pavilion Hotel could be built with the coming of the railway down to the harbour in 1843. In 1851, Thomas Farley surrendered his lease of the Jacobs shipwright area back to Lord Radnor. Soon building work took place and the London and Paris public house and hotel was built. It is now named Gillespies.

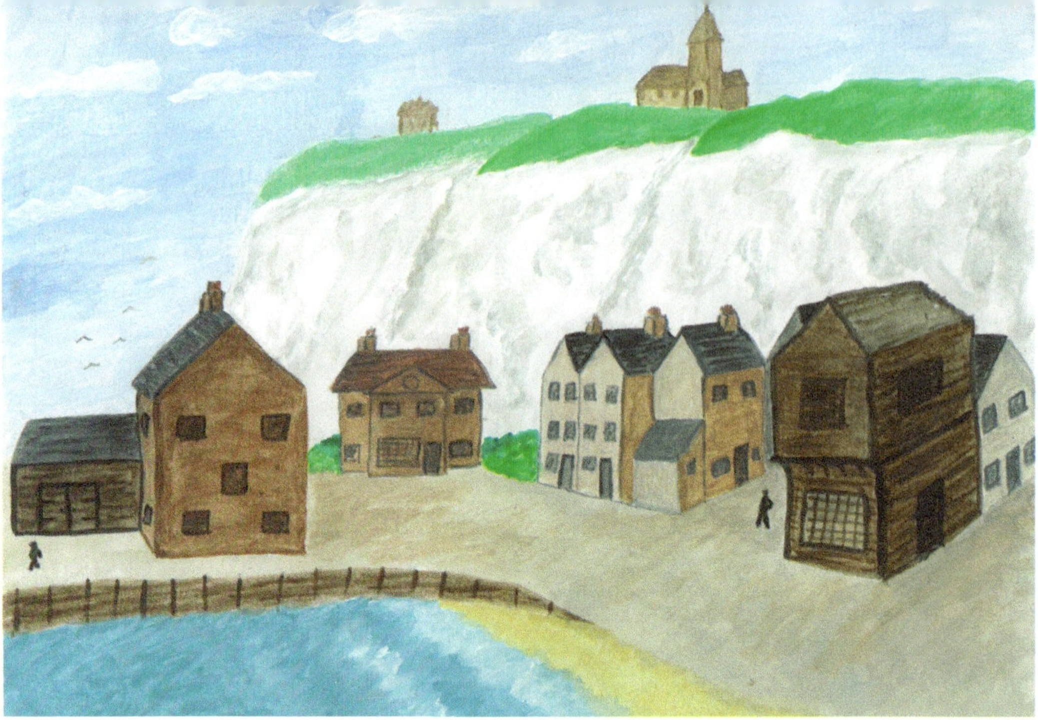

From Ship Building Sheds to a Hotel

Above: This is an artist's impression of what the area looked like before the Pavilion Hotel was built. To the right of the picture was the Smithy, now called Gillespies, on Harbour Street. The next street with the man in was Gulston Street, now South Street. The next house could possibly have been The Saracens Head, near The Princess Royal. The first building on the left is the carpentry sheds, standing on the land Thomas Telford bought around 1809 for use with the coming of the railway.

Below: An aerial view showing the Grand Hotel Burstin, once The Royal Pavilion hotel, and Gillespies on the lower right of the picture. Comparing the two pictures, I hope the reader's imagination can conjure up how the area possibly looked in the 1700s.

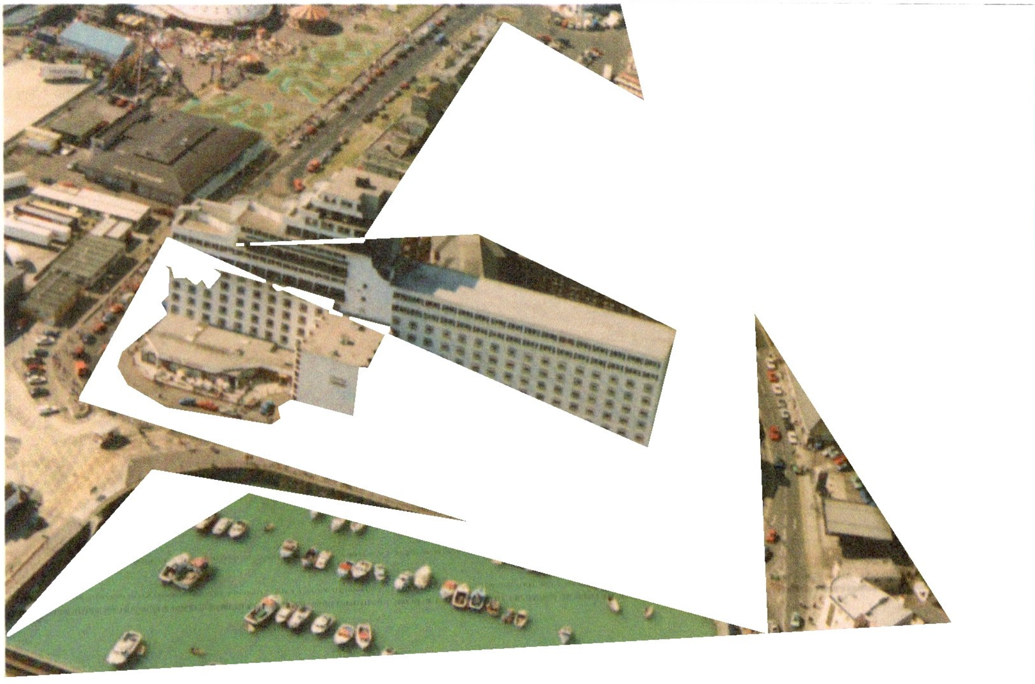

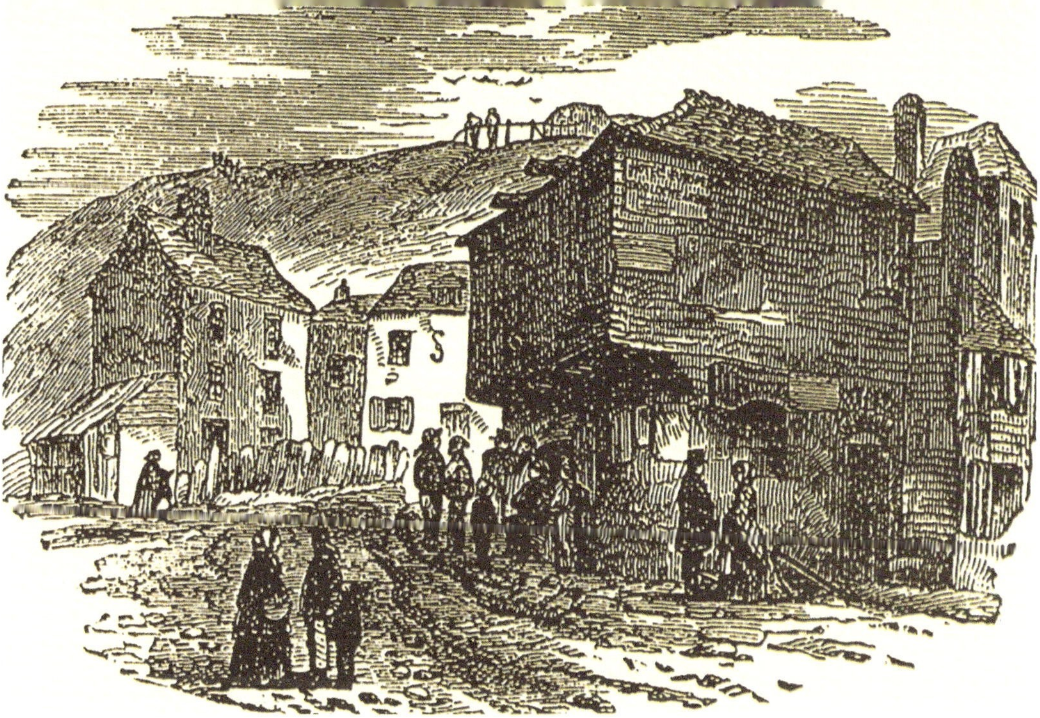

Spies in Our Shangri-La?

Above: This picture was etched in around 1850, by S. J. Mackie who in the 1800s would visit towns and villages to write about their good and bad points. He would also etch interesting buildings, and wrote about this Smithy saying, 'It spoilt the look of the area belching out black smoke'. Within a couple of years it was demolished and replaced with the London and Paris Hotel; only in recent years it was renamed Gillespies. It is featured in the larger picture (*below left*) taken in 2013.

Below left: On the left-hand side is part of The Grand Burstin Hotel and on the right, Gillespies.

Below right: A close up of The Shangri La, built in 1894 overlooking Gillespies. It had been reported on television that in the First World War this building was the German Consulate. From the room at the top you can see up and down the channel with ease.

It has been newly discovered that there was in fact no German Consulate in Folkestone; it was actually situated in Dover from 1900 to 1914. The Consul was Sir William Crundall who was also elected the Mayor of Dover thirteen times. He primarily held the post as he persuaded Kaiser Wilhelm to get German liners to dock at Dover. Today there is still a German Consulate in Dover.

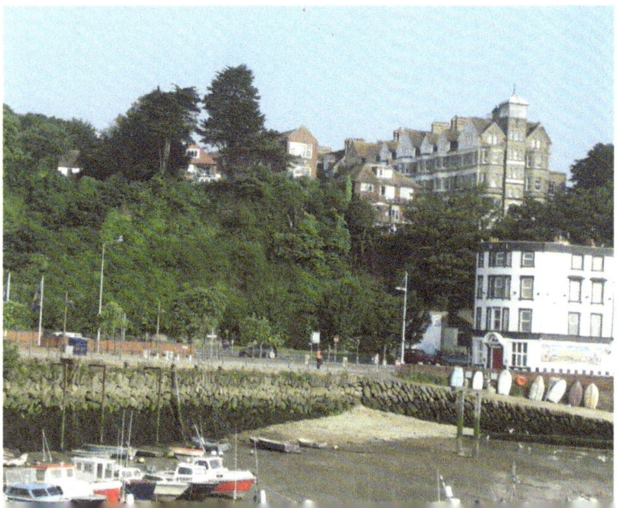

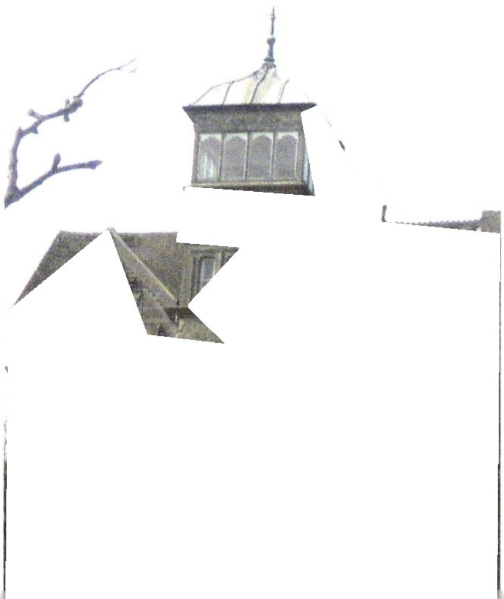

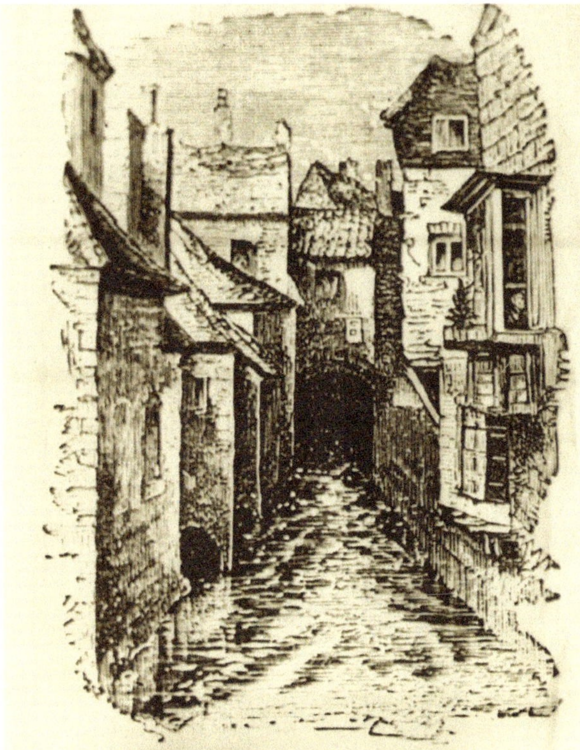

THE PENT STREAM IN 1856.

Harbour Street, Possibly Early 1800s

Above: The Pent Stream that ran from the distant hills down to the sea. What we know today as Harbour Street ran in between the houses, which were narrow streets.

Below left: All that was left worth saving of South Street and Harbour Street was three public houses – the only buildings remaining today. Two were knocked into one and named The True Briton and The Harbour Inn, which is now called True Briton and Gillespies.

Below right: The large restaurant in Harbour Street was demolished in around 1950; the rest of shops and cafés in South Street were also demolished leaving an open area as it is today, shown on the next page.

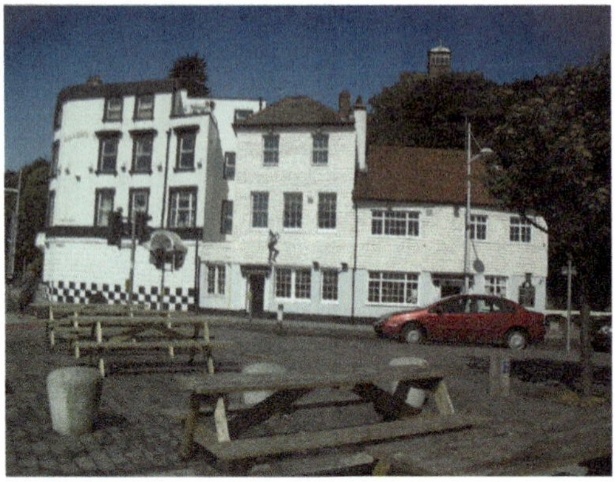

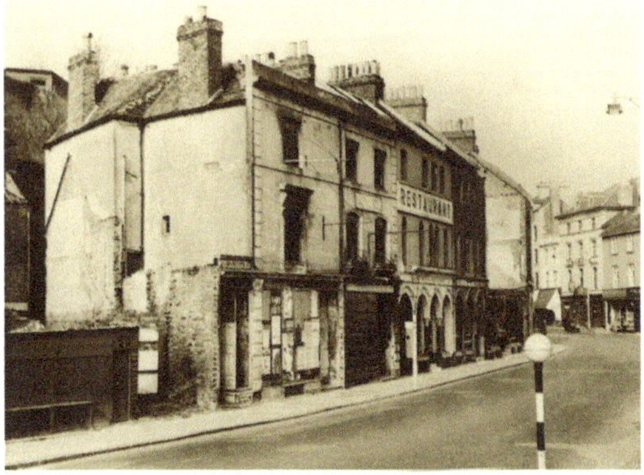

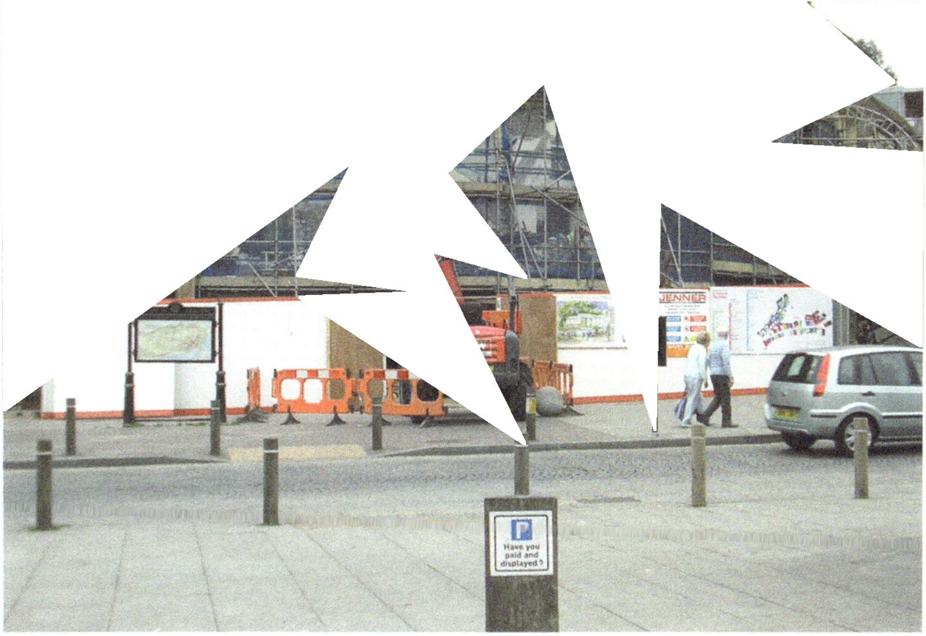

Secrets of Smugglers Discovered

Above: The renovation to Nos 2–4 South Street in 2010 reminded me of an article written in 1866 in the *Folkestone Chronicle*. When this area was being demolished, it stated the workmen found papers hidden in the loft relating to names of Folkestone smugglers from the mid-1700s. I wondered what happened to them. My memory was jogged in October 2010 when a hole appeared in the back of the building, shown in the picture below. I enquired about it and told the workers that a lot of old houses in this area had hidden rooms and they said they would inform me of the archaeologist's report. I went back two days later, greeted with a wall of silence – nobody knew anything about it and the hole was bricked up. Then I was told it was a coal chute from the top of the cliff, but there were no coal marks in the hole and no way could coal be tipped from the top of the cliff. I never did find out any more about the hole.

Below: The hole in the wall that looks like an old doorway to somewhere. In the picture above you can just see it through the scaffolding.

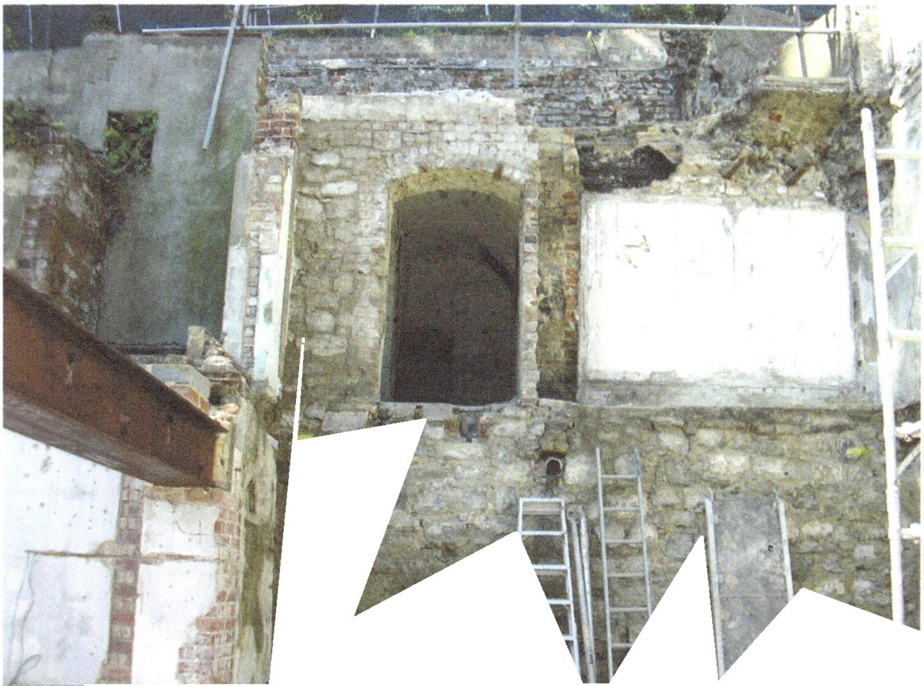

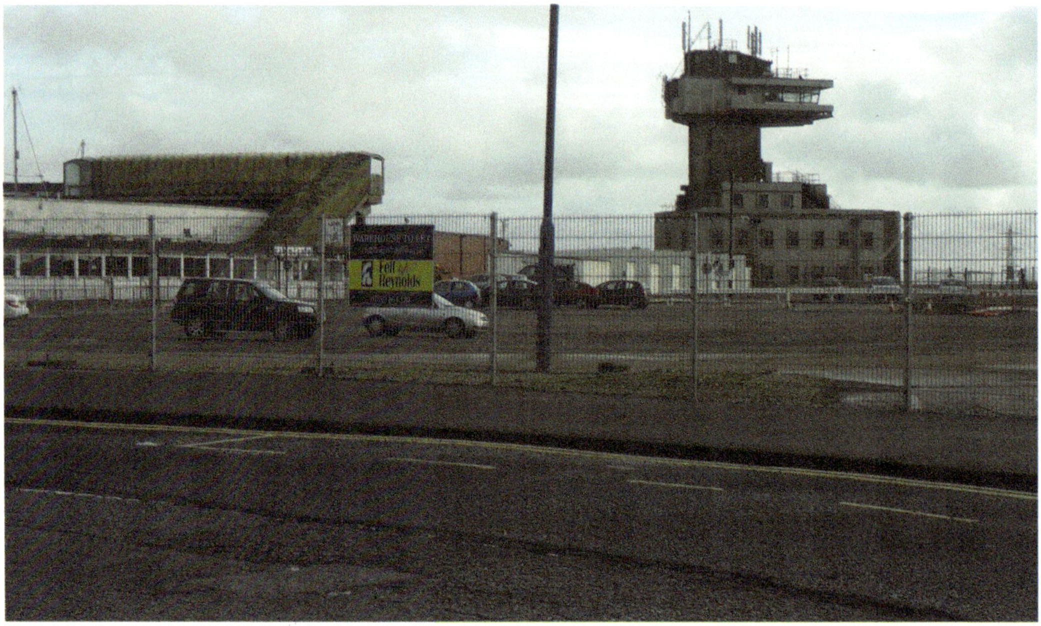

Here One Day, Gone the Next
Above: The Pilot Lookout Tower was built in the 1970s and became unsafe to use after only forty-or-so years of use. This is how it looked in January 2014.

Below: The seagull standing guard over the demolished Pilot Lookout post, now a heap of rubble, in August 2014. We do have some large seagulls in the area; we only wish the holidaymakers wouldn't feed them! The large seagull is used as an information bureau in the summer months when various events take place.

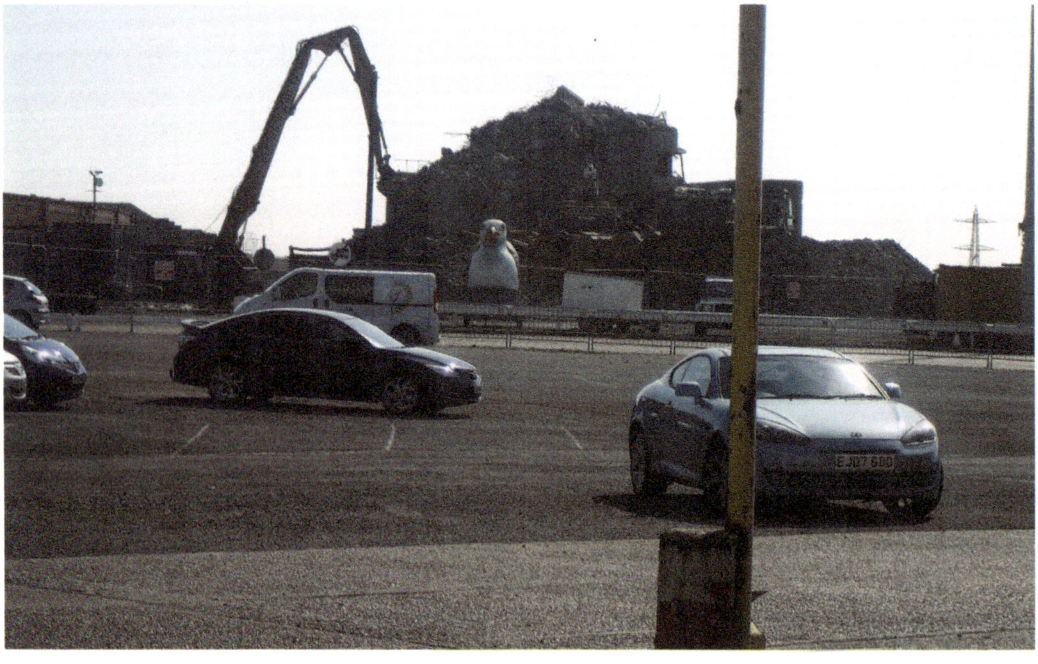

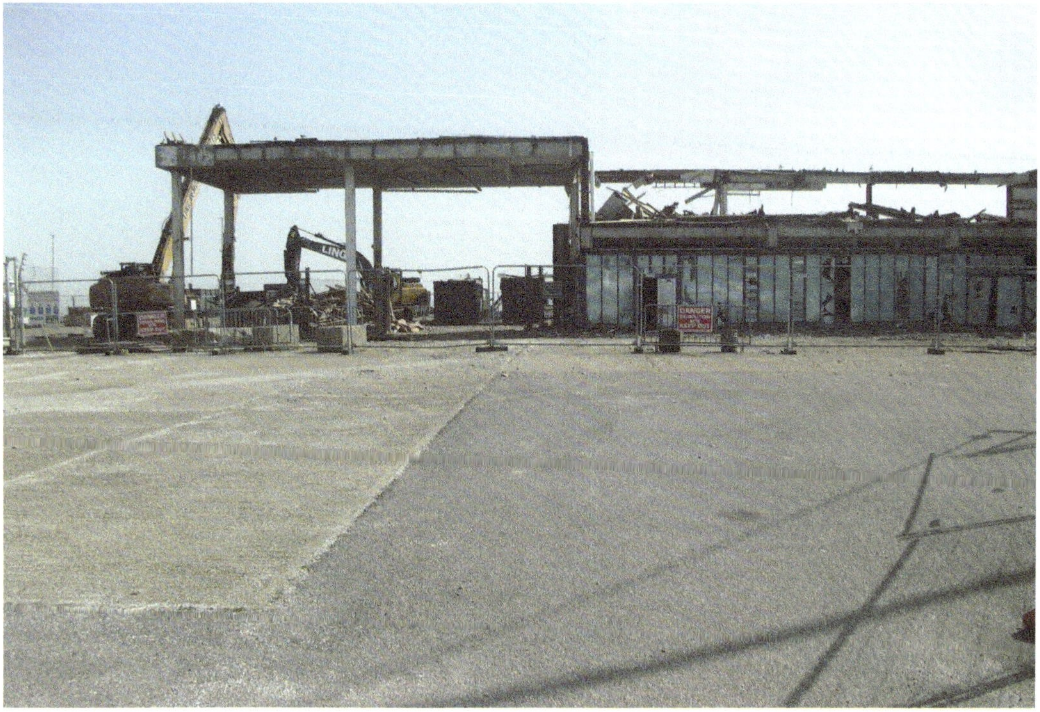

Last of the Harbour Buildings

Above: The last of the harbour buildings to be cleared from the site – a huge task for Walker Brothers but they managed it on time.

Below left: The harbour on 4 August 2014. The ground was cleared and tarmacked over and made into a car park. This was finished in readiness for the unveiling of the memorial arch by Prince Harry who afterwards walked down the Road of Remembrance to the harbour in memory of the troops that came this way on their journey to France in the First World War. This picture was taken from the East Cliff overlooking the harbour; if you had good eyesight you could see Prince Harry standing down there.

Below right: So not to disappoint, the lower right picture is Prince Harry speaking to various ex-military personnel.

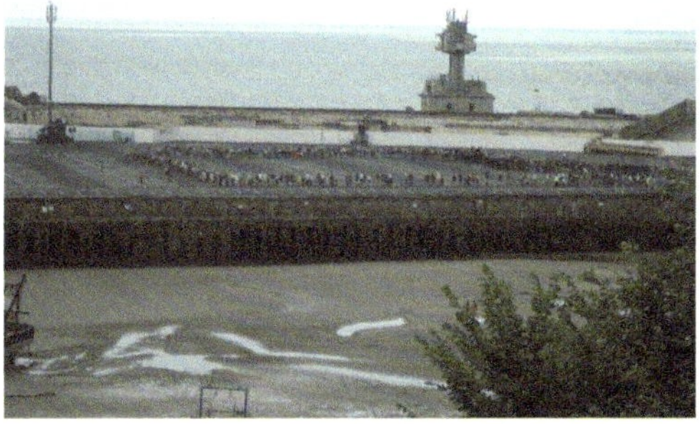

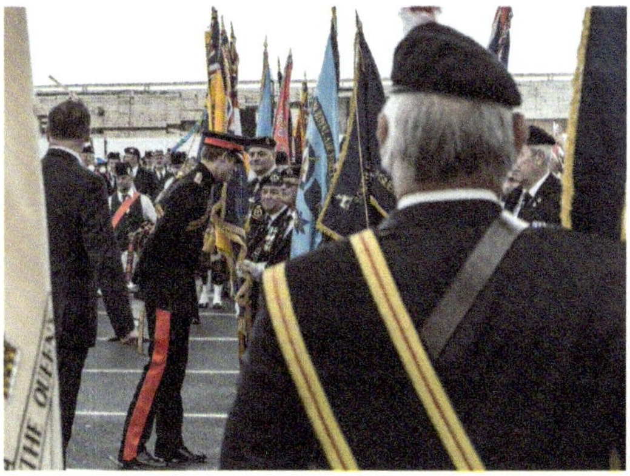

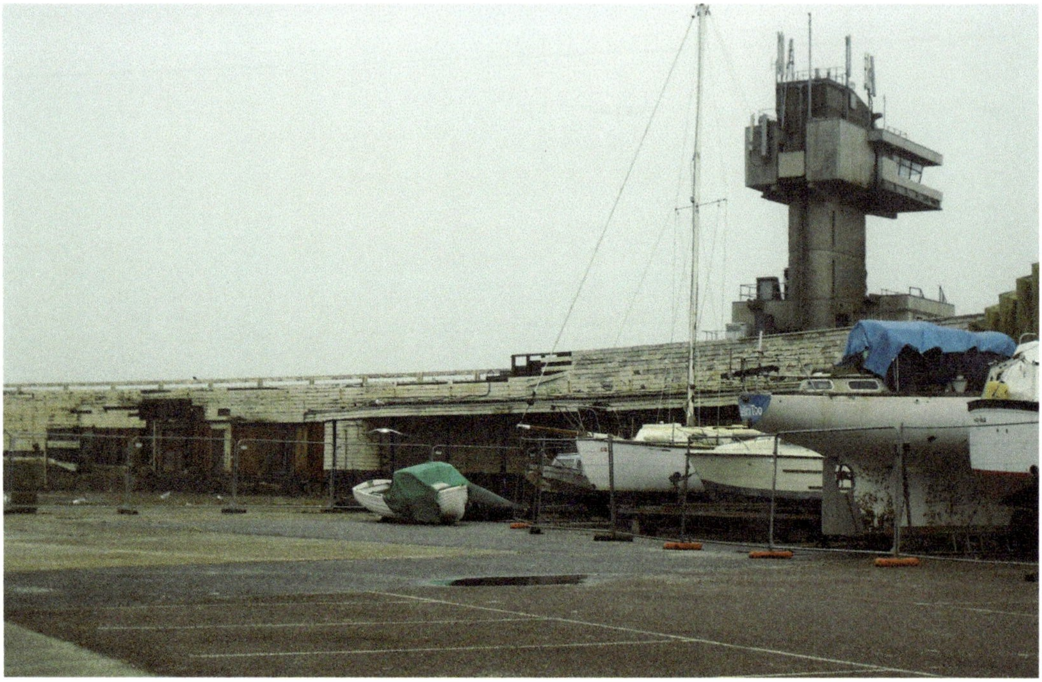

Old Tatty Buildings Ready to be Destroyed

Above: The picture above shows the Pilot Lookout building and the old harbour buildings being demolished in the spring of 2014. All this area of the harbour was cleared and tarmacked in readiness for the 4 August visit of Prince Harry.

Below: The last remains of the former transit shed on the harbour site that had been empty for many years. It was occupied by the Folkestone Youth Project until the winter storms of 2014, which made the structure unsafe.

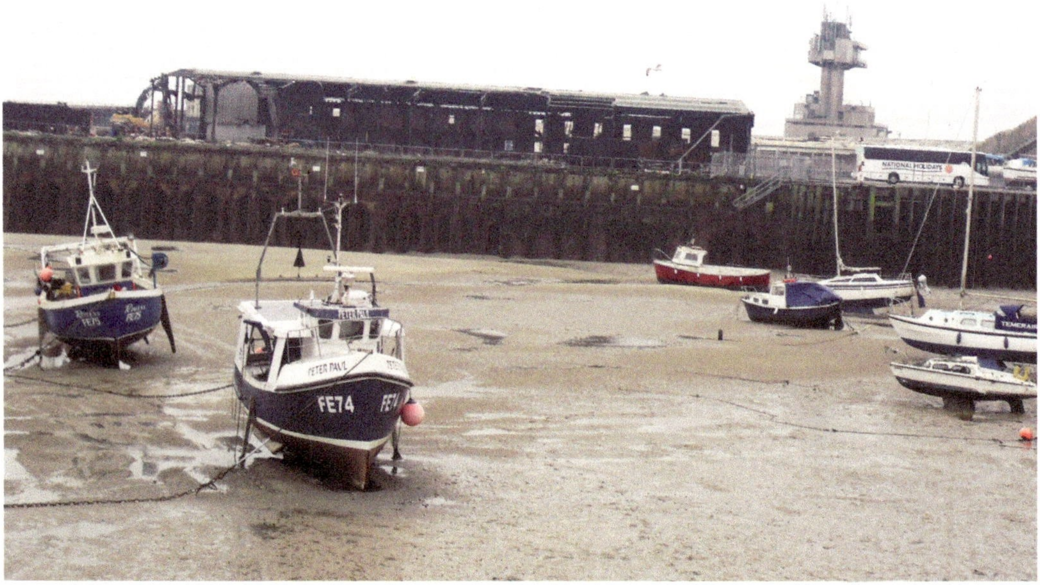

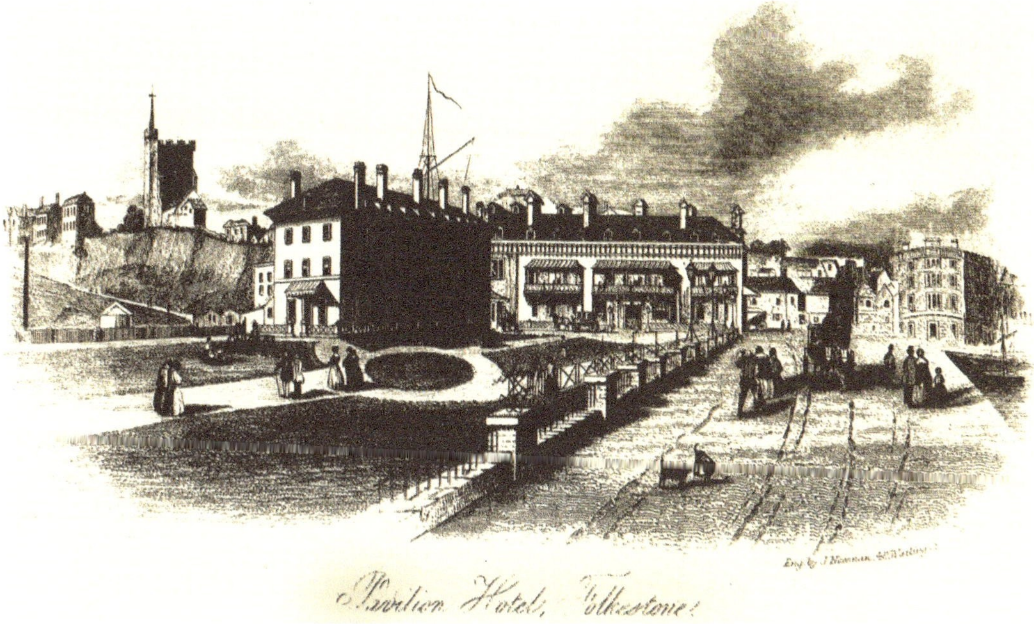

At Last, a Decent Hotel

Above: A welcome view of a nice hotel instead of the tarpaulins that were draped over the Jacob's Shipwright building sheds. This etching of the Royal Pavilion Hotel that replaced the Jacob's Shipwright sheds was etched around 1853; the building to the far right is the London and Paris Hotel. S. J. Mackie reported in the late 1840s that 'it bellowed out dirty smoke and was unsightly to have a smithy by the harbour'. It is believed that the London and Paris Hotel was built in around 1852.

Below: The Royal Pavilion Hotel early 1900s, sold in the 1950s and demolished in 1981/82. Notice how different it is to the picture above. Over the years the building was expanded to accommodate the influx of visitors, not only from abroad but England as well, who came to Folkestone for a breath of fresh sea air.

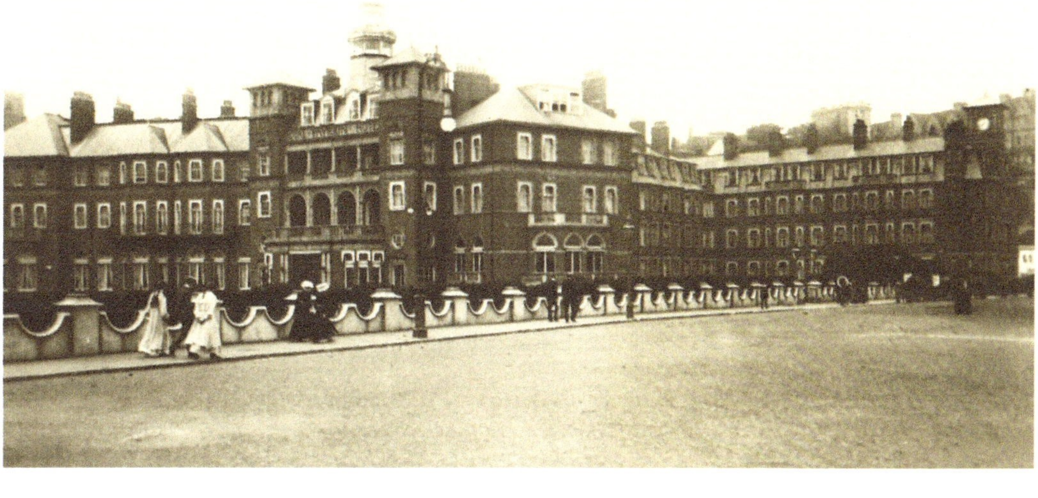

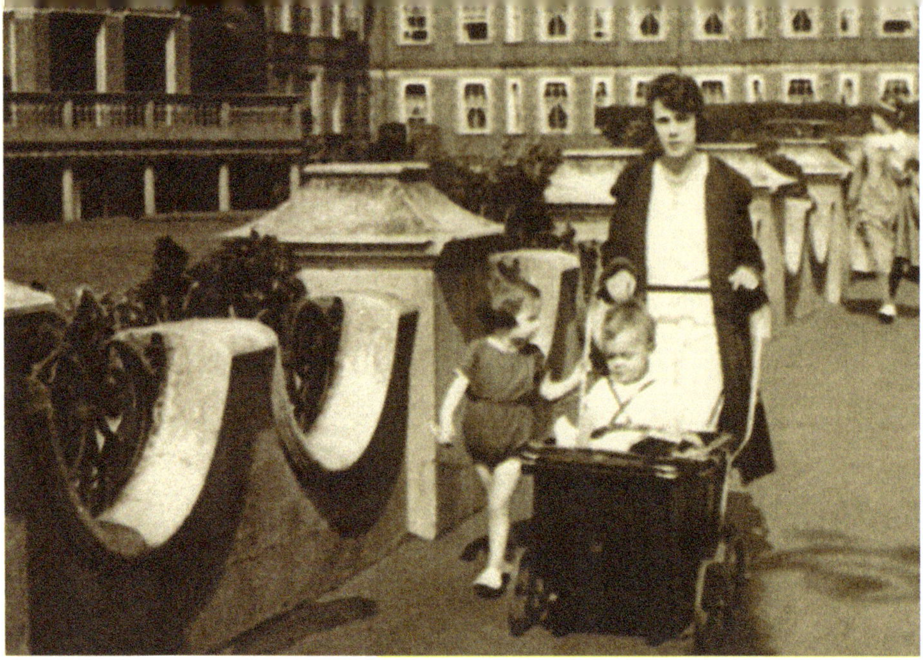

Taking a Stroll

Above: Elsie Mary Milton (née Huntley) walking with her children Rosemary and Peter past the Royal Pavilion Hotel around 1936. Shortly after this was taken Elsie and her husband Leslie moved to Coventry. Sadly Elsie died in 1939 and Leslie later died in 1942 and the children were adopted. Leslie's father had a wet-fish shop in South Street before the Second World War. However, it was around sixty years later that Rosemary discovered her family were from the Milton fishing community.

Below: The Grand Burstin, the tent-like object at the top of the building, is part of the 2014 Triennial art display that takes place in the town every three years from August to November. It was Alex Hartley who created the *Vigil* and it was said that from August to November the tent would be occupied as a lookout, which was exactly what the artist intended it for.

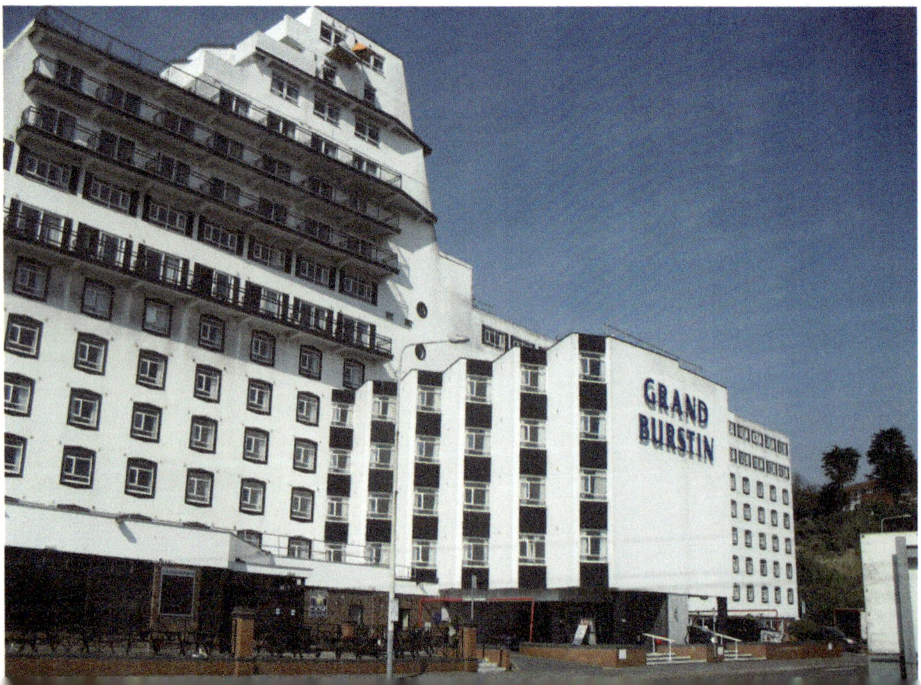

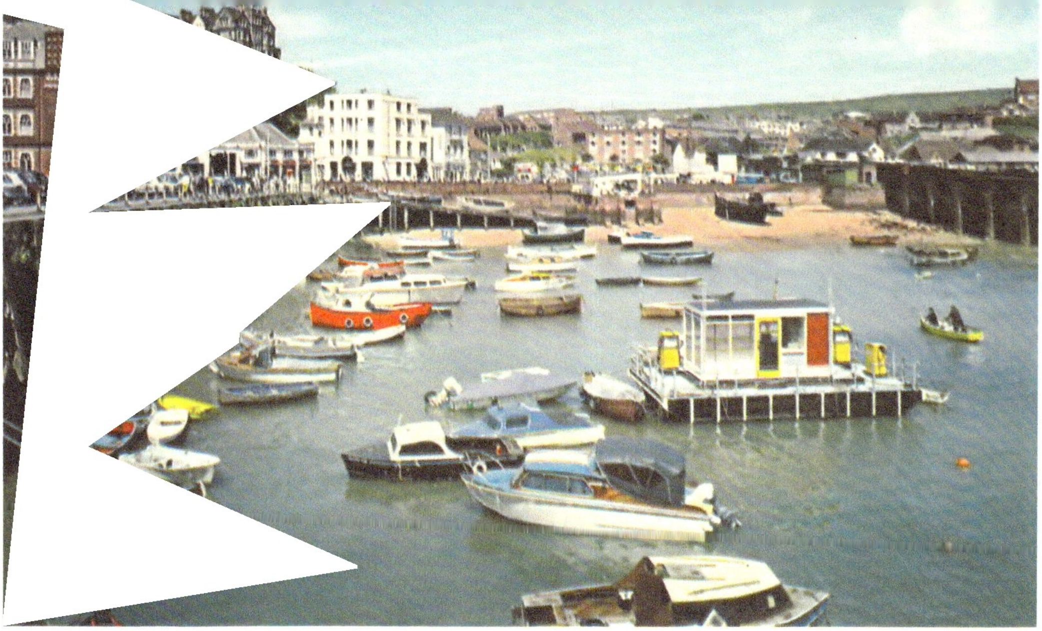

A Petrol Station in the Middle of the Harbour

Above: A new 3,000-gallon marine refuelling pontoon became operational in the harbour, pictured July 1963. Mr and Mrs Morris, Boat Chandlers and Service Dealers from Morris Marine, New Romney, said they would give a twenty-four-hour service (apart from when the tide is out) to fishing boats, yachts and power crafts, with fuel, oil and many spares from aboard the pontoon.

Below: The shed in the picture, taken in 2015, is the Marine Fuel Store, situated in The Stade. It is in easy reach for the fishermen and yachts to refuel their boats. The notice on the fuel store is a contact number for people who need fuel.

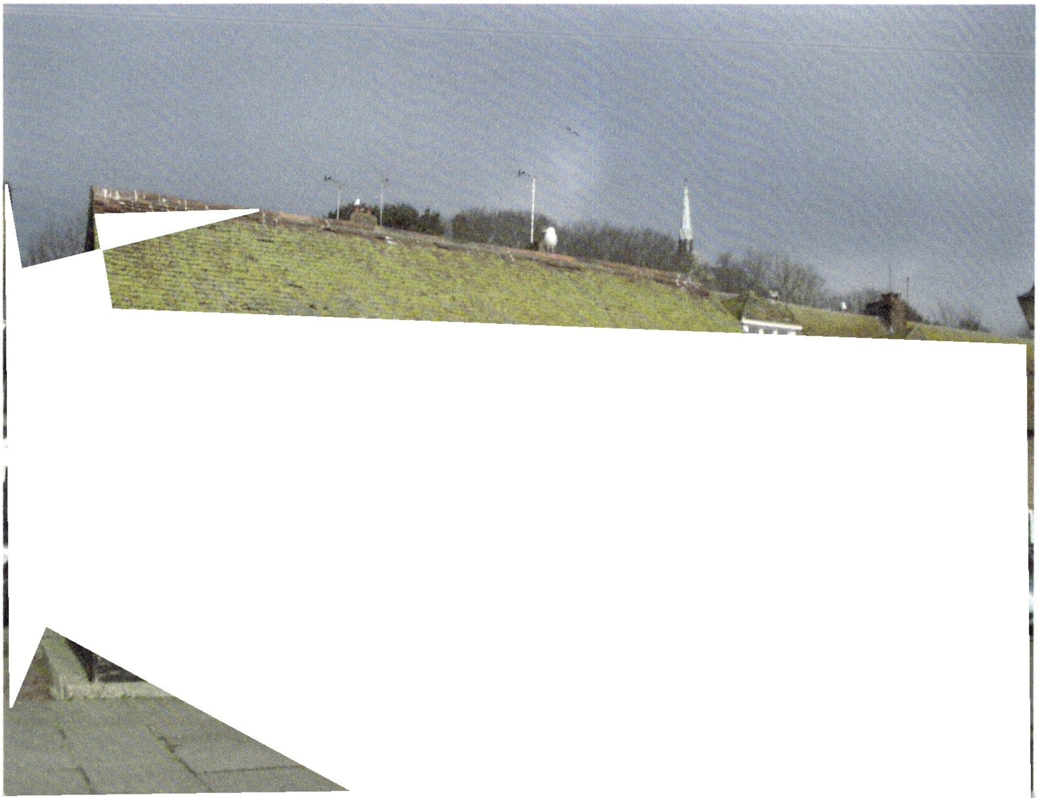

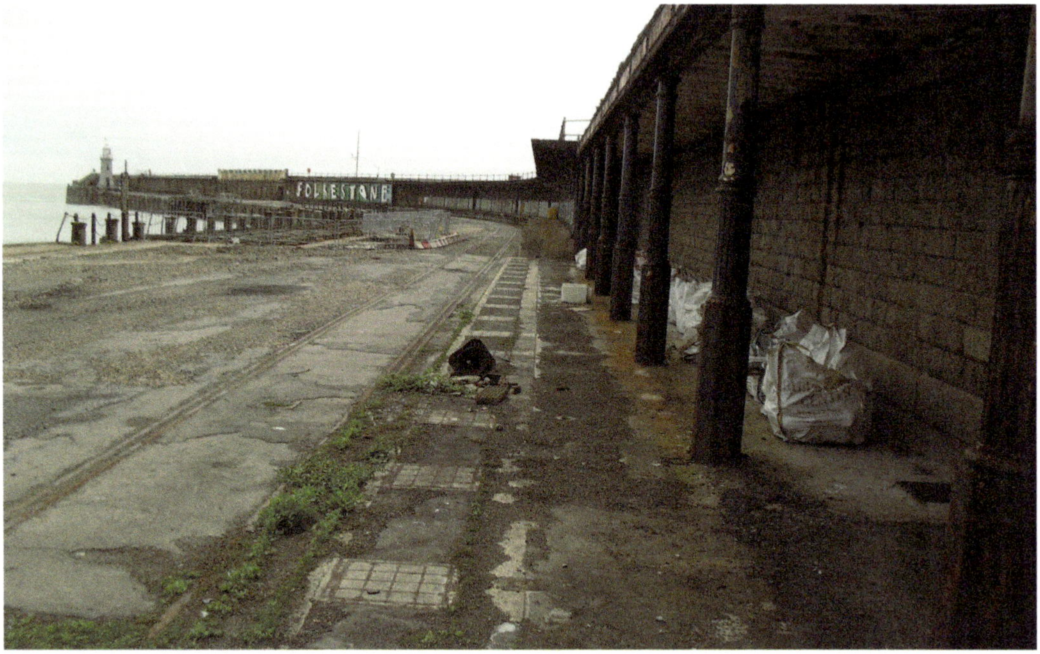

What Will I Become?
Above: Shown in 2011, a derelict train station awaiting its fate.

Below: Walker Bros Construction Co. renovating the Harbour Arm, in April 2015, through the Sir Roger De Haan Charitable Trust. After many months of work planned, it is destined to be open for the early summer trade and for the people who like to take their rods onto the top deck of the arm to fish. Note the black metal supports above, all painted up and the area now filled in.

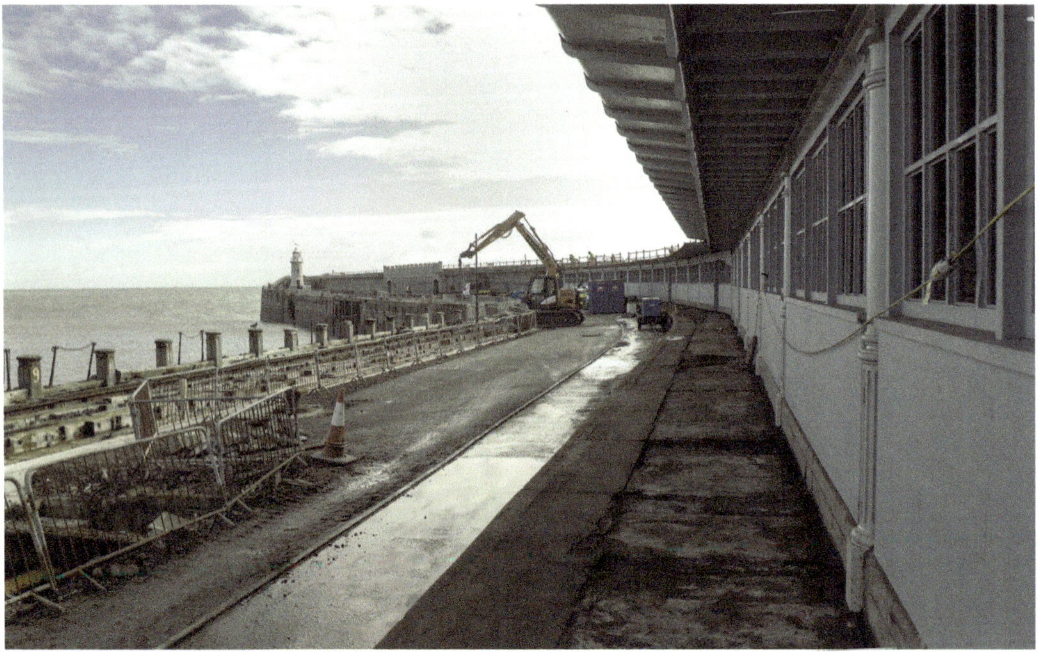

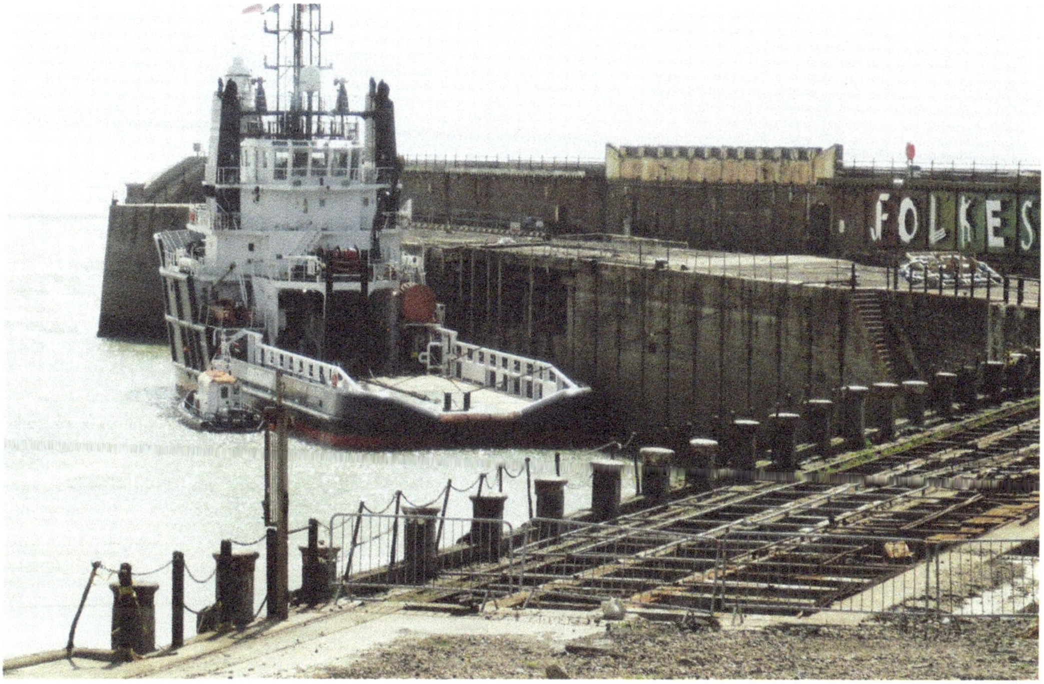

Renovation of the Harbour Arm
Above: Taken in 2011, a sad, dangerous-looking site.

Below: Taken in 2015, the same area in the process of being renovated through the Roger De Haan Charitable trust. The harbour will once again be a place for folk to be proud of, albeit, not with Cross Channel ships or steam trains, but walkways for sea views and a café. There might possibly also be a museum depicting the use of the harbour that played a large part in the First World War, ferrying tens of thousands of troops to the front.

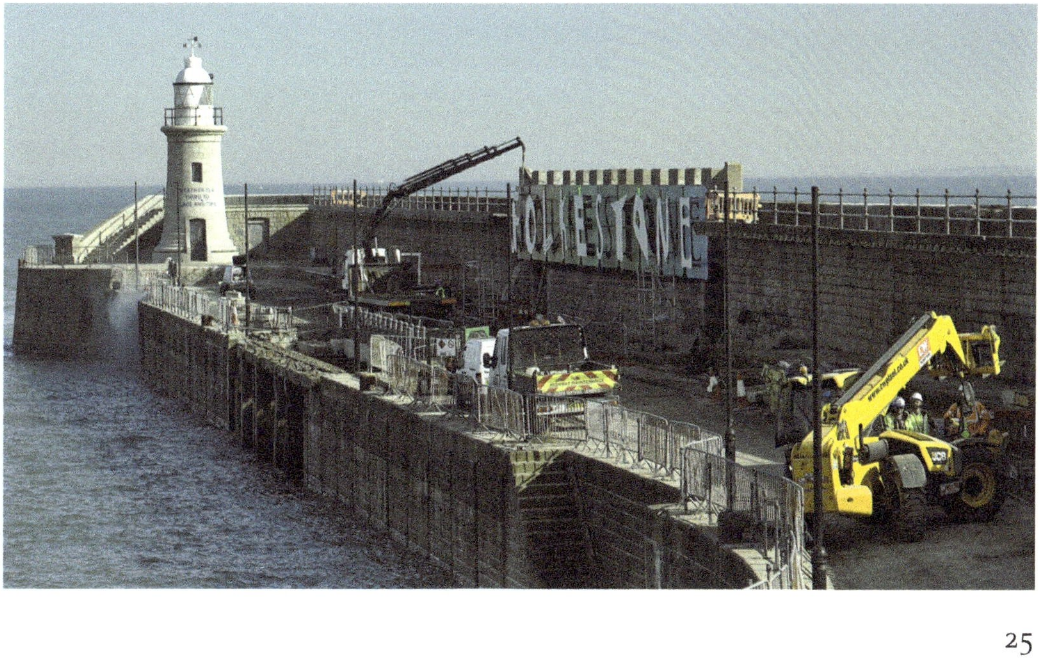

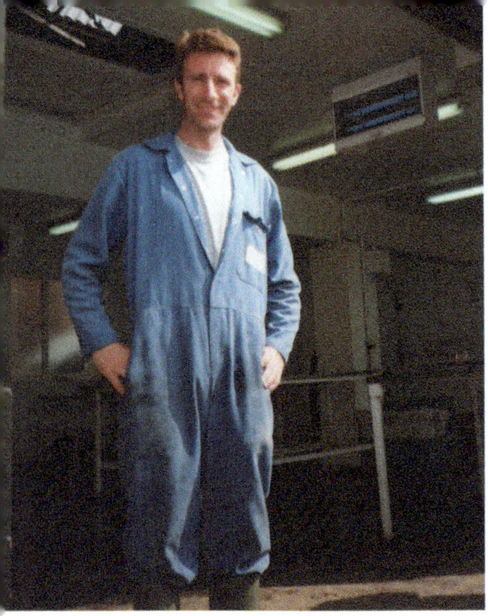

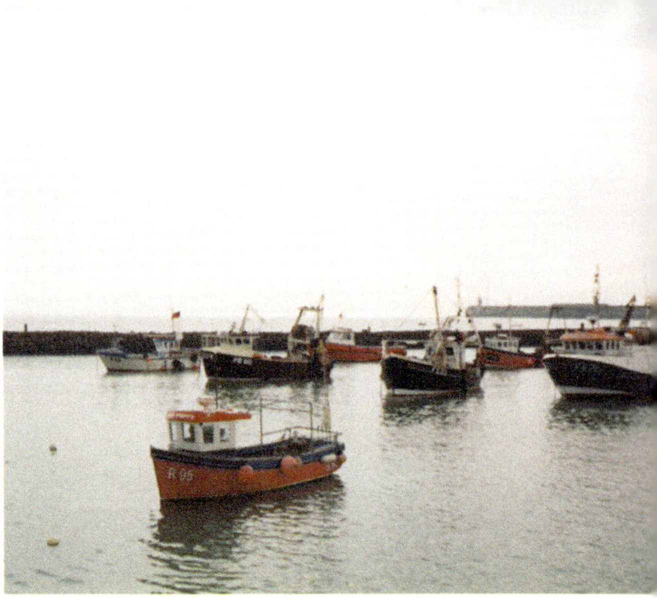

Fishermen's Dilemma

Above left: This image of Jessie Milton (born 1965) was taken in 1999. Jessie is a descendant of a long line of Miltons who have fished from Folkestone since the mid-1600s. Now sadly, with the depleting fishing fleet that are now allowed to fish, Jessie is the last of the Milton family to fish for a living and now spends his working days in The Folkestone Trawlers wet-fish shop, on The Stade, skinning and gutting fish for sale in the shop and for hotels.

Above right: Jessie's boat *The Poppy R95,* in Folkestone Harbour which has now been sold off to a fisherman and used out of Hythe.

Below: View of the Folkestone fishing fleet in the 1920s, now depleted due to the government quotas to help preserve fish stocks. This has spread discontent among the fishermen, saying so many fish are thrown back as quotas are reached; such a shame as dead fish are no good back in the sea when they can be for our use.

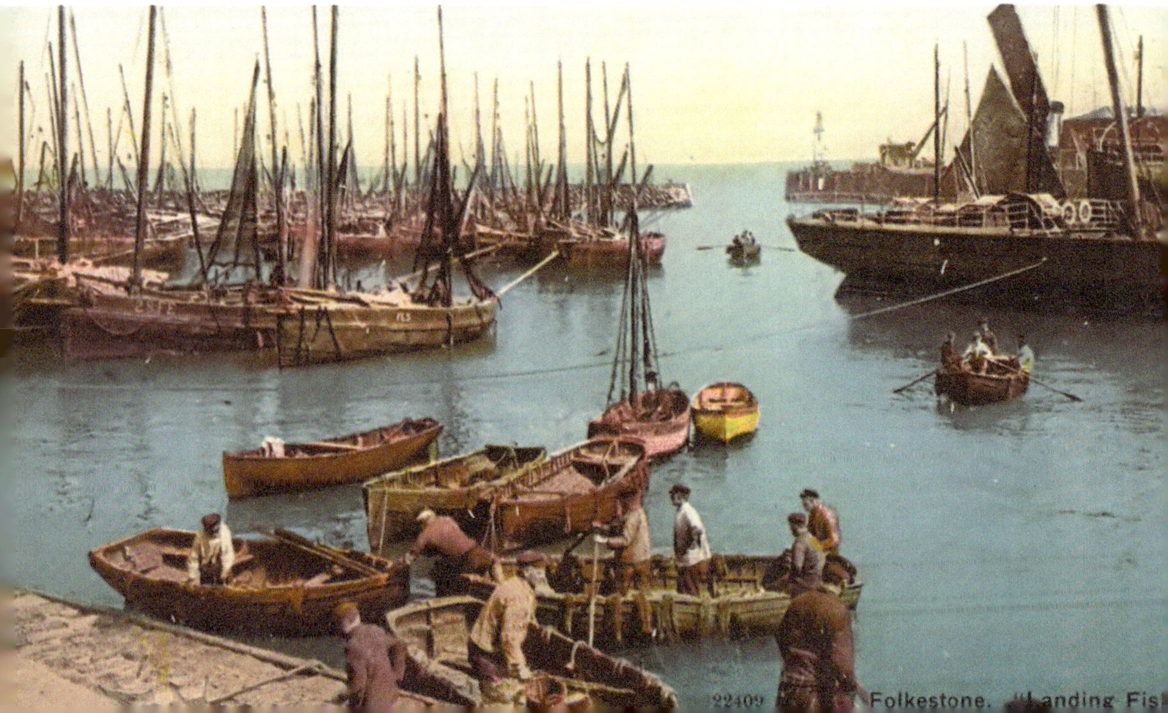

Folkestone Goalie, 1923

Right: Bill Goodman from East Street. His love of football paid off when he became goalkeeper for Folkestone in 1923 and played in the team for many years. Bill also worked for the Folkestone Corporation at the Chalk Pit, Canterbury Road. From one of his football contracts in 1929 he was being paid £2 a week and an extra 5*s* to play midweek.

Below: Rebuilding the Folkestone football team in 1923, the goalie in the middle of the picture with the dark jumper is Bill Goodman. By 1927 he was in the first team and was chosen for the county and won the championship. In 1930/31 Bill had his benefit match and a report on him stated that he gave his finest display in his ten seasons with the club and had the safest pair of hands they knew. When playing against Huddersfield, the goalie opposite to Bill ran down the field to shake his hand. Despite many offers from northern teams to leave Folkestone and go professional he refused and played only for Folkestone.

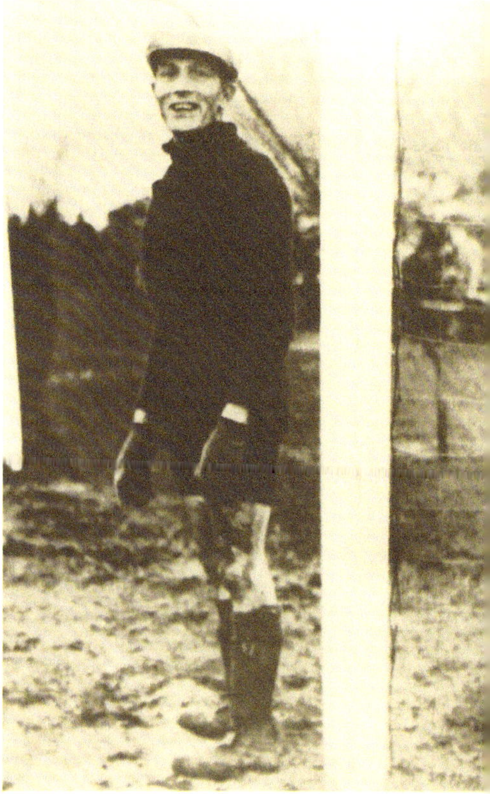

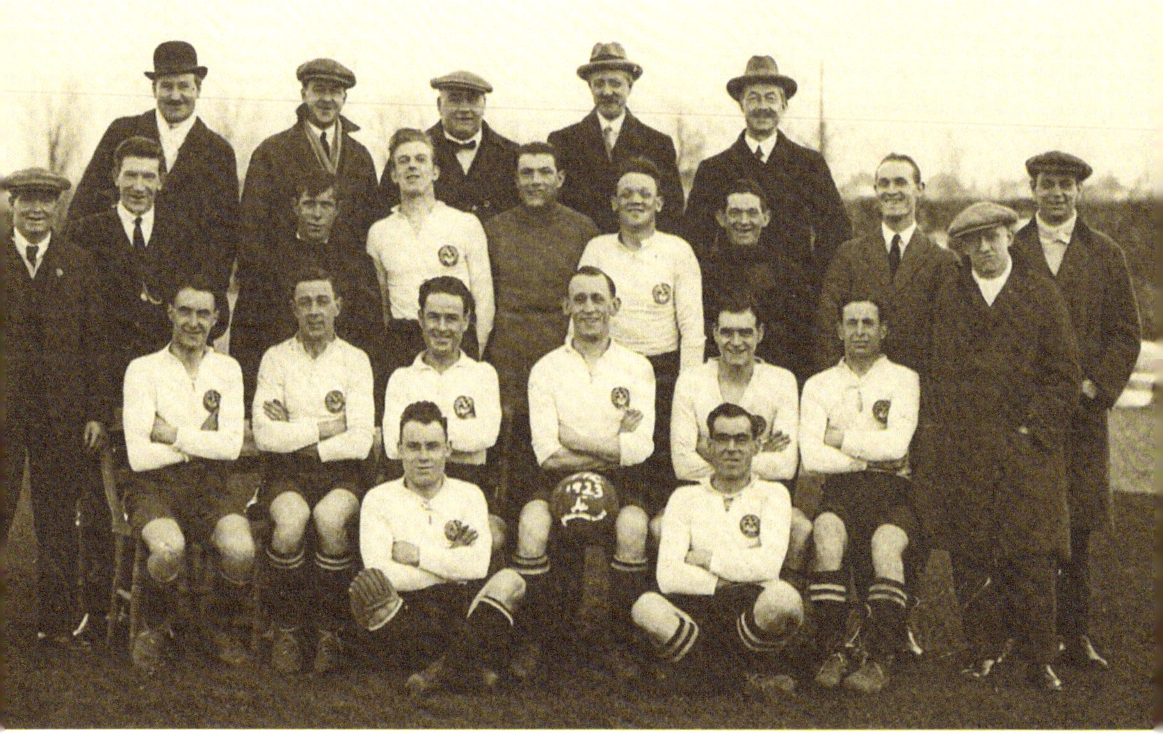

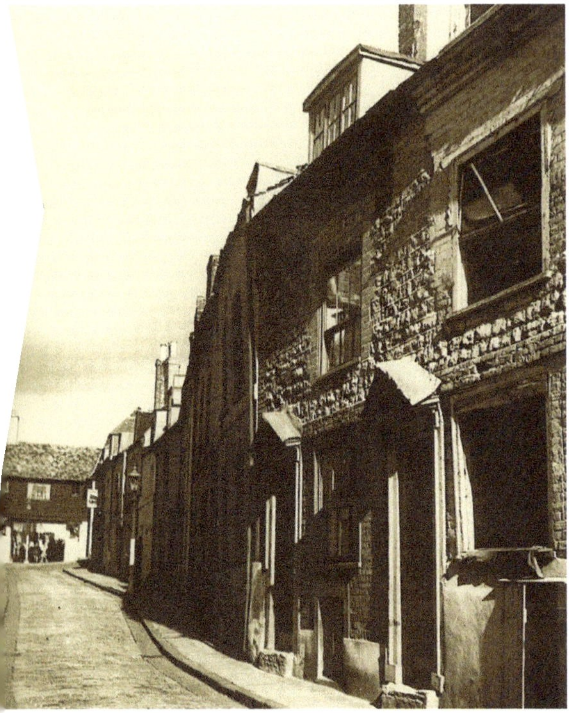

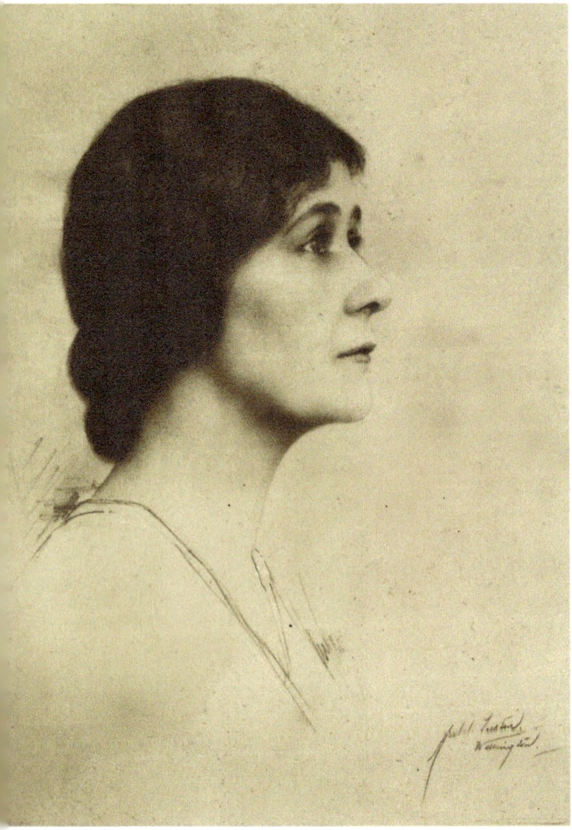

From Folkestone's Poor Fishing Quarter to Australia's Bright Lights

Left: North Street, built in the 1690s, as it looked before 1940. Part of the old fishing quarter of Folkestone, which was bombed during the Second World War and rebuilt into flats in the 1950s. In the late 1890s William Harvey Marsh and his family lived at No. 24 with his wife Elizabeth (née Milton) and their five children, born from 1883 to 1900. Sadly, Elizabeth died in childbirth in 1900 and William in 1908, meaning the eldest of the girls looked after the younger children. Alice Abbott Marsh (1887–1972) later went to Australia and married there in 1911. But what a tale this lady told and lived all her life...

Bottom left: I was told her story by Alice's granddaughter. It sounded as if Alice was a ladies' companion who travelled Europe and saw many interesting places and ended up in Australia where she married as Elsie and lived her life out as Alvisio Le Faye. It wasn't until after her death that her granddaughter decided to trace the family tree, starting with her marriage certificate which stated she was Elsie Marsh instead of Alice. Her deceased father, William, was a fisherman from Folkestone. After much research it was revealed that Alice married the very talented Emanuel Aarons, a musician and composer who toured and played in Australia and New Zealand. The name Alvisio, it appears, was Elsie's stage name. Was this lady ashamed to be a daughter of a fisherman? She kept her secret by pretending she was a French gypsy. She would tell tales saying 'you haven't lived until you have danced in a Gypsy camp to their music'. However, Alice was possibly of gypsy descent: her grandmother was said to be of gypsy origin but was born and lived in Chatham, Kent, in a house in the 1820s.

So Alvisio was our Alice who went to Australia on a help scheme with the Salvation Army, and by all intents her husband went along with her alias. Alice's daughter Anita, who had a suite of music written and dedicated to her by her father, would not accept her mother was anything other than French and born in France.

Would You Like a Brandy Sir?

Right: The Three Mackerels at The Stade. This old pub was where Richard Sanders, a fisherman, and his wife Betsy lived. She ran the pub when her husband was at sea. It was reported that to deceive the revenue men Betsy would walk around the fish market with a large basket of washing, with bottles of brandy concealed under the clothes. The Three Mackerels was demolished in the 1930s, along with other buildings in the fish market area, in a slum clearance purge. When the old building was being demolished the workmen found a secret panel and behind it was a room to hide their secret booty – bottles of brandy. The building that replaced it was The Odd Fellow's Arms, now named The Captain's Table.

Below: The picture of The Three Mackerels' replacement was built in the mid-1930s and is now named The Captain's Table. To the front-left of the picture is the Smokehouse restaurant. The tall building next to it is the take-away part. Opened in 2011, it has accommodation above, which is let out to summer visitors.

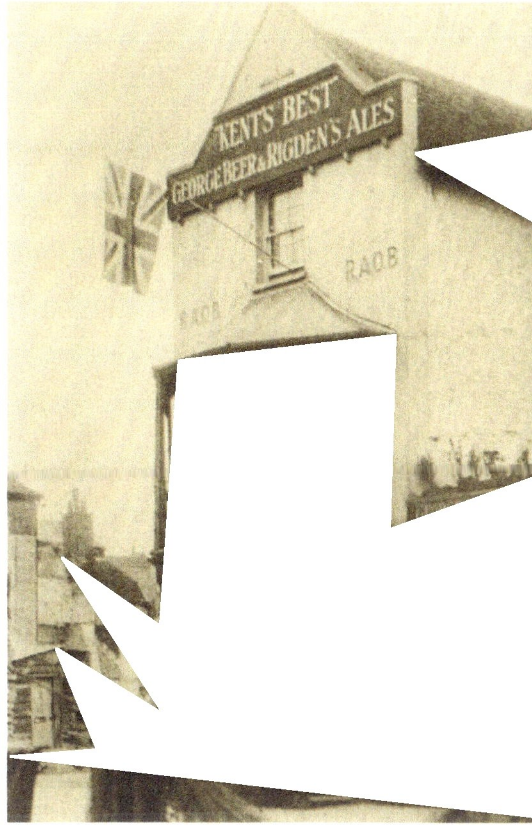

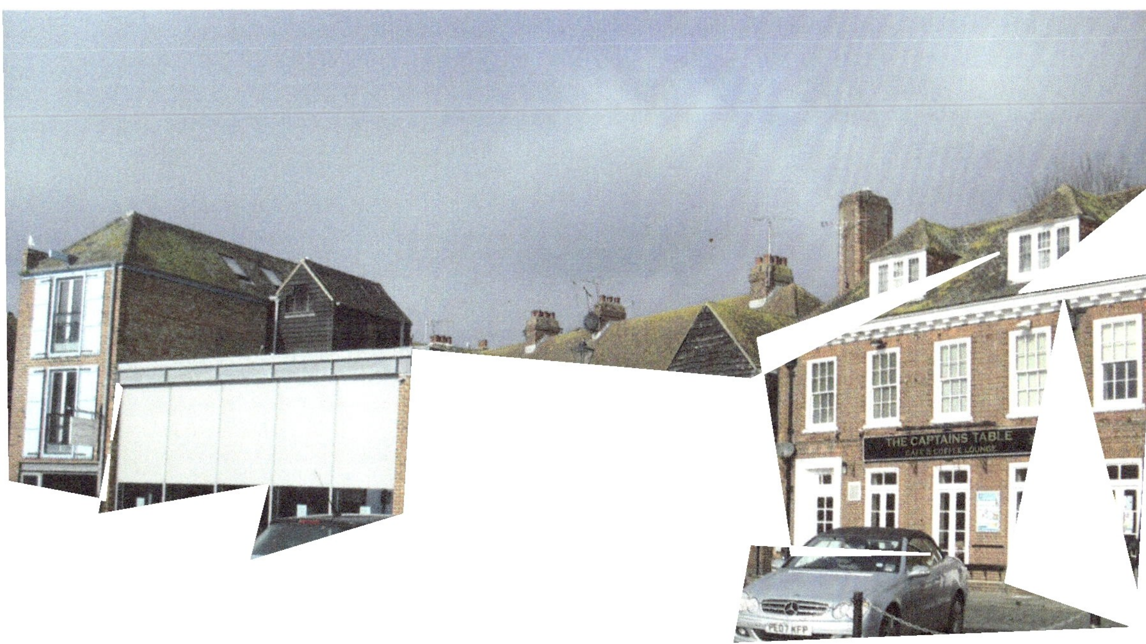

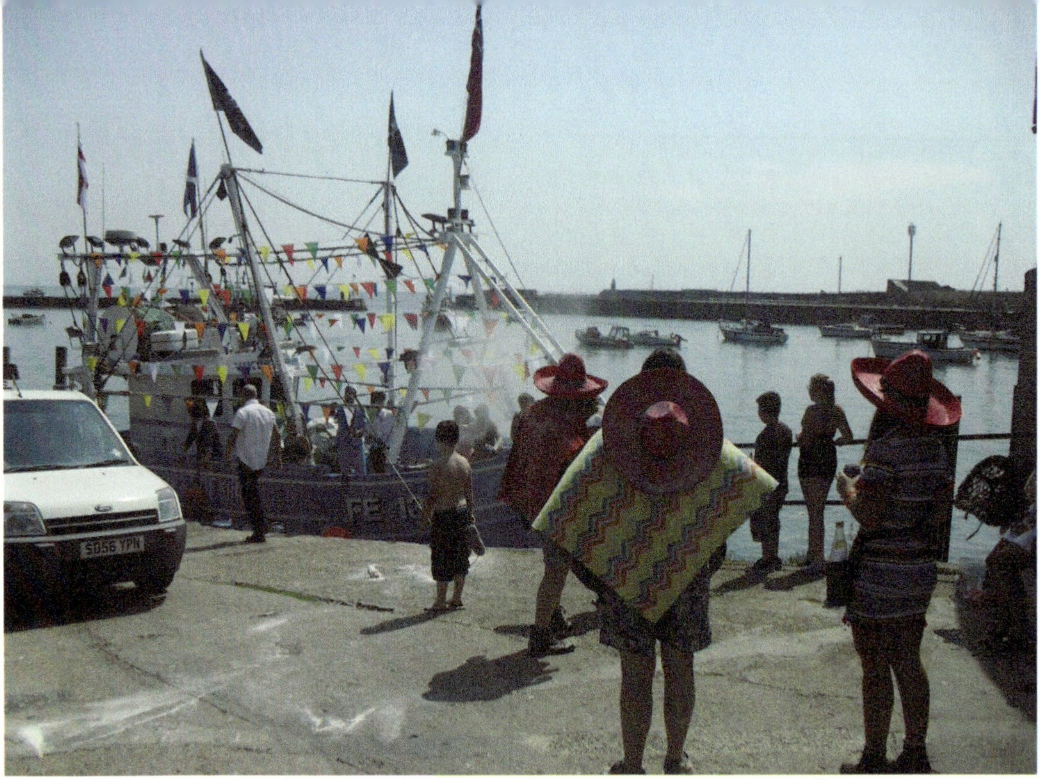

Pirates in Our Harbour!

Above: The fishermen of Folkestone hold an annual fancy-dress boat race. This picture, taken on 26 July 2014, is of one of the first boats back that year. They sail out of the harbour and then race back again. On the way they have flour fights and plenty of camaraderie. The people on the boat above threw some flour as it docked in the harbour, covering everyone who was close to them.

Below: Two smaller boats just arriving back into the harbour are having a flour fight before docking. It was a nice day, which it made it all the more enjoyable for the contestants and visitors alike.

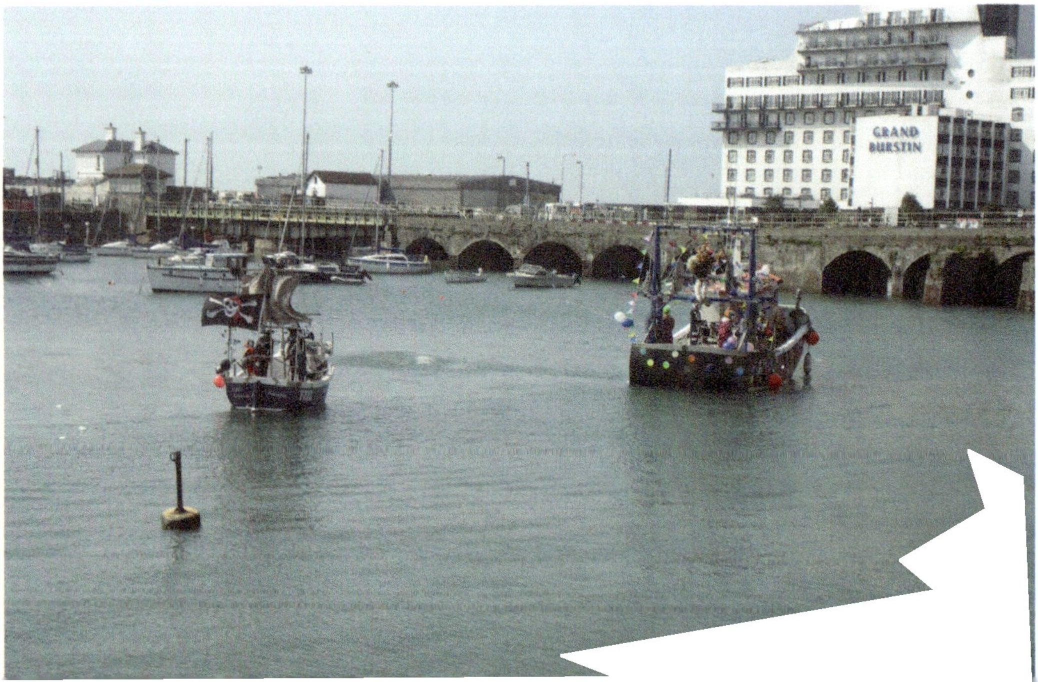

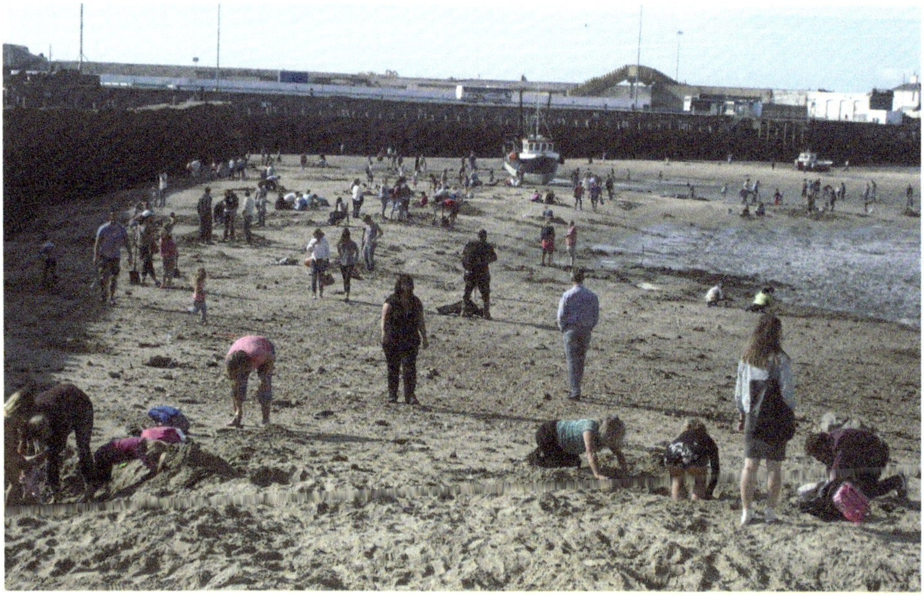

Digging for Gold; Better than Fracking for Gas!
The two exhibits shown here were part of the 2014 Triennial Art Festival.

Above: People digging for gold in the sand in August 2014. As part of Folkestone's Triennial events, Michael Sailstorfer, an artist, buried thirty pieces of 24-carat gold worth around £250 each as his artistic entry for the people to find and keep.

Bottom: Sarah Staton's sculpture *Steve* glances back to famous twentieth-century predecessors. Sarah felt that the edible plants around *Steve* and plenty of seating made it welcoming for the twenty-first century.

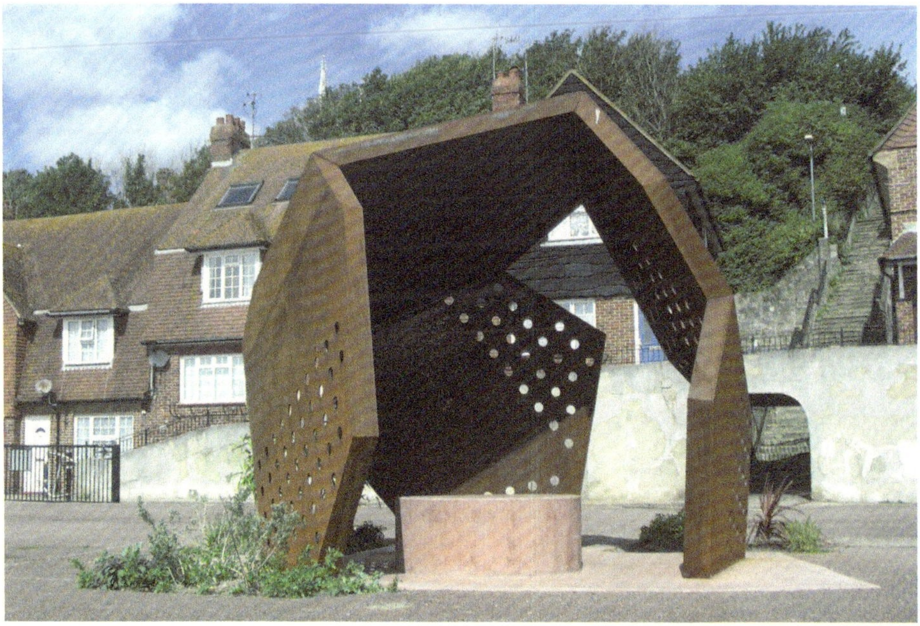

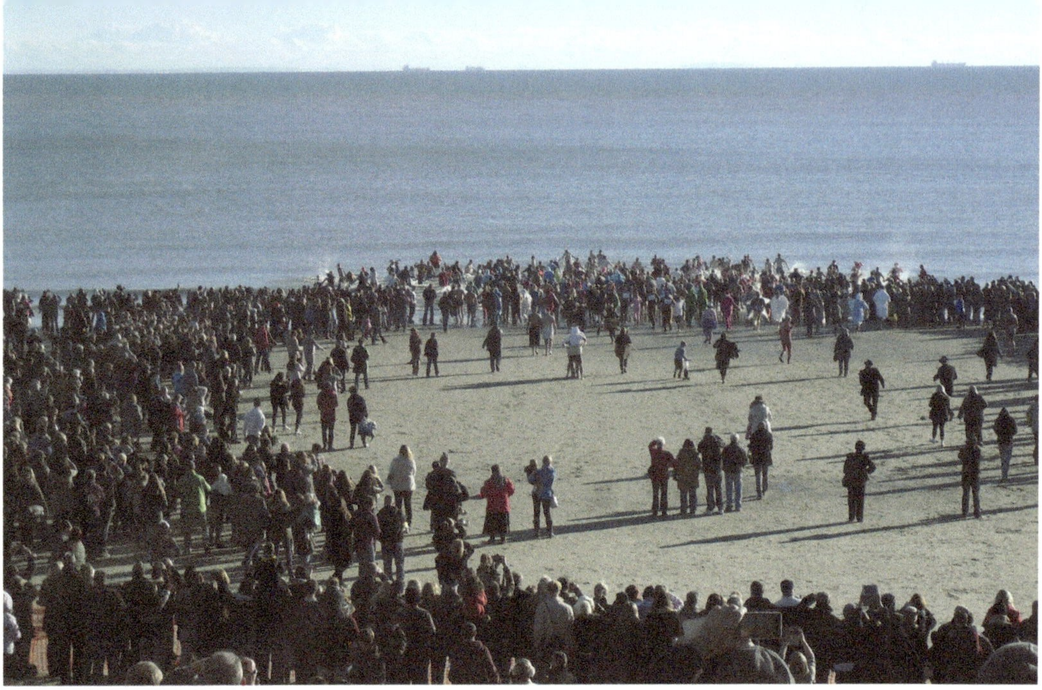

Fancy a Boxing Day Dip?

Above: The traditional Boxing Day fancy-dress dip organised by the Folkestone Lion's club to raise money for local charities. Before the horn blows to signal people to run in to the sea, the organisers ask who is the oldest and the youngest swimmer, and then they judge what is the best fancy-dressed person or group. Everyone who participates receives a medal for their effort. Every year everyone wonders what the state of the sea will be. Last year, as with many other years, I watched this event and the sea has always been very calm.

Below: A picture of the same area, a week previous to the event in 2014. What a difference you can see in the sea; I sure wouldn't want to swim in the sea if it was rough like this.

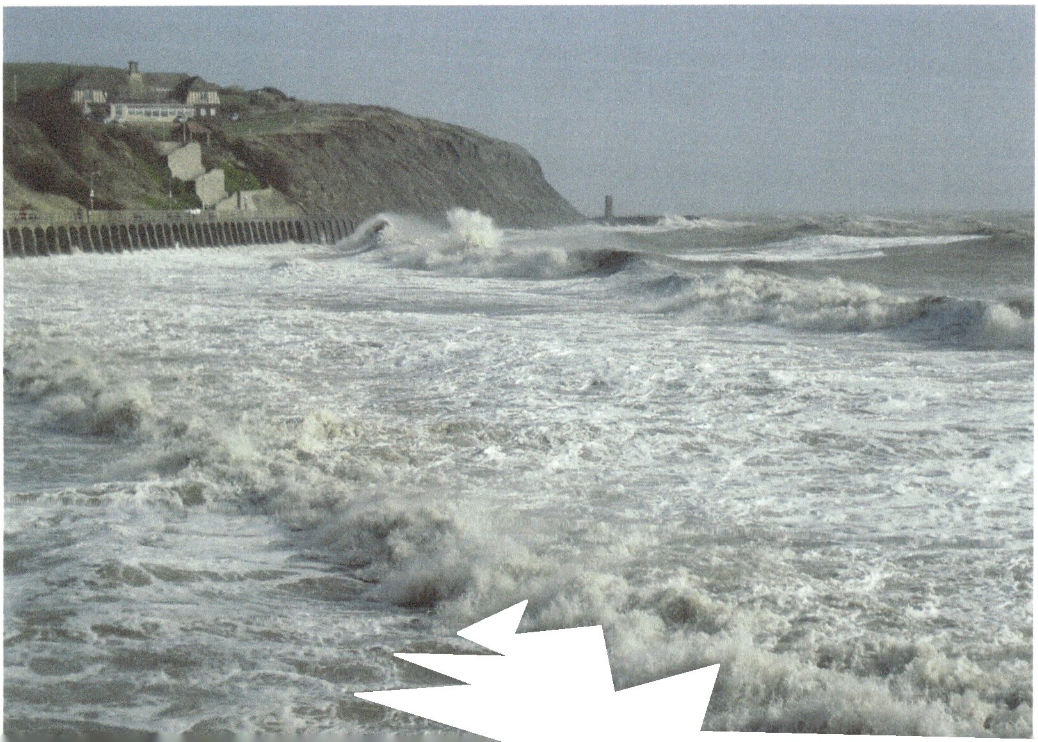

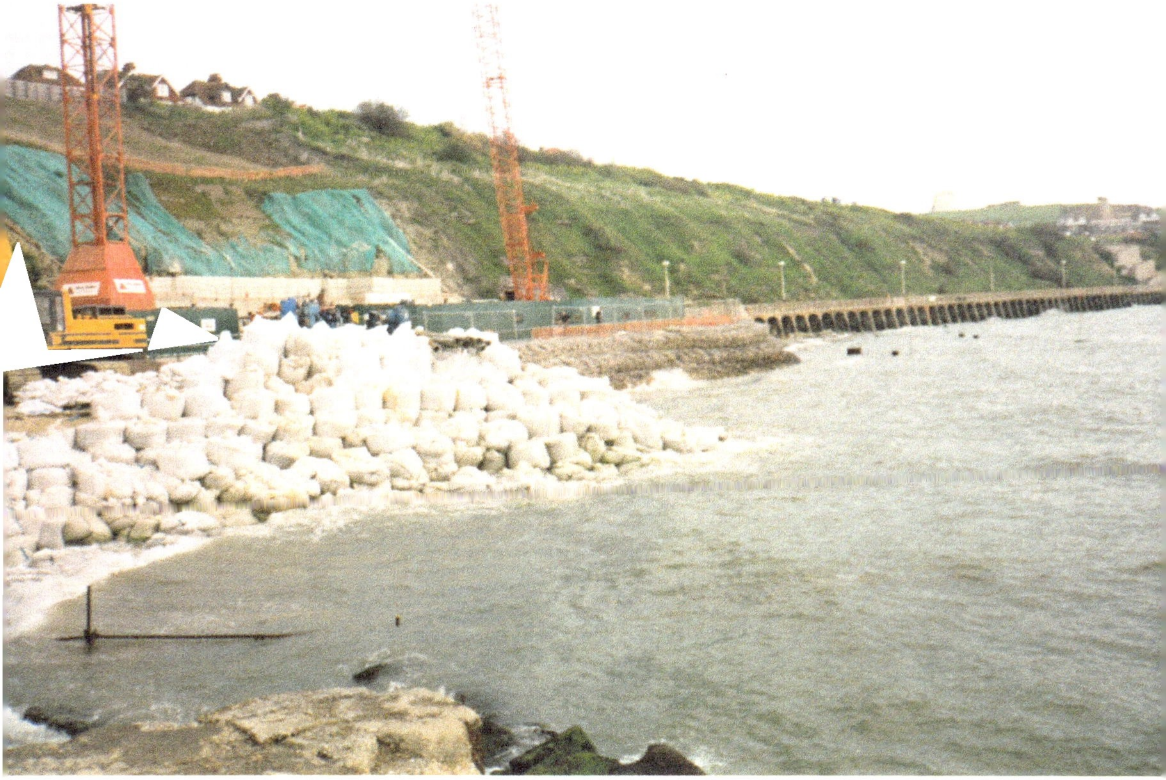

What Are They Doing to Our Sands Bathing Area?

Above: Southern Water preparing to build a new sewer outlet under the sand area of Folkestone in 1998. The old sewer pipe outfall was considered not far enough out to sea so a new treatment works was built on the Old Junction railway-marshalling site. It continued down to the seafront.

Below left: The sewer trap, in February 2000, ready to be covered over.

Below right: Here you can see a ship laying the sewer pipes that eventually went much further out to sea for health and safety reasons. Before the sewer was put into operation an ex-paramedic told me he went down the pipe from its source to the end on a motorised cart. This was to assess if it was feasible in case paramedics had to go down there to attend anyone working in the pipe.

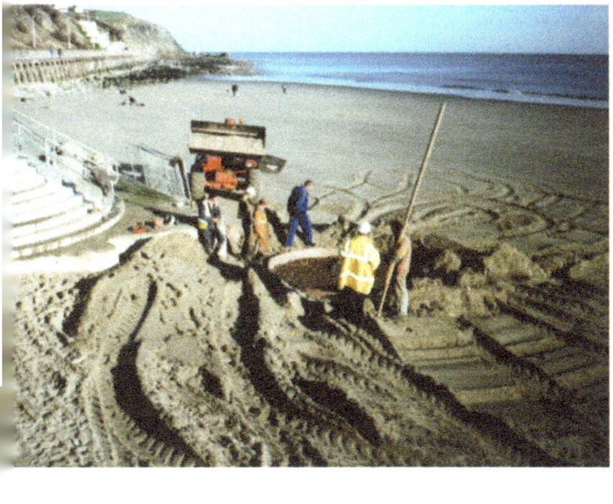

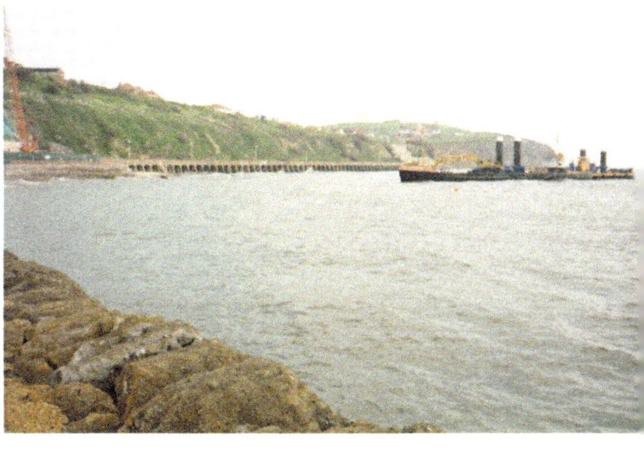

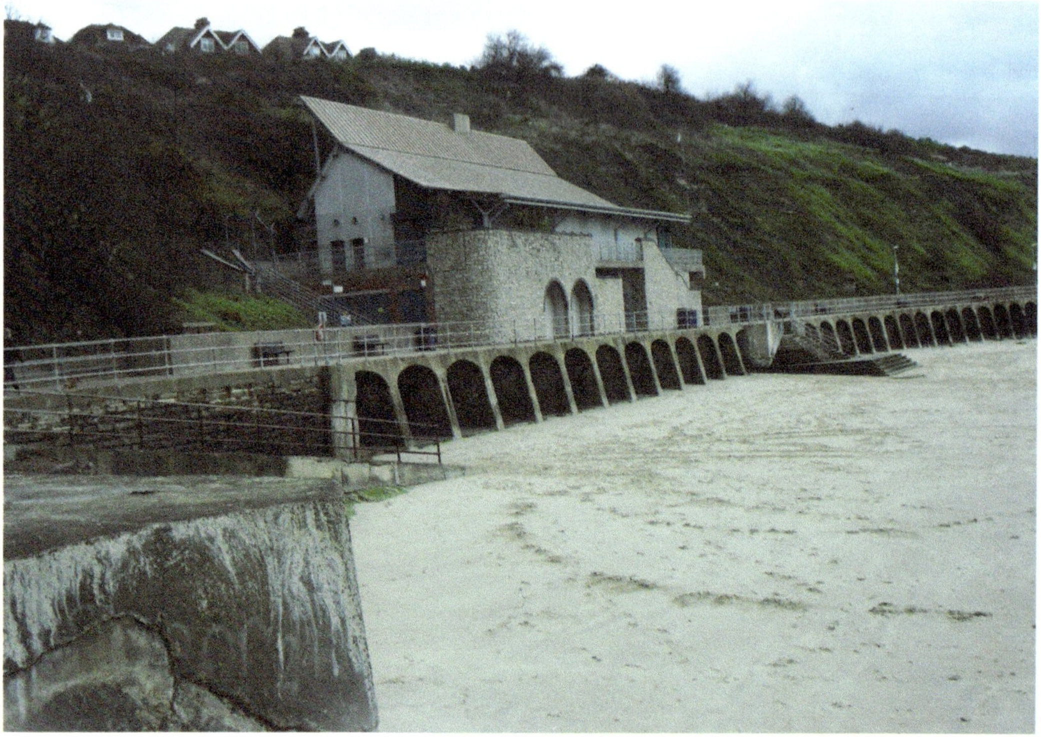

Our Very Own Mermaid

Above: The building finished in 2000, with a café and toilets, fronting the sewer works that continues out to sea for about 3 miles. There is a nice flight of steps leading down to the sands.

Below left: Just a few yards from the modern sewer building is this old sewer outfall, that had metal railings, covering the door shaped areas. From an Ordnance Survey map of 1895 it shows a sewer pipe leading from this projection under the sand, running about fifty feet down to the sea, in line with the East Head wall.

Below right: With the second Triennial of 2011, Georgina Baker, a Folkestonian mother of two, was chosen to model for Cornelia Parker to make a bronze mermaid, in the pose of the little mermaid in Copenhagen. The statue was purchased for the people of Folkestone with money from the Art Fund and the Roger De Haan Charitable Trust at a cost of £25,000.

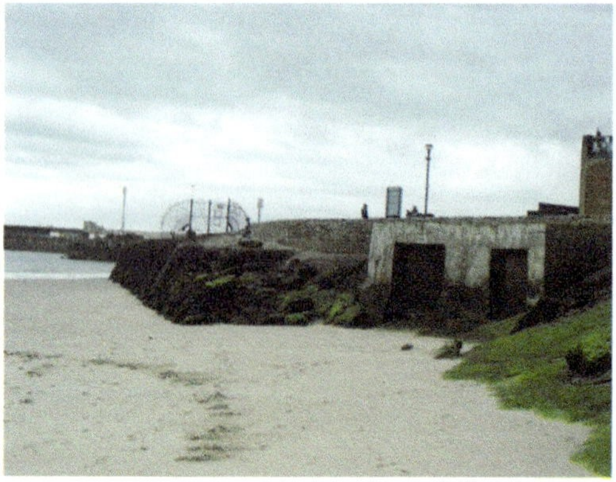

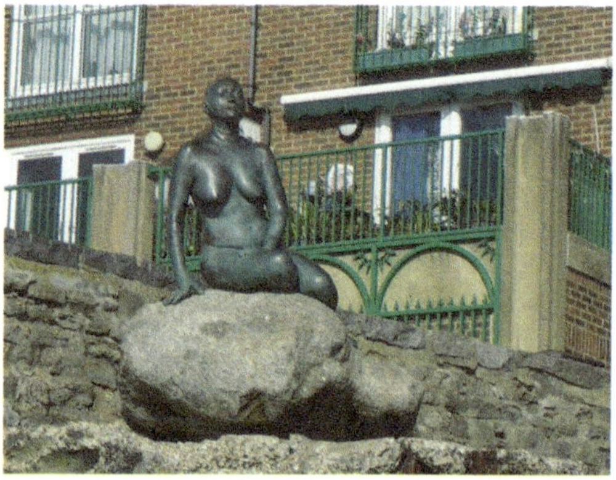

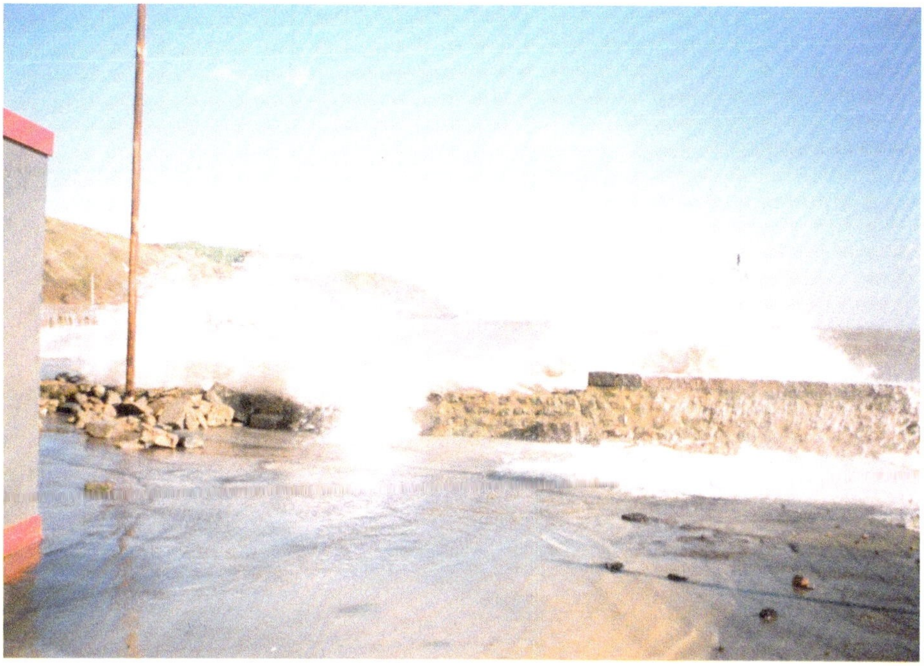

Exciting but Dangerous
Above: The rough seas in January 1990 at the Folkestone Sands area. Note the sea as high as the cliffs pounding Coronation Parade.

Below: A few minutes later the sea breaching the wall leaving debris a good 20 feet along the path. As you can see from the photograph I had to run quickly out of the way. It was quite frightening to have brick particles being hurled around you.

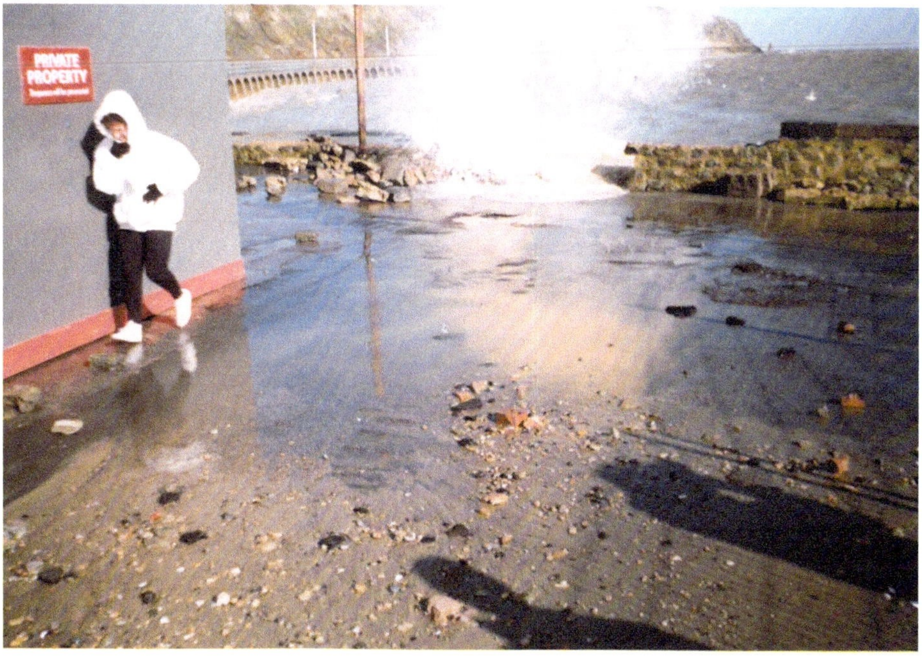

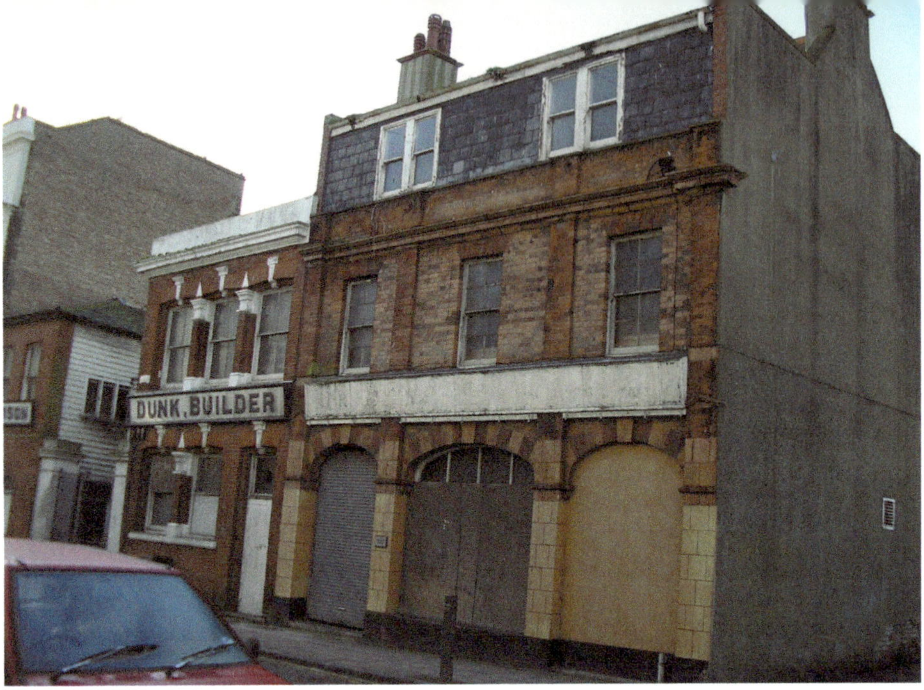

From Builders to a Theatre

Above: Dunk Builders Nos 45–47 Tontine Street; next door at No. 49 was a Fremlins Beer retailer and in the 1980s a cake shop. This area was demolished around 2003 and plans for the theatre were produced in 2006. Dunk's was an old family firm trading in Folkestone since the 1850s. They built St Saviour's church in 1895 and helped with H. G. Wells' mansion in Sandgate. They also built many schools in Dover and Canterbury after the Second World War. In 1999, the receivers were called and forty men were made redundant. Sadly, Dunk Builders came to an end.

Below: The Quarterhouse Theatre venue that replaced Nos 45–49 Tontine Street, which opened in 2009. It holds all sorts of venues for the arts: theatrical, musical and the annual Folkestone's Book Festival in November, with many well-known authors as well as local authors. Its metal facing shape is meant to replicate seashells, but the locals call it 'The Cheese Grater' as close up that is what the metal looks and feels like.

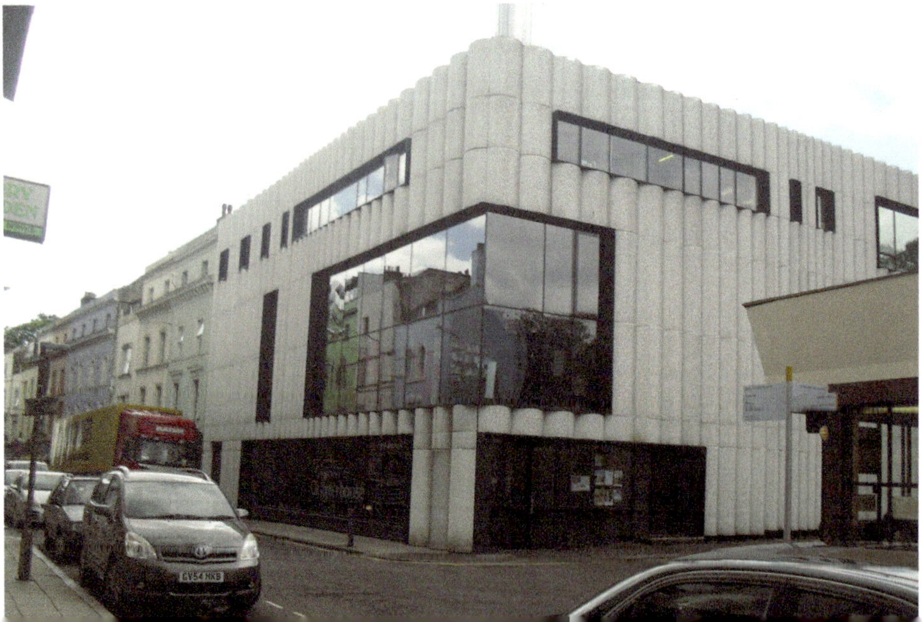

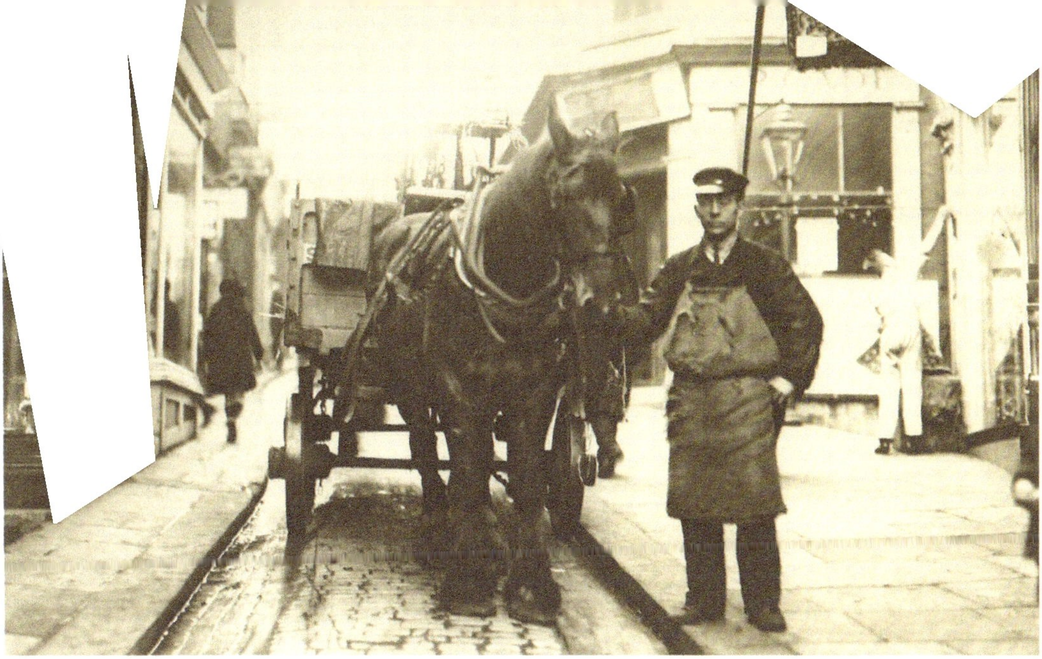

Tale of the Horse

Above: Robert Garnham with his horse and cart, in the Old High Street, on his delivery round in the 1920s. Robert, born 1889, went into the army when the First World War broke out and was sent to Ypres. When they had to go over the top he was shot in the knee. Luckily he was rescued and sent back to England where he was discharged as being unfit to serve. He recovered sufficiently to get a job at the Junction Station parcels department and a horse and cart was provided for him to make the deliveries to shops, hotels and the public. Robert lived at No. 105 Blackbull Road and would often pop home for a cup of tea when on his rounds. One day after his cuppa he went out to find the horse gone. On looking up and down the road he saw the horse at the horse trough at the bottom of the road having a drink.

Below: The view Robert would see today at the bottom of Blackbull Road standing outside his house. The red car is where the drinking trough used to stand.

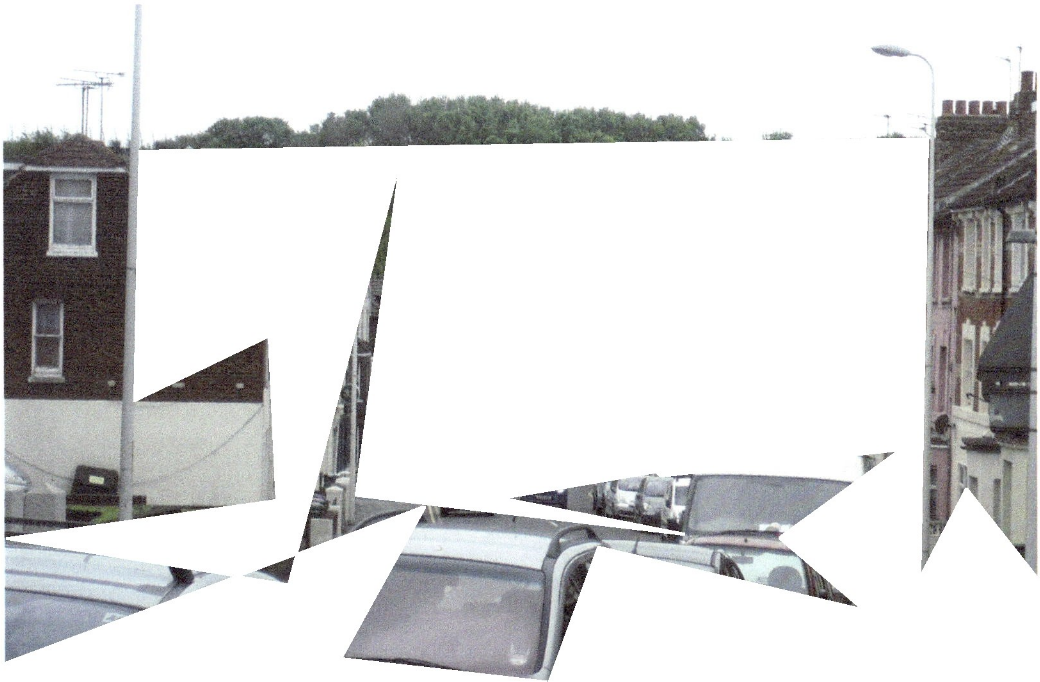

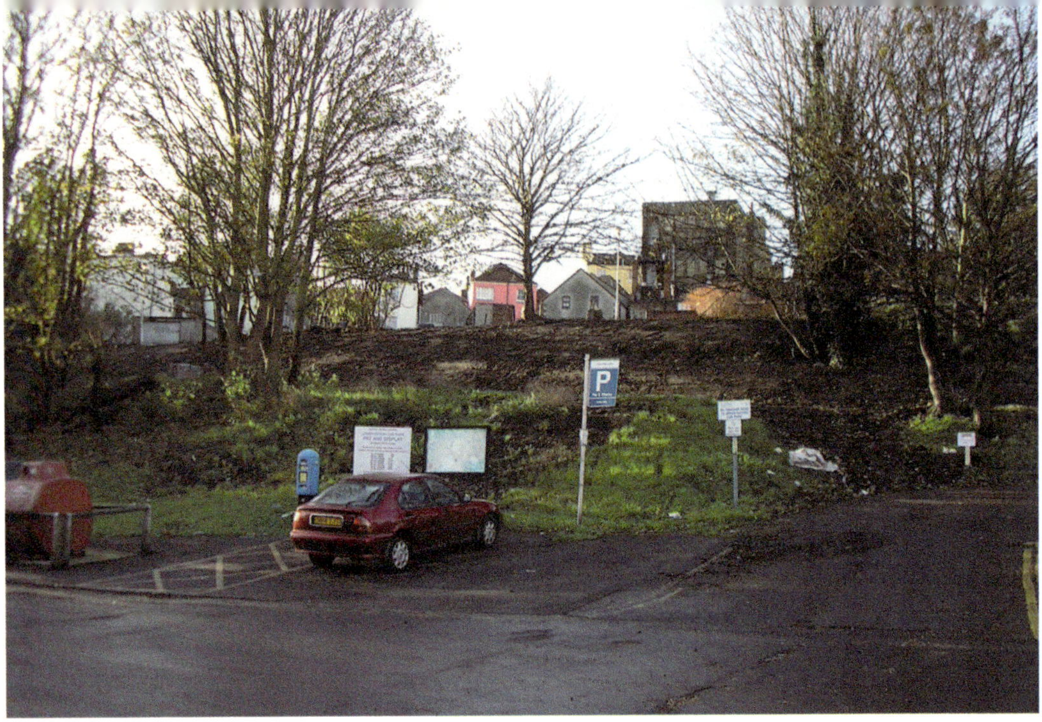

At Long Last, Payers Park Landscaped

Above: Mill Bay looking up to Payers Park in 2000, such a steep hilly area, unused for many years. When the third Folkestone Triennial was being organised, it was suggested that the area be made a permanent park for the public's use. The park was developed in partnership with funding from the Roger De Haan Trust, Kent County Council and the Heritage Lottery Fund.

Below: The park was finished on time for the start of the Triennial in August 2014 and the grand opening was performed by the following, from left to right: Cllr Pamela Carr, Chair Shepway District Council, Kent County Council Cabinet Minister for Economic Development, Mark Dance, Chair of Kent County Council Peter Homewood, Leader of Shepway District Council David Monk, Sir Roger De Haan, Lewis Biggs, curator of Folkestone Triennial.

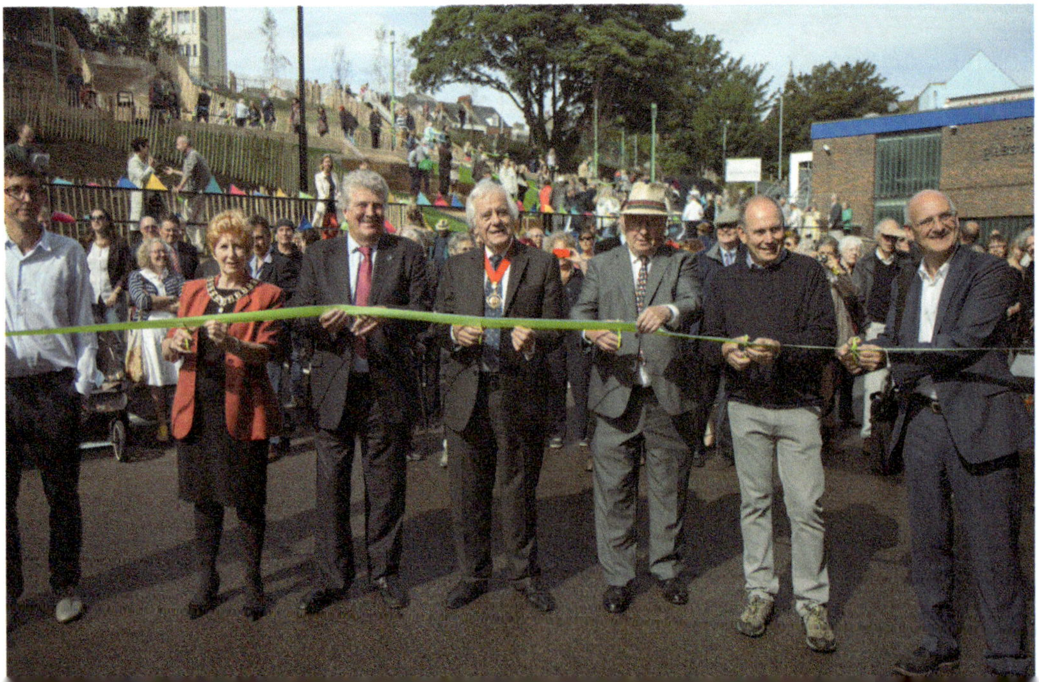

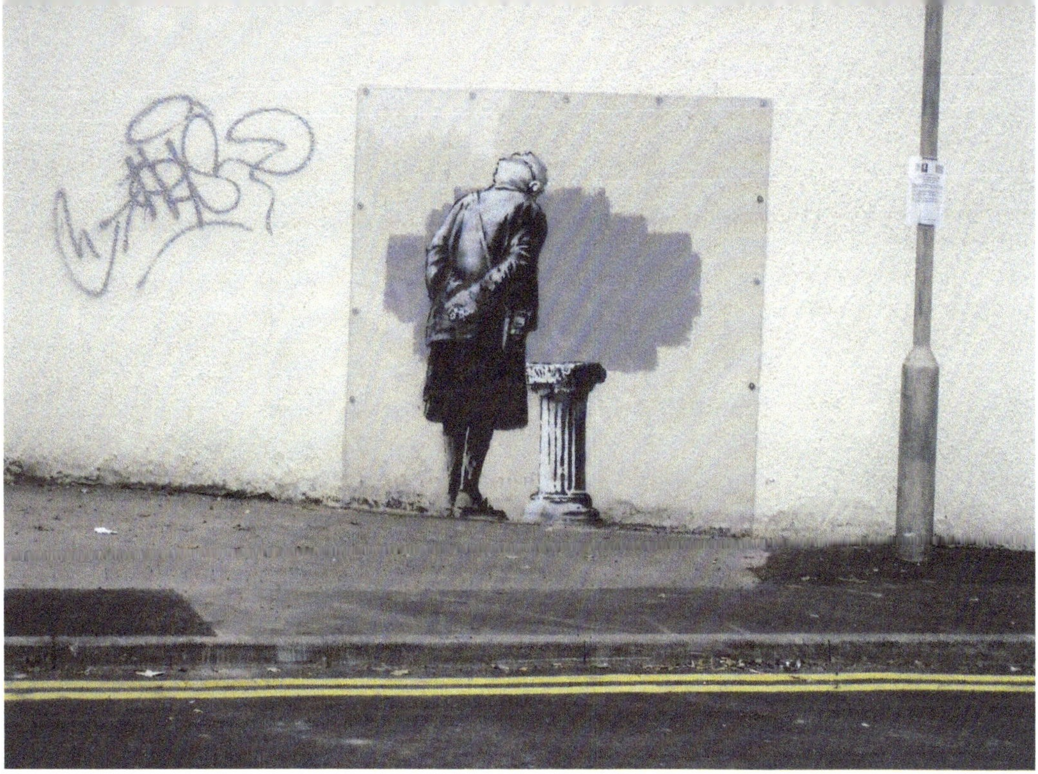

Exciting Late Addition to the Triennial

Above: A Bansky piece, which he called *Art Buff*, appeared overnight in September 2014 on a wall in the Payers Park area. Shortly after Shepway Council covered it with a sheet of protective perspex. On Banksy's website he referred to it as 'part of Folkestone Triennial. Kind of'. On 30 September, much to the locals disgust, the *Art Buff* was removed and sent to America for sale it was expected to sell for about £450,000. Pest Control, the agent who verifies Banksy work, said the *Art Buff* had not been authenticated and that the work was for the people and not to be sold. Banksy had picked up on the vibes of the people wanting it to remain in Folkestone, but the *Art Buff* remains in New York's Keszler Gallery and with the hopes of the Folkestone people, it will be returned as a permanent site has been suggested for it.

Below left: I couldn't resist standing beside the *Art Buff*, deep in thought as well, wondering if graffiti artists would deface it.

Below right: After the *Art Buff* was removed another sign appeared in its place, from a local graffiti artist.

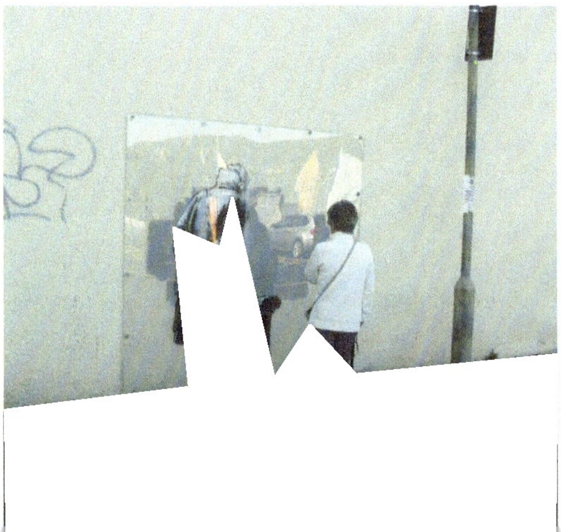

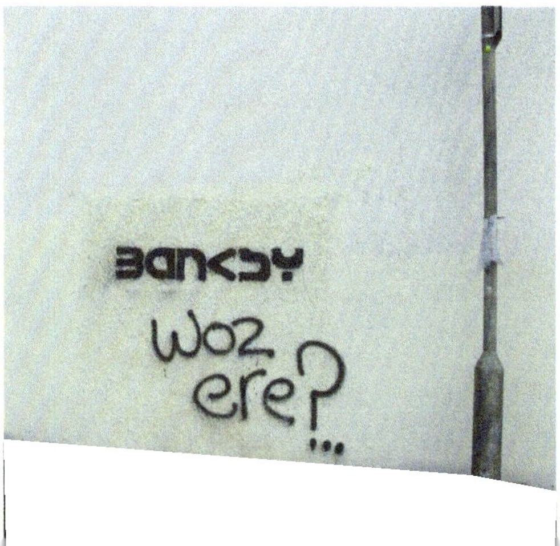

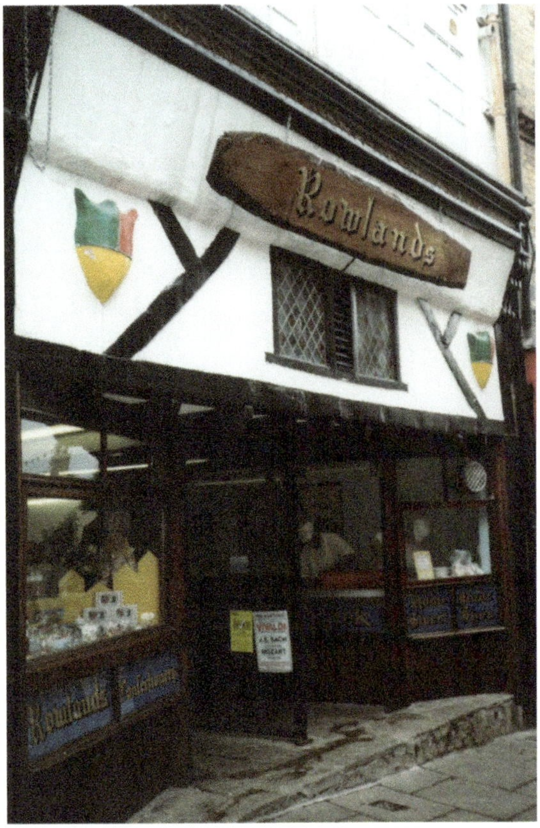

The Demise of Our Rock Shop

Left: Rowlands Rock shop at No. 17 the Old High Street was a fascinating shop, where we could watch John Brickell and his son Daniel making rock. Often a little window would open and you were given a sample. Sadly when the property was taken over in the regeneration of the High Street the much-loved shop front was destroyed and a new one replaced it.

Below: No. 17 is now occupied by The Great British Shop Ltd, with many gifts all made in Britain.

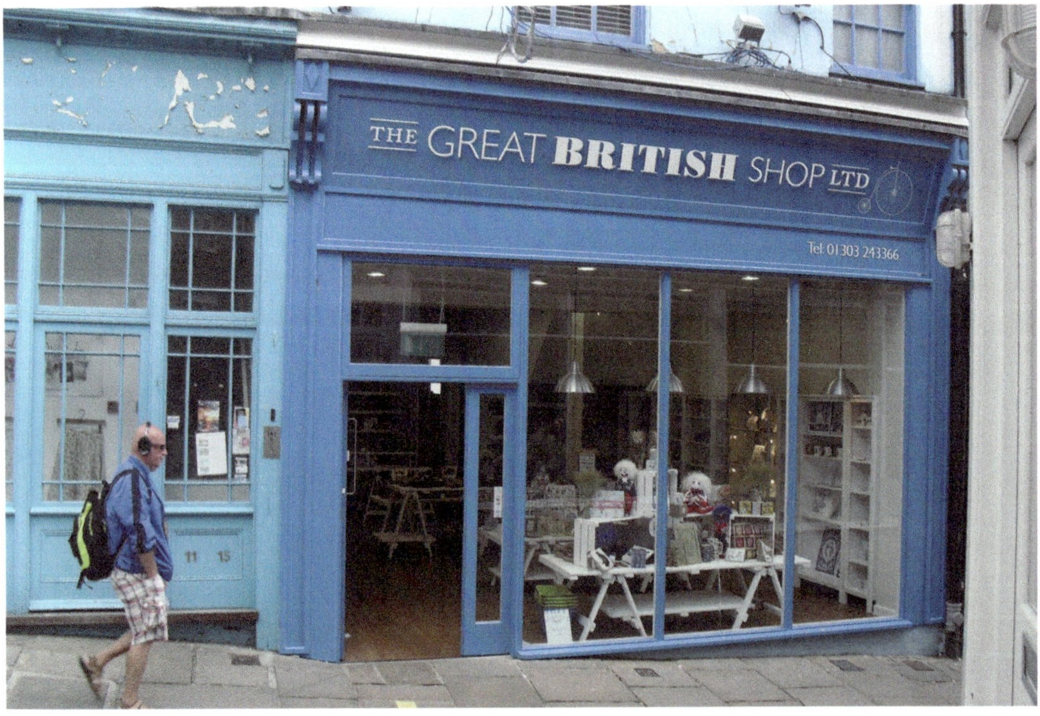

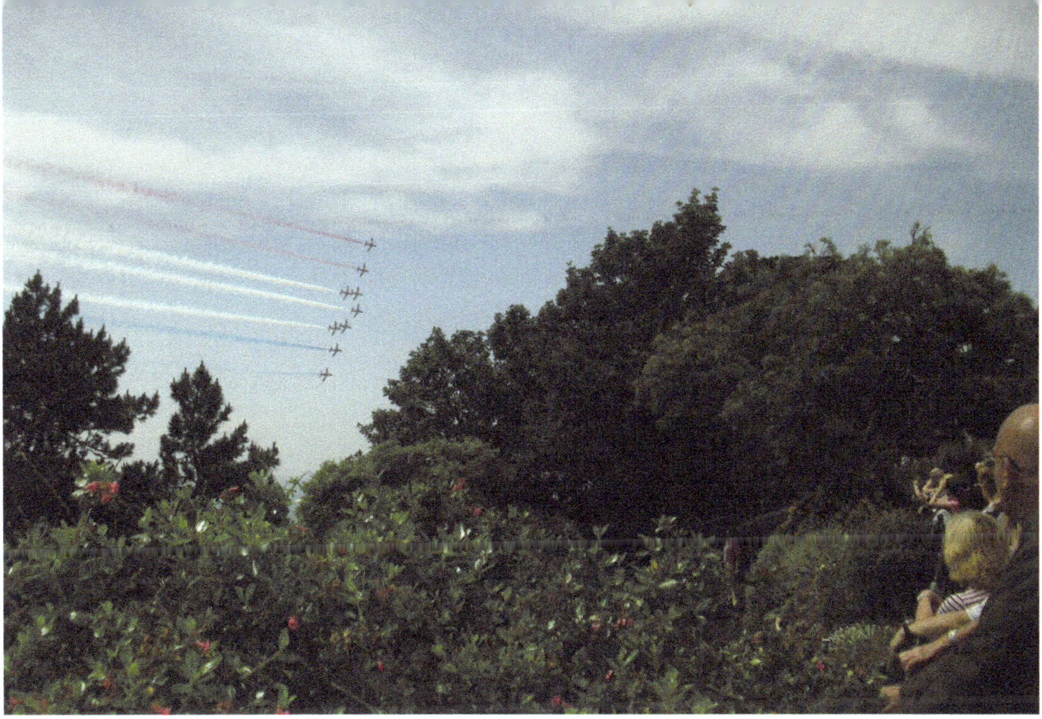

The Last Visit of the Red Arrows – Folkestone Air Show, 7 June 2014

Above: Folkestone hosted many events during 2014. This lovely shot of the Red Arrows was taken on the Leas at the air show. Sadly this would be the last show held at Folkestone due to financial reasons.

Below: On the same day there was a fair ground situation on the seafront, where at one time Jimmy Godden had his amusement park. This remained for the pleasure of the community for a few days. Just like old times having amusements for the locals and visitors alike.

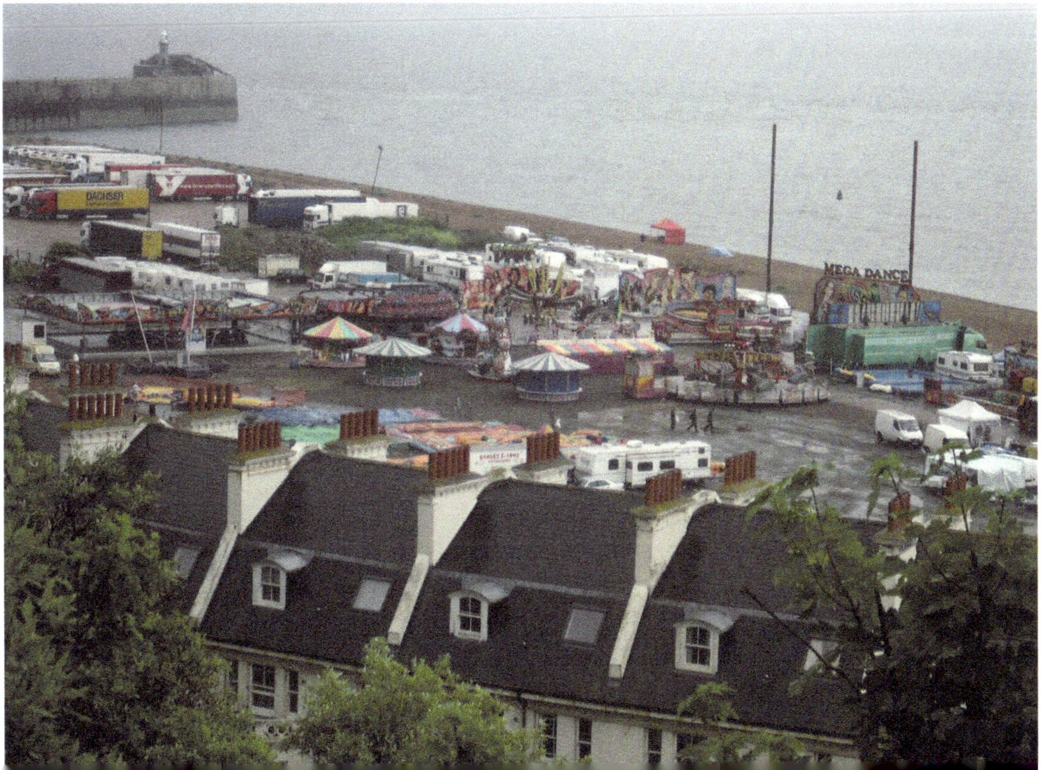

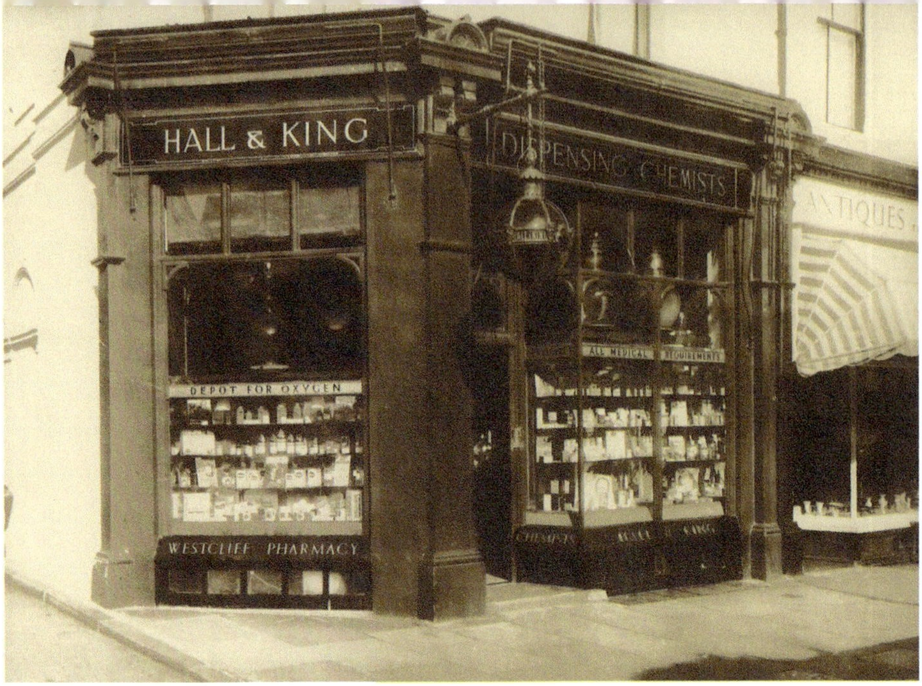

Where Has My Victorian Shop Front Gone?

Above: No. 24 Bouverie Road West, Hall and King's the chemist had traded here under the name of Robert Hall from the mid-1880s, until Mr Williams, a computer repair man took over in recent years. When he took the shop over, on the shelves up high, you could still see the old coloured apothecary bottles and the large ball outside hung on a metal rod that went right through the shop. Sadly the ball disappeared years ago to Deal Theatrical Co. and hasn't been heard of since.

Below: April 2015, a new shop front appeared at No. 24 Bouverie Road West. What a shame this has replaced the splendid old Victorian one in the photograph above. The only original feature remaining is the pole that the ball was attached to – perhaps too difficult to remove, I guess.

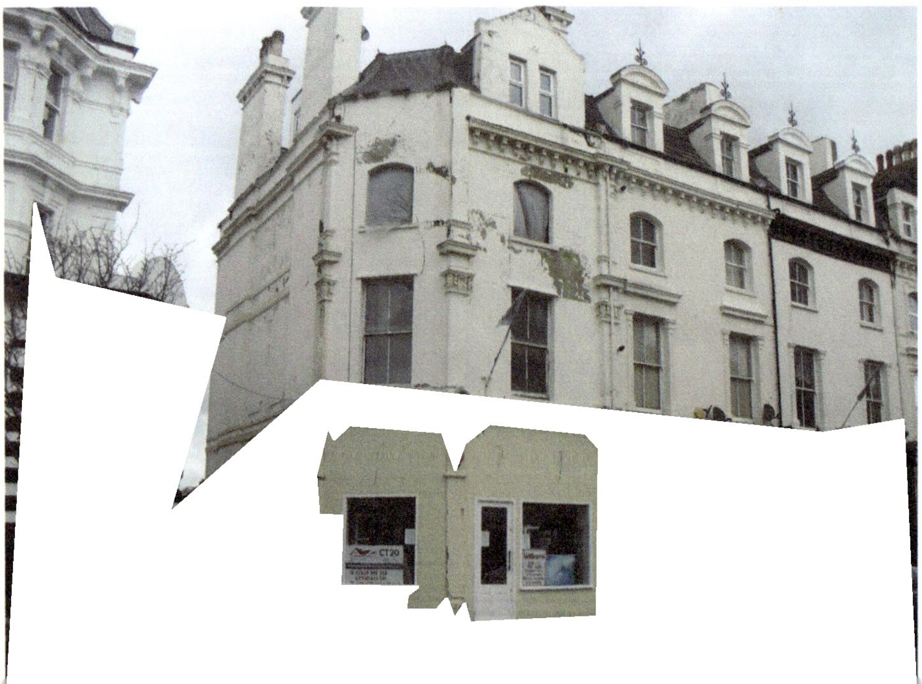

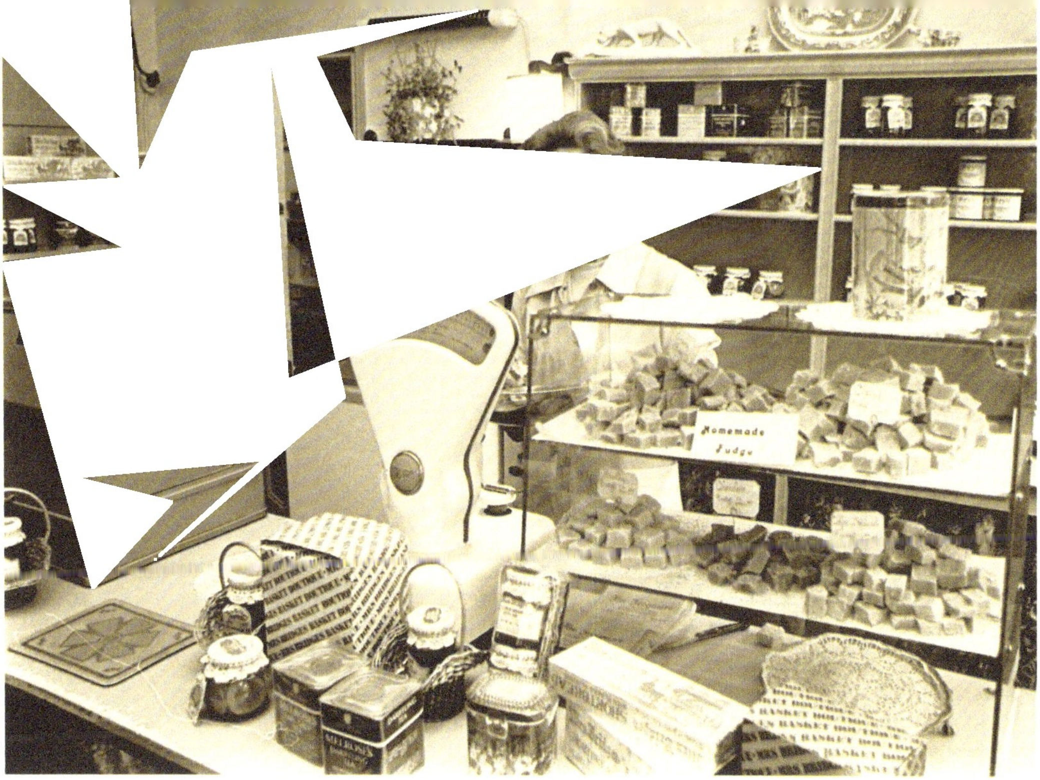

Would You Like Some Home-Made Sweets?
Above: Mrs Mitchell serving at the Frogmore luncheon and tearooms, No. 128 Sandgate Road, in the early 1960s. This was Sam Rockett's Tea Rooms also selling home-made cakes, jams and sweets. Mrs Mitchell said Sam Rocket was a lovely man to work for.

Below: At No. 128 Sandgate Road, in September 2012, the business is now a Pizza Hut. In the 1970s No. 130 was the Halifax Building Society and No. 132 was George Ellis the dental surgeon. Practically all the shops at this end of Sandgate Road are different from what they were forty years ago; alas a sign of the times. The specialist shops are no longer needed and included high-class grocers, the West End Dog Shop, tearooms, men outfitters and high-class shoe shops. However it is no longer financially viable for them to trade.

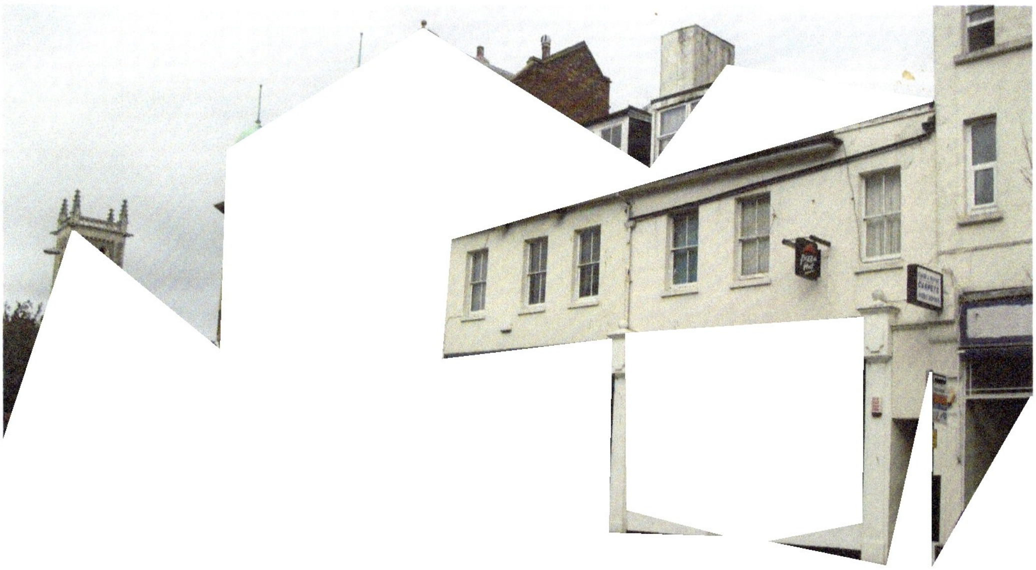

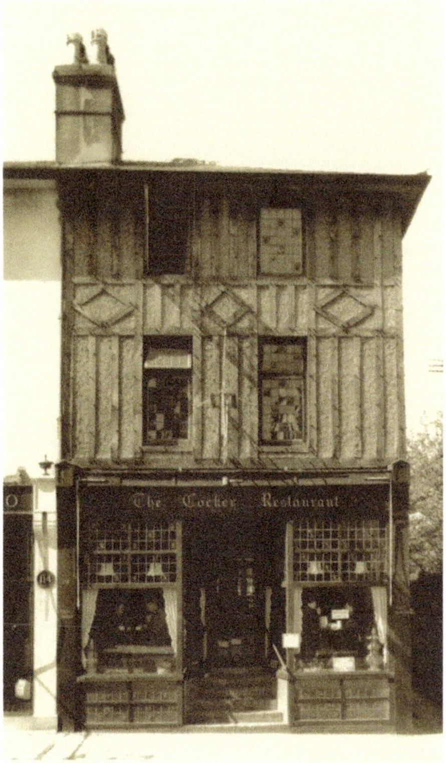

Plate of Cakes and a Pot of Tea

Left: The Cocker Tea Rooms, No. 112 Sandgate Road, was opened in around 1938. This was a very popular tea room and considered to be in the elite part of the town. It was for people who wanted to feel special, and dare I say, felt it was nice to frequent the partaking of tea and cakes.

Below: Papa's the fish and chip shop in 2014, is at No. 110 Sandgate Road, once Finlay and Co. Ltd tobacconists. The Cocker Tea rooms were situated where the gap is today. The gap between No. 112 and 114 Sandgate Road leads to Sainsbury's supermarket and the Town Walk shops.

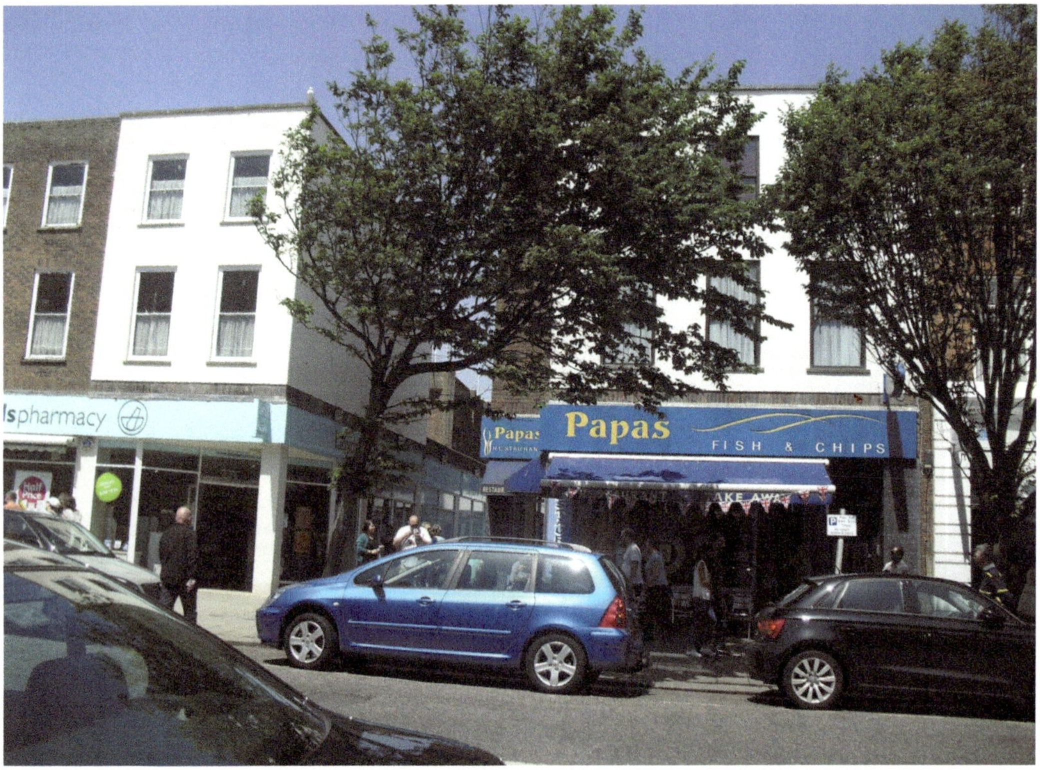

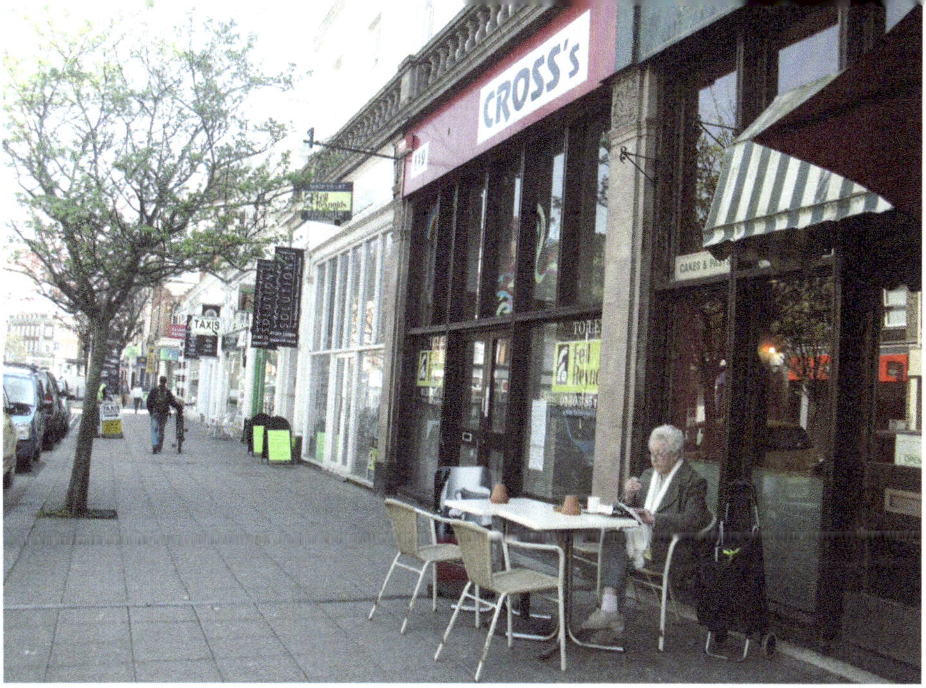

Two More Shops Closing Down

Above: Cross's the stationers, sadly closed on 19 March 2015, having been trading in Sandgate Road for 115 years. They first opened at No. 91 Sandgate Road, and a few years later moved to No. 79; in 1986 moving up the road to No. 119, but as the lease was up they decided not to renew it. Their Ashford shop still remains open to this day. Sitting outside Le Café is Miss Gwen Gould who said she didn't mind being in the photo and was interested in local history being recorded for posterity. A Folkestonian lady, Gwen was born in Dunn's Alley and her ancestors were the Hall family from the fish market.

Below: Pickwick's of No. 2 Church Street, another unique shop with the lease expired and not being renewed owing to lack of trade. Linda and Charles Carmichael have been trading there for twenty-five years and are naturally sad to be leaving. You can still see them at their shop in Cheriton High Street, Rochefort's newsagents, where they have been for the past fourteen years and hope to go on trading for many years to come.

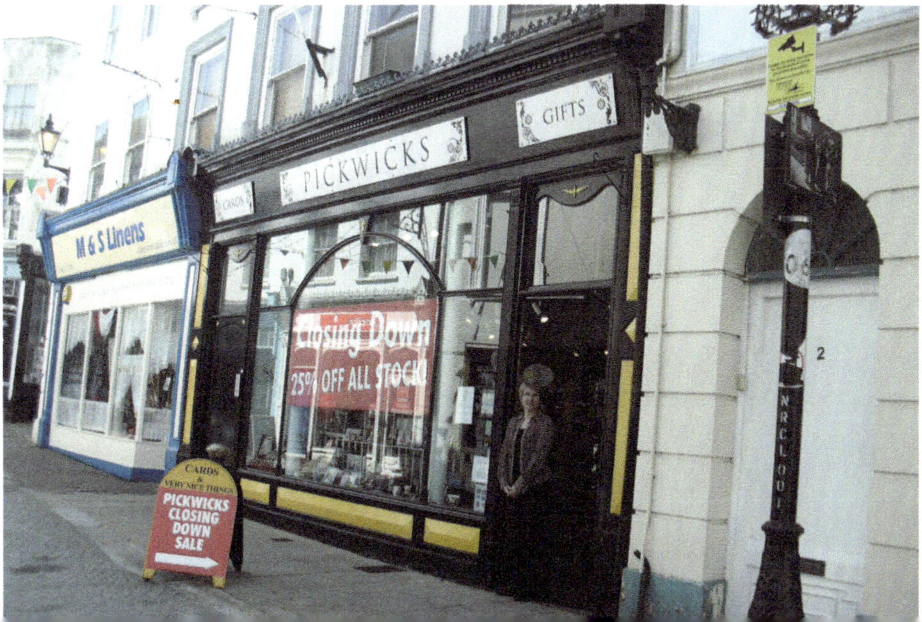

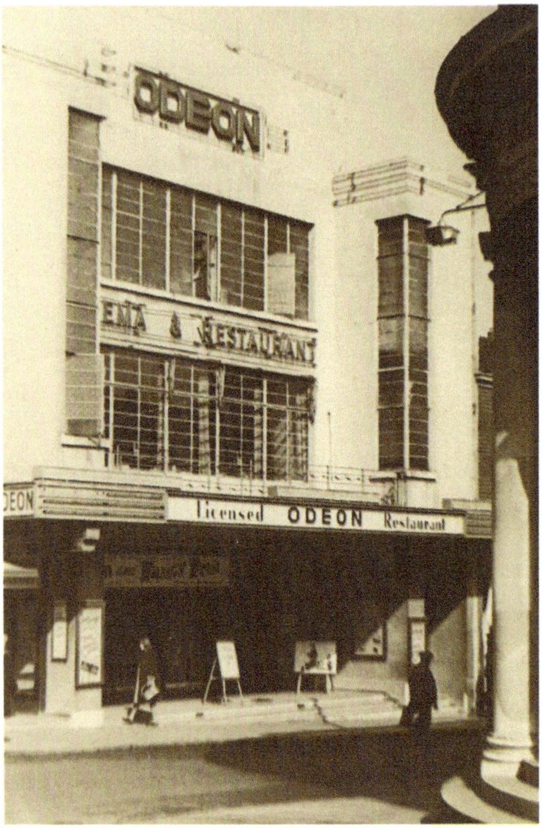

Our Odeon Swapped for a Chemist

Left: When I was given this photo of the Odeon cinema and bar, it brought back memories of a tale told by my aunt. She was an usherette during the war and was up on the roof on her evening break when there had been a bombing raid. She said her parents' house had been hit and the manager had replied 'How stupid you can't see Sydney Street in the dark from here'. She said she knew it was bombed and was off home, much to the disgust of the manager. When she got home it had been hit and only the staircase was left, but she was pleased to find that no one had been in the house at the time. When this picture was taken in March 1947 the film showing was *Fun and Fancy Free*, a Walt Disney production. The Odeon closed on 26 January 1974.

Below: In this photograph taken in 2014 you can see that Boots now occupies the building. The old building was demolished and rebuilt to suit the needs of the chemist.

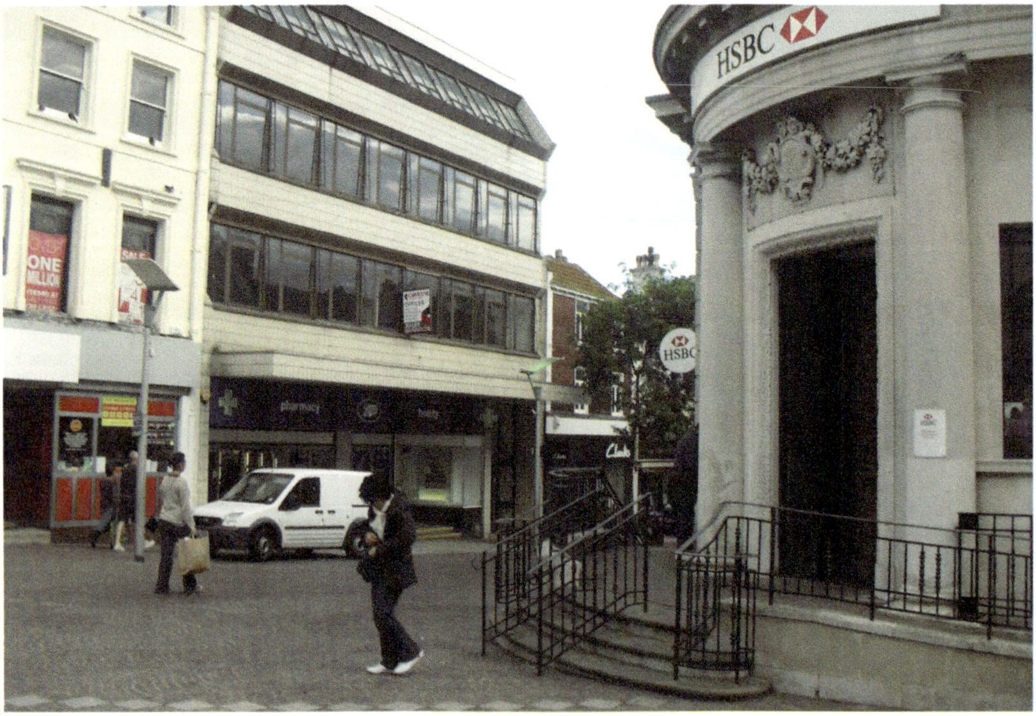

We Have Traded for 120 Years in Same Shop

Right: Leonard John O'Clee outside his jeweller's shop at No. 27a Sandgate Road in 1895. Today it is No. 35 but still the same shop – the road numbers having changed over time. Before 1895 John H. O'Clee had a shop at No. 5 George Lane and traded there for approximately six years. Was this Leonard's father or relative?

Below: James O'Clee, Leonard's great-grandson, following in the family tradition. James tells me that none of his children wished to go into the jewellery business as it is not as lucrative as in the past.

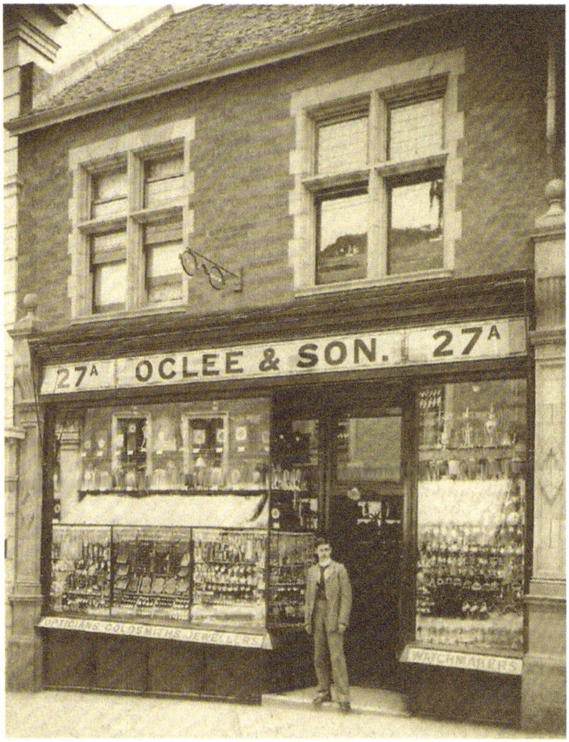

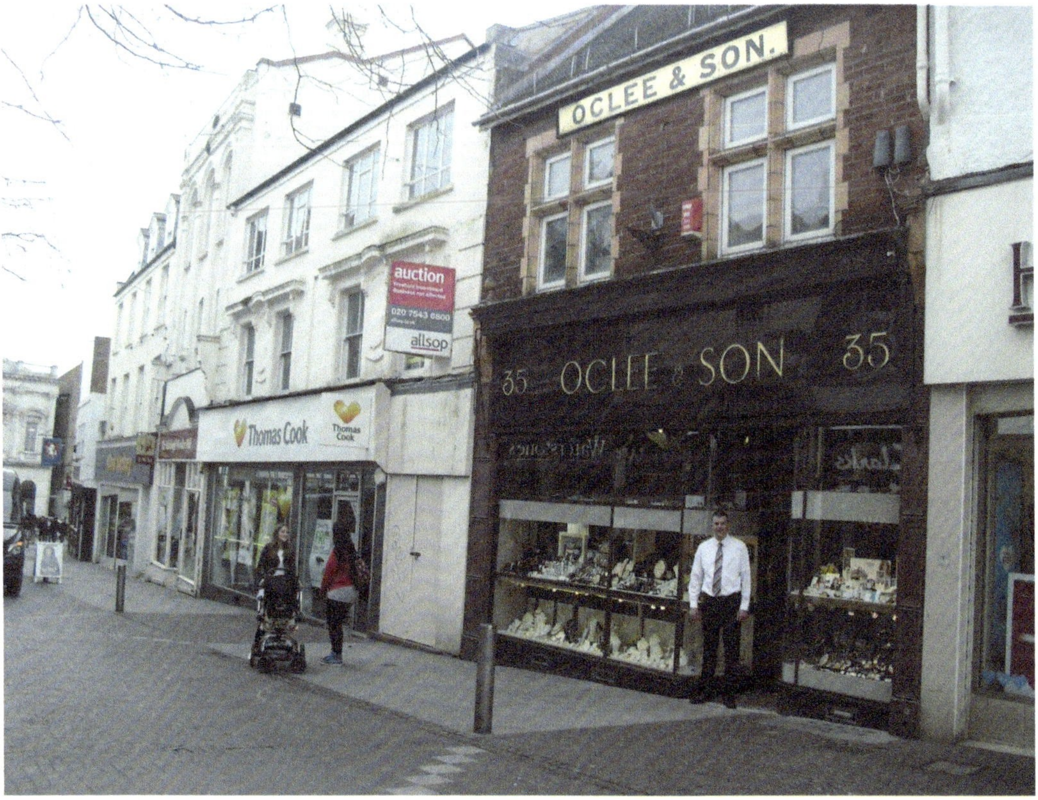

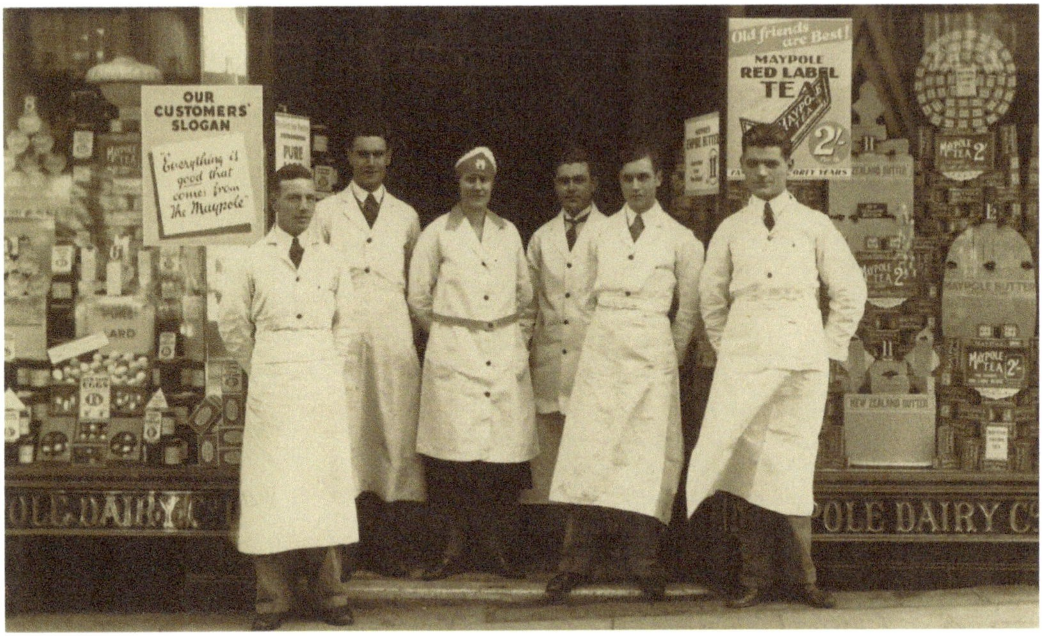

The Maypole Grocery Shop at No. 23 Sandgate Road, in the 1930s
Above: The gentleman at second left is Albert Davies, who worked there until the war, when he became a fireman and also rented the shop featured on page 67.

Below: The Card Factory at Nos 23–25 Sandgate Road in 2014. In the 1930s it was The Maypole, Walton fruiters and John Sainsbury Ltd. In the 1970s it became one shop Nos 23–25 Sandgate Road. Curry's Ltd then sold bicycles and some electrical goods if my memory serves me right.

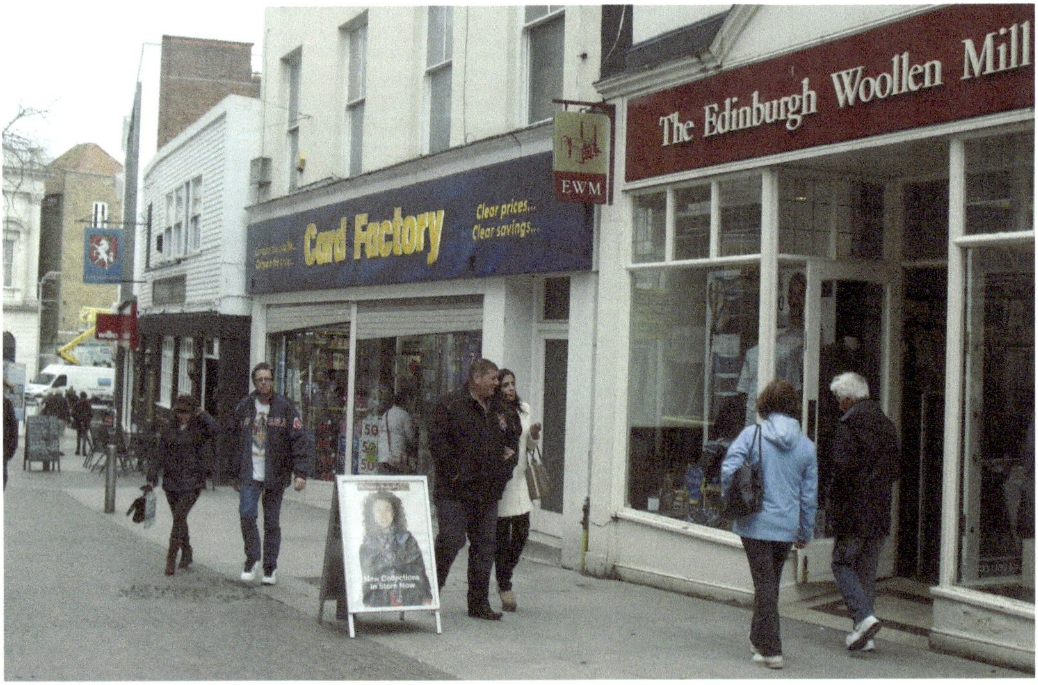

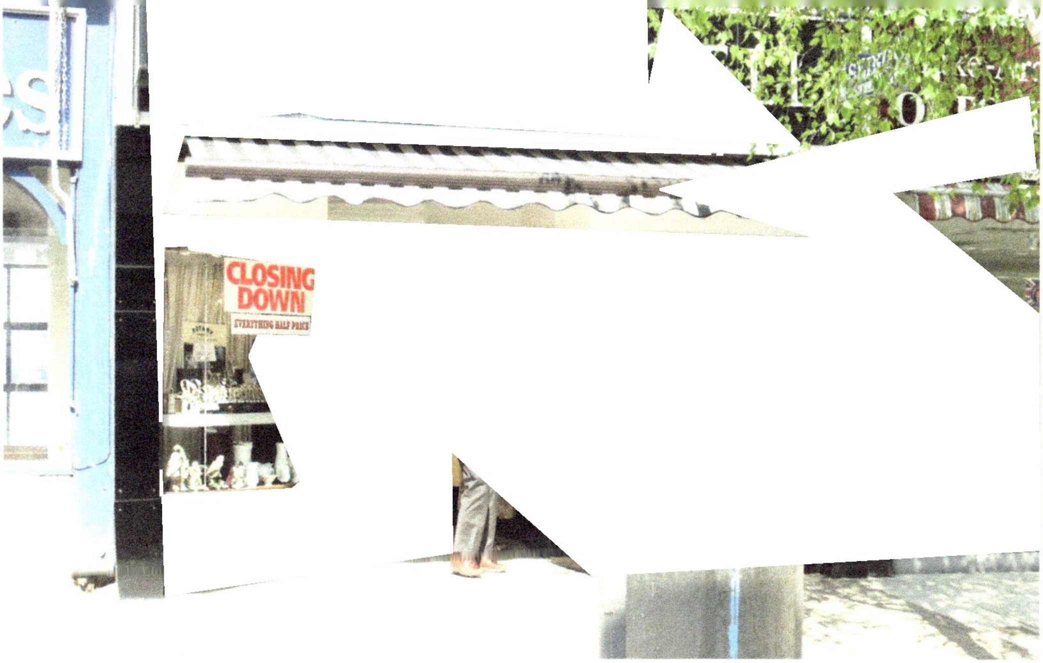

Another Trader Leaves Us

Above: John Angel the jewellers that traded at No. 24 Guildhall Street from around 1955 to 2011. This shop took over from George Goldsack who had previously been trading for around fifty years. Inside the shop when John Angel's took over was a casement clock that George Goldsack had made when he owned the shop. I wonder where that clock is now. When I was doing some family tree research for a relative of George's, who was living in Canada, he was thrilled when I sent him a photo of the clock. On enquiring at John Angel's Dover branch, I was informed the clock was sold with the shop, along with the other items.

Below: T. D. Electronix took over the shop when John Angel's closed, which is also a family business.

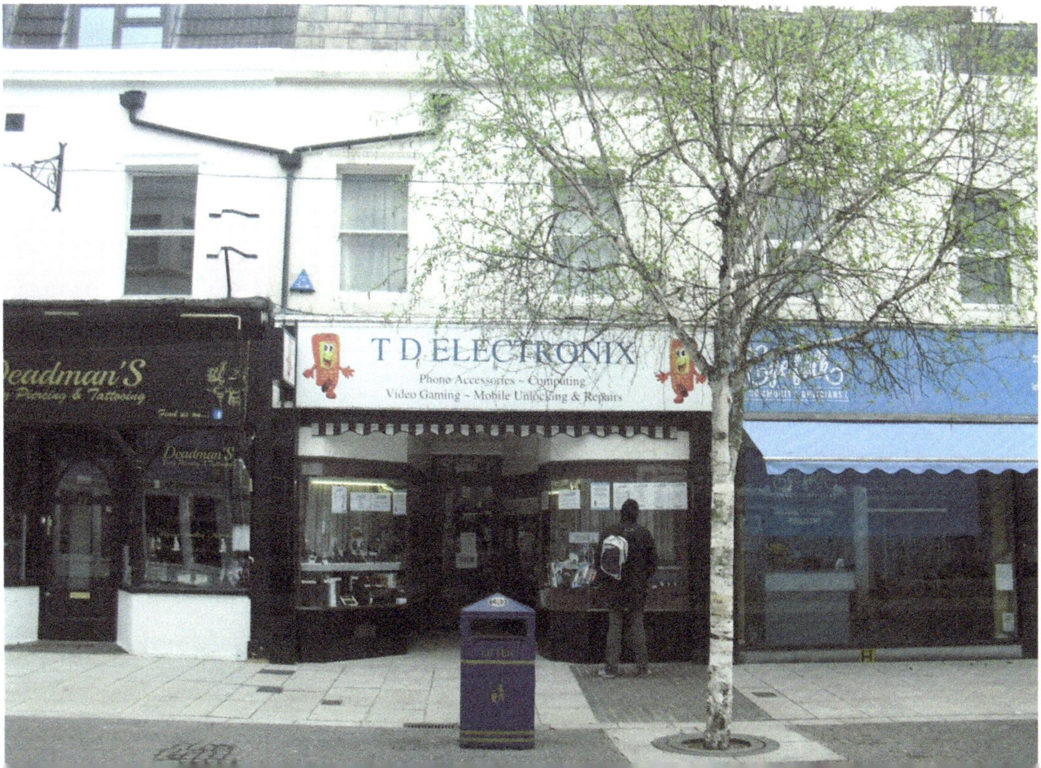

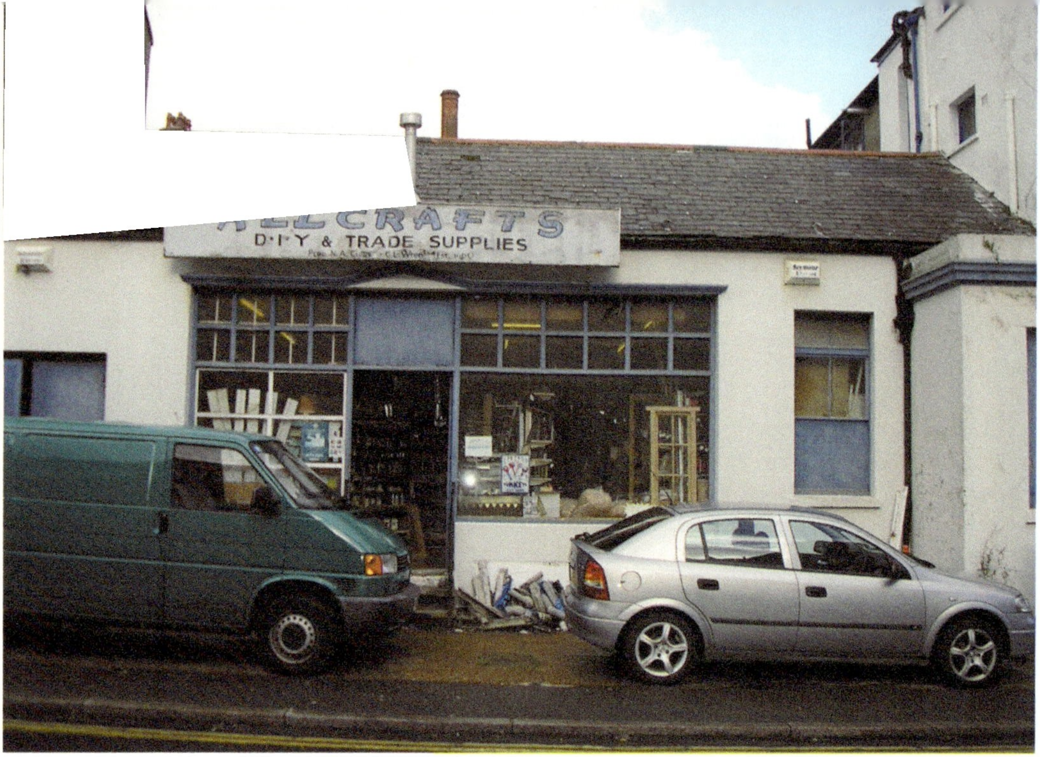

Allcrafts DIY Gone but Not Forgotten

Above: Allcrafts DIY supplies, in 2002, was situated at No. 2 Victoria Grove in Folkestone. It was a small shop in the town, very handy for various supplies and much missed when the shop closed. It was used by local builders and the general public. The personal service one received made the shopkeepers special.

Below: After being closed for many years Allcrafts was demolished and in 2014 a block of flats was built in its place – a bright new building that will house some of the many people needing accommodation in the town.

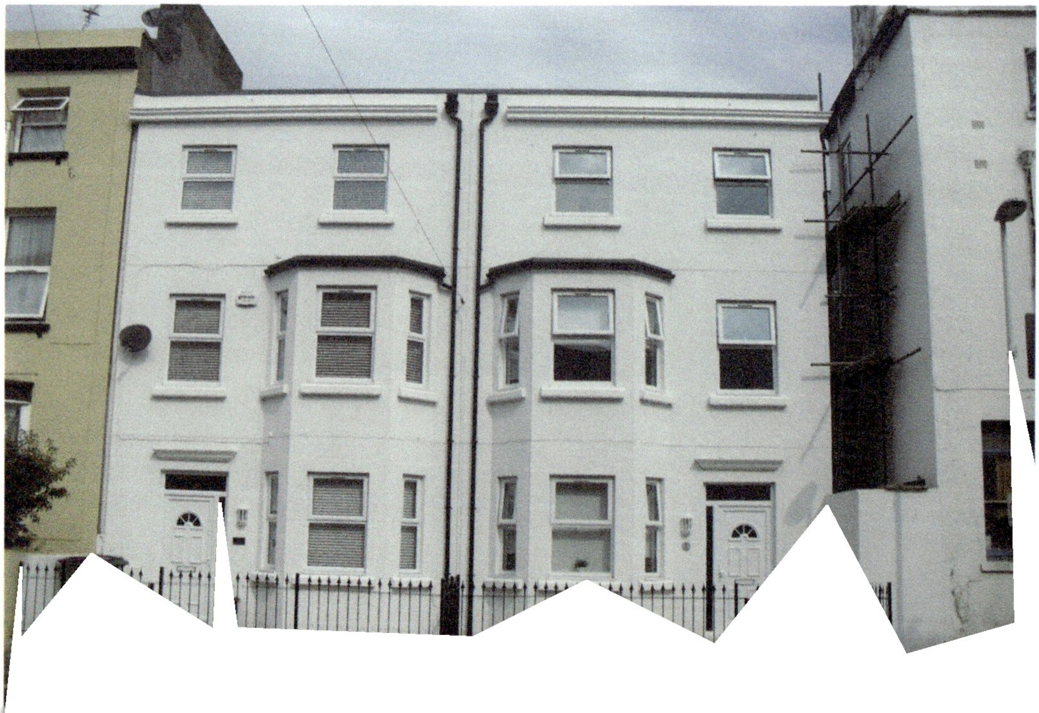

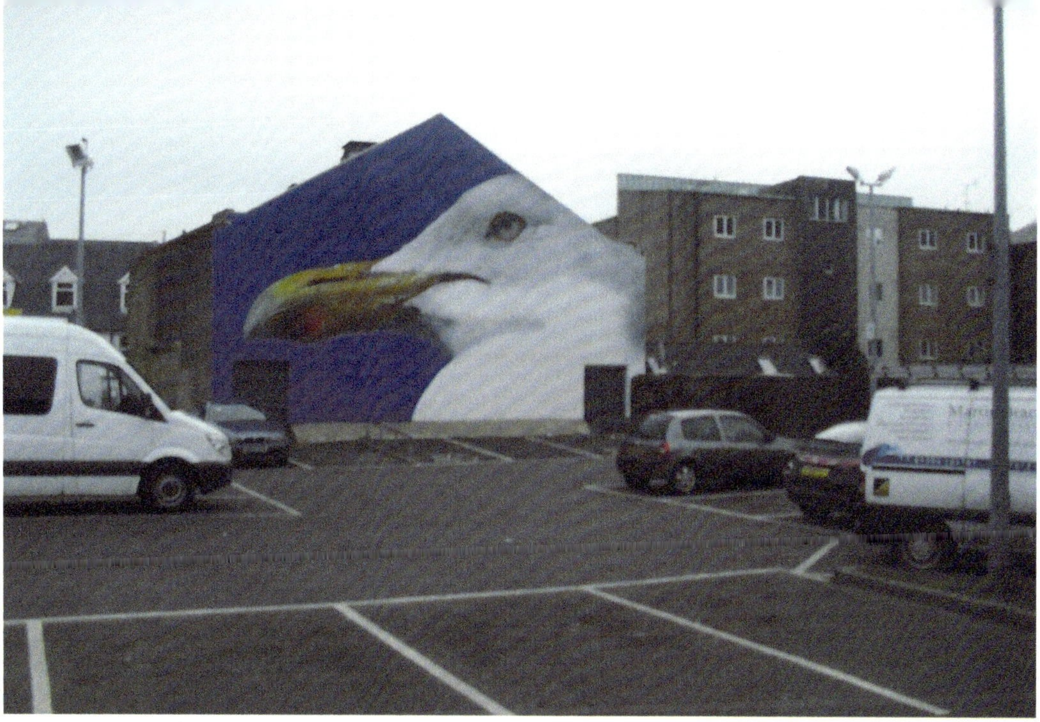

What a Large Seagull

Above: The seagull was painted in St Eanswythe Way as some artists thought many locals hated the birds and they ought to be appreciated. It is a good likeness but people do get fed up with the mess they create, dragging bags out of bins to find food and taking food from people's hands.

Below left: Also in St Eanswythe Way is the graffiti picture; commissioned of course, which is painted on the side wall by the back of the Town Hall. It does brighten up a dull wall; but perhaps they should have covered the entire wall even if it was just in one colour.

Below right: A close-up of the picture to see the artistry of the piece seeing the picture in real life is quite amazing trying to imagine the artists on a scaffold getting it all in prospective.

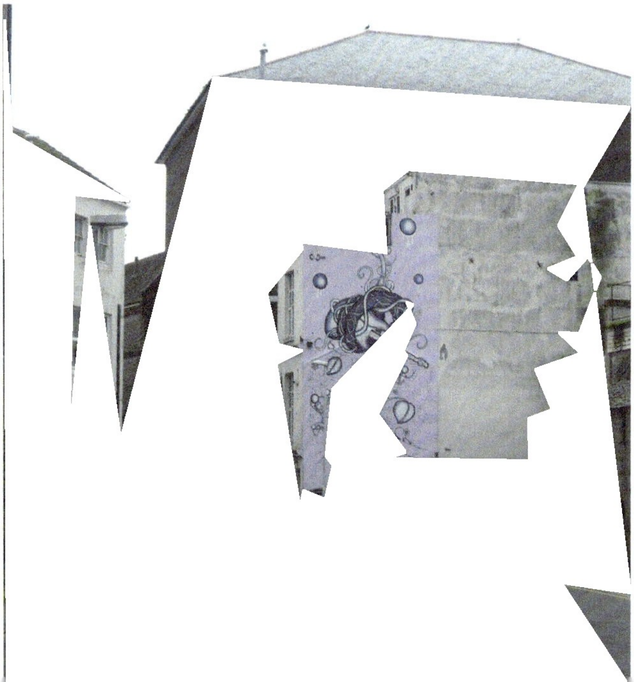

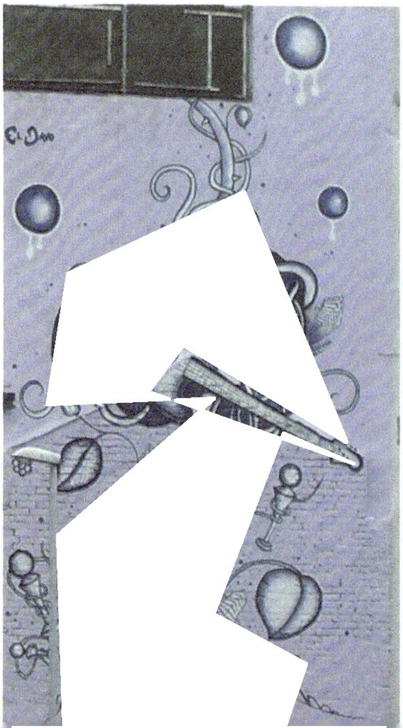

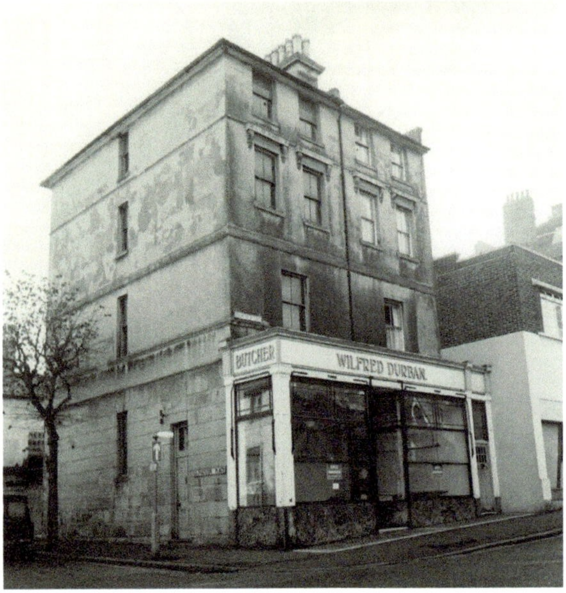

Fun and Games at 4A Bouverie Road East

Left: Durban's the Butcher at No. 4 Bouverie Road East, in around 1970. The little door next to the shop window was No. 4a Bouverie Road East. What an amazing place that was: Mr and Mrs Gray and Mrs Morley lived there a good forty years, before they were rehoused, as the building was to be demolished. No one would believe the many famous actors, singers and dancers stayed there over the years, when they were appearing at the Pleasure Gardens Theatre. The reason that the stars stayed there was because Mr Gray worked at the Pleasure Gardens Theatre along with two of his sons. It started in the early 1950s when some of the cast had no digs and he invited them to stay as his very large house. Some of the famous names were Bill Maynard, Freddie Frinton, Kings Brothers, Old Mother Riley and Kitty, and Malcolm Vaughan. I was told the Coldstream Guards often stayed there so they could be together. One actually slept in the bath one night, saying, 'It was home from home and the grub was good.'

Below: Next to the white-painted building was the Gun Tavern with a cottage attached, but sadly it's no longer there. One of its residents said she could hear the darts being thrown into the board and assumed the board was hung on the dividing wall from the pub to her house. The Gun Tavern opened in 1843 and closed in 1974, and during that time it had eleven landlords. On the opposite side of the road where, the taxi is, Durban's the Butcher's was situated.

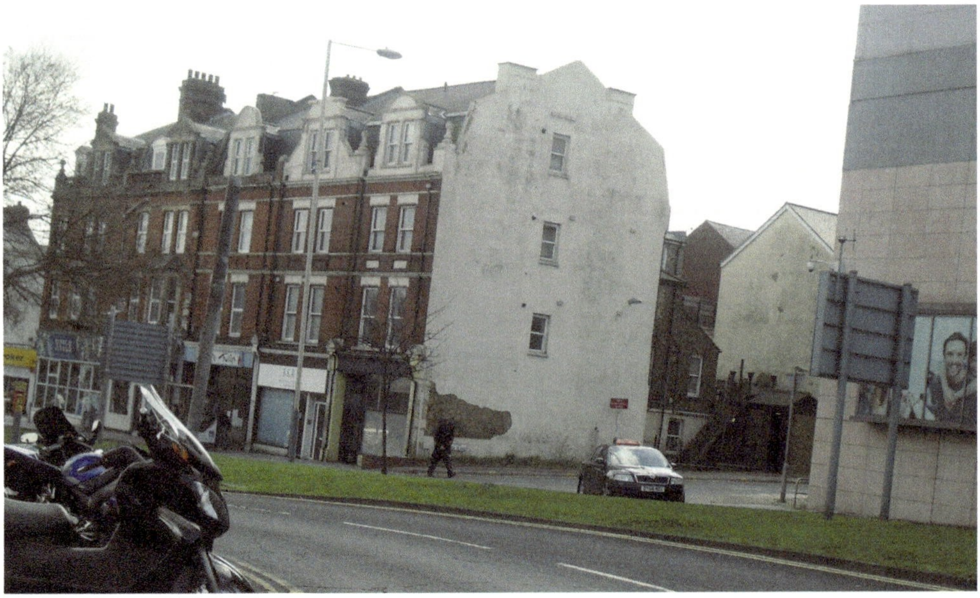

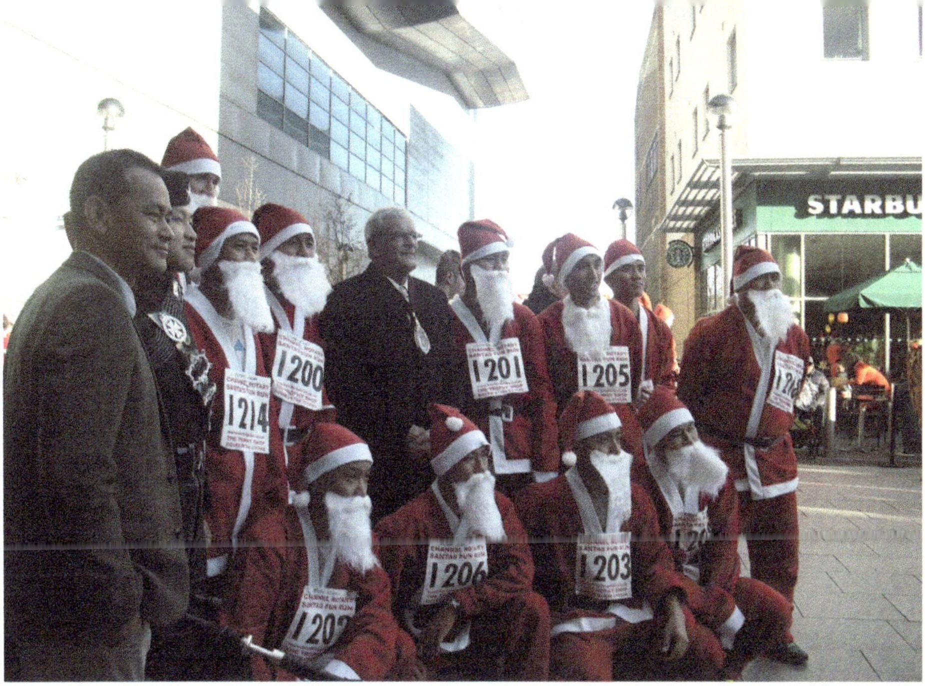

Who Said Santa Doesn't Exist?

On the 14 December 2014 the eleventh annual Santa run, organised by the Folkestone Channel Rotary Club, took place to raise money for charity. This year it was thought to have raised in excess of £4,000. This is a race for anyone who wanted to take part.

The picture above has some of the Ghurkha soldiers from Shorncliffe camp who willingly support all the events Folkestone puts on. In the middle of them is Alan North, Folkestone's mayor, before they left Bouverie Place shopping square.

Below: Some of the competitors as they are making their way past Debenhams in Sandgate Road, as you can see this race is for anyone who wishes to take part – even some dogs were dressed as Santa.

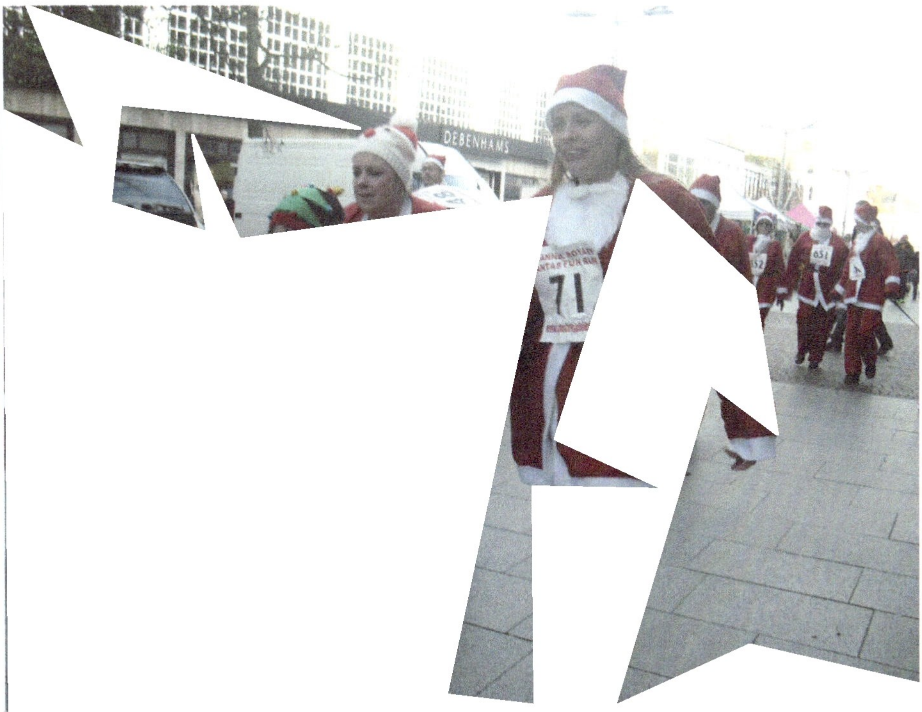

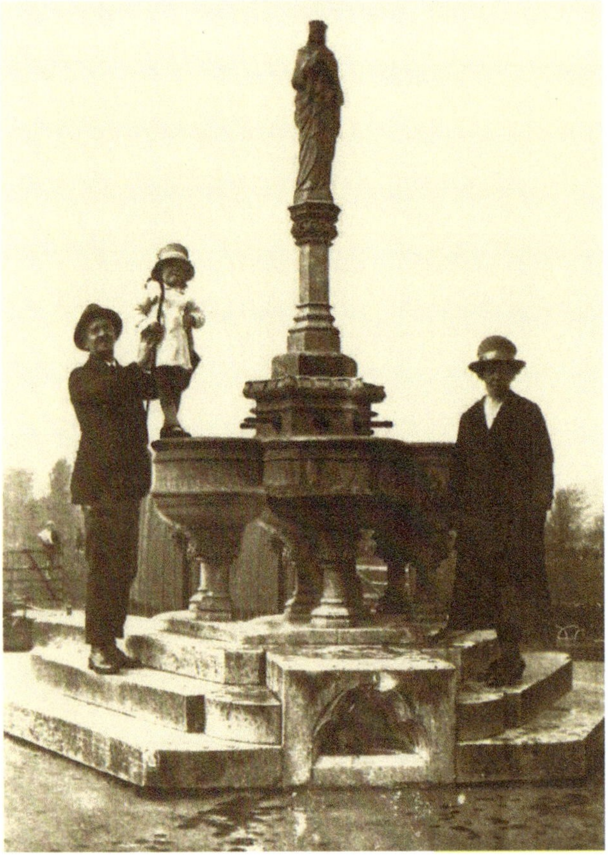

Will the Statue Be Replaced?
Left: The picture taken in the 1920s of Mr and Mrs Sheppard with their daughter Joan, showing how the Radnor Park fountain once looked. Joan, who lived with her parents in Mead Road said, with a hat like that she looked like a storm trooper minus the boots.

Below: This picture is how the fountain looked in 2014. Frank Bond a local historian is hoping to get funding to get the fountain restored. The statue of St Eanswythe that sat on the top of the fountain was allegedly destroyed by an ex-soldier in the 1960s.

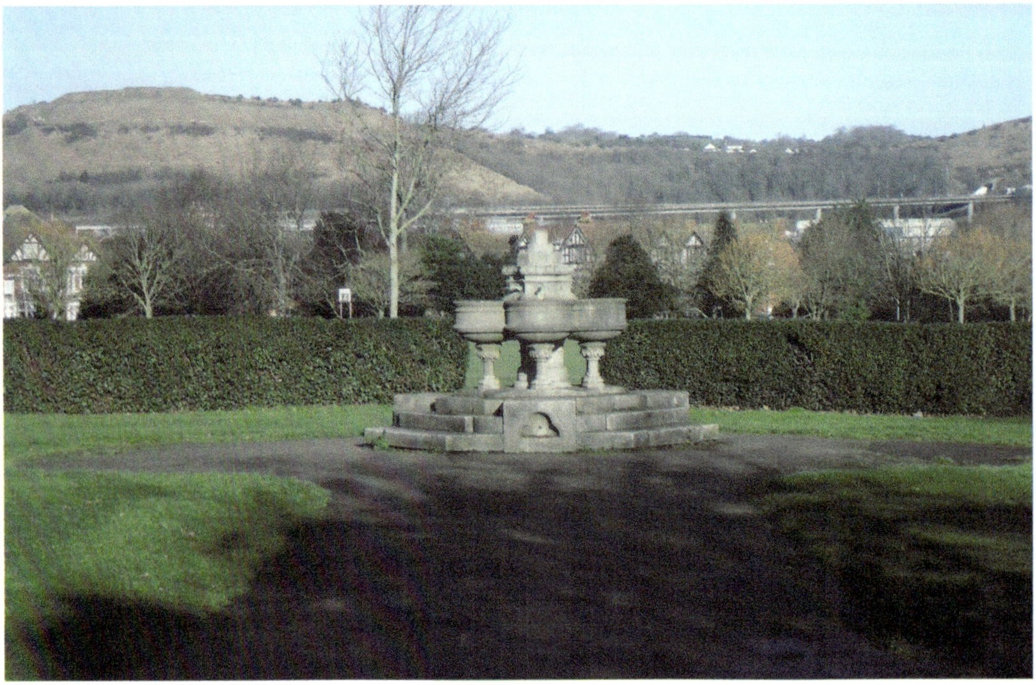

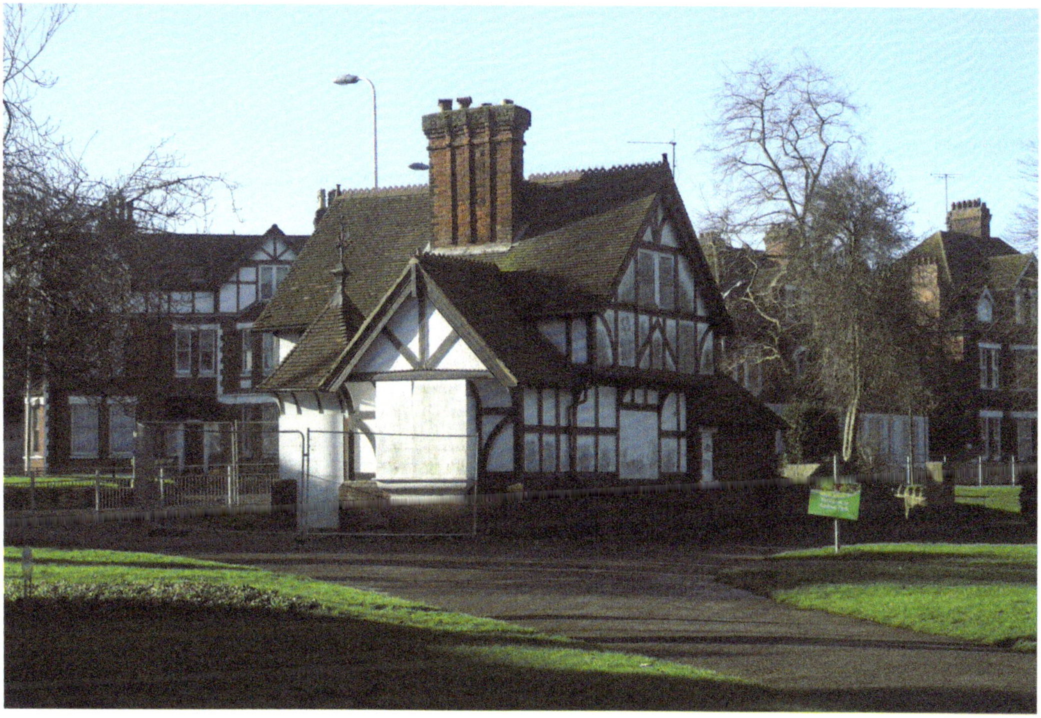

A Treasure Waiting for Restoration

Above: The beautiful old park keeper's lodge, situated on the edge of Radnor Park, was built in the late 1880s and with William Attwood the first occupant in 1885. In 1951 Claude Noble lived there with his wife and son David, Claude being the last to leave in 1990 when he died. Claude had worked for the Folkestone Corporation and he was in charge of the tree gang that looked after Folkestone's trees.

Right: Eagle-eyed Bob Mouland, trying to keep our heritage intact spotted, the old finial on the lodge looking like the tower of Pisa. The Folkestone Parks and Pleasure Grounds Charity are having meetings to decide the lodge and finial's fate – being empty for many years it is deteriorating badly. The finial is now at the Hawkinge cemetery awaiting renovation.

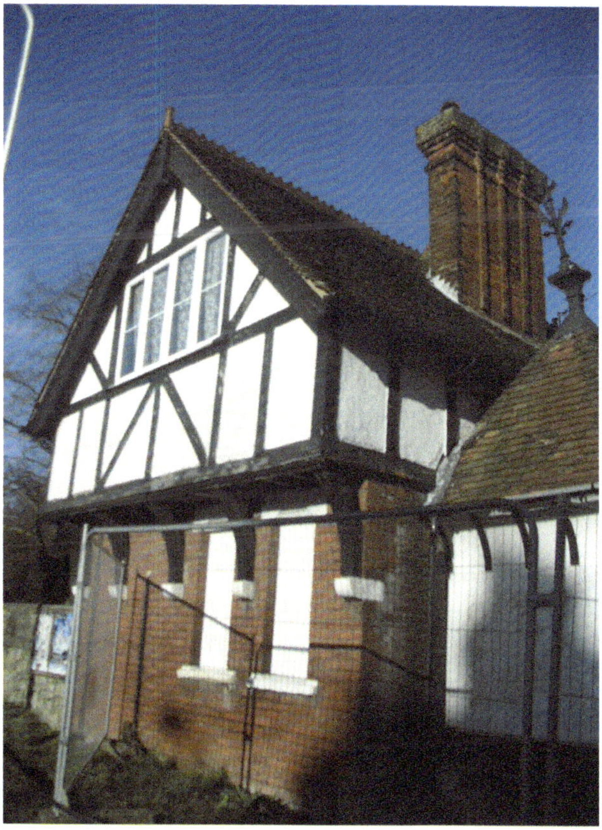

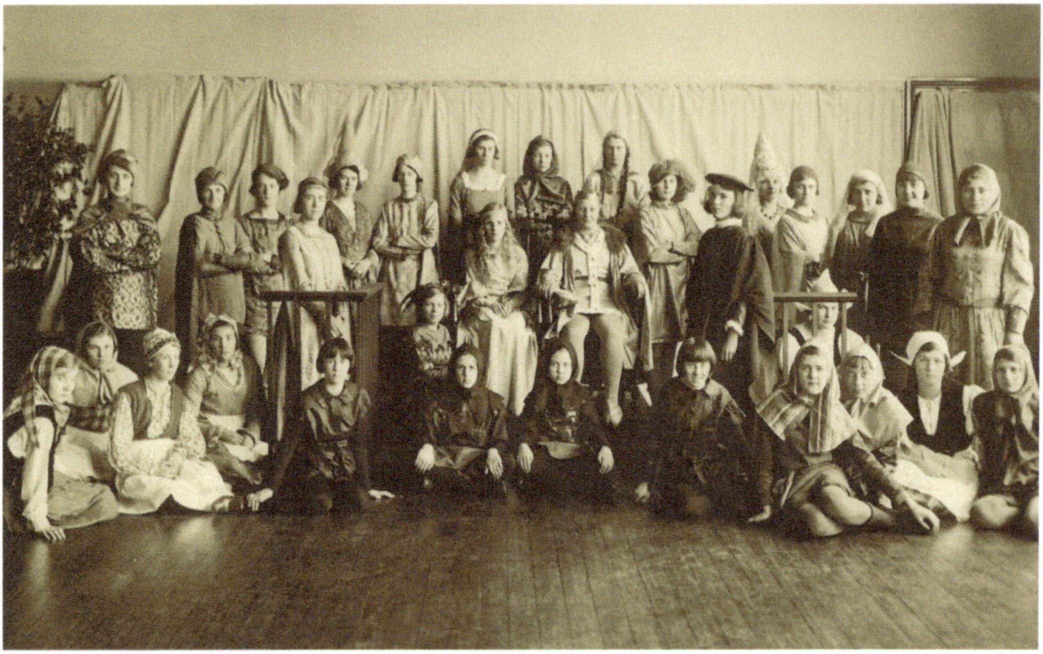

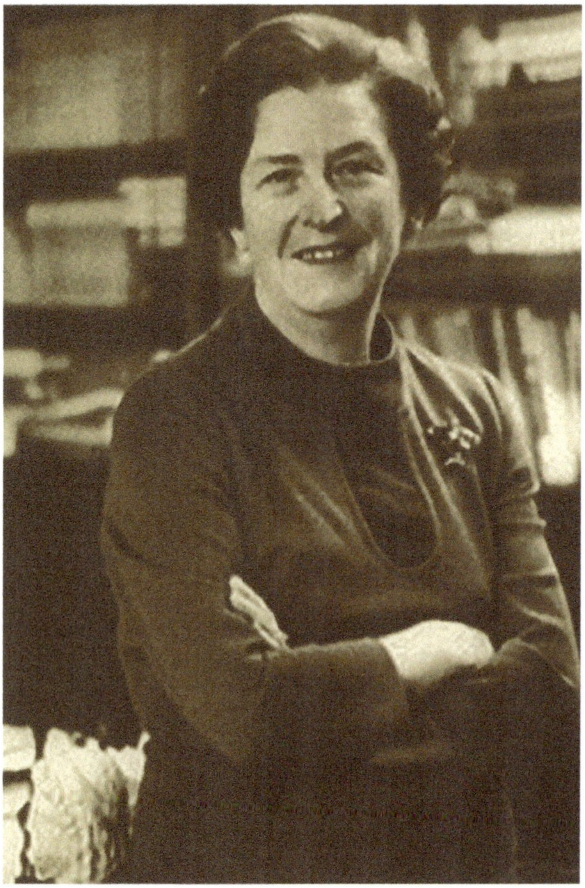

The Goose Girls Pantomime in 1933

Above: The Folkestone School for Girls in Coolinge Lane, Folkestone, who put on this pantomime. Joan Simpkins (née Sheppard) is sitting on the floor at the Kings' feet and Sheila Sherlock is the girl with the Dutch hat on.

Left: Dame Sheila Sherlock (1918–2001) was the main creator of Hepatology, starting in 1940. After sixty years of her career, she became one of the world's most famous names in clinical science. Her exciting lectures kept everyone on their toes; her best known book was *Diseases of the Liver*, published in 1955. She was supported by her distinguished physician husband Dr Gerry James, born in Dublin and brought up in Folkestone. She attended Folkestone School for Girls in Coolinge Lane and gained a place at Edinburgh University.

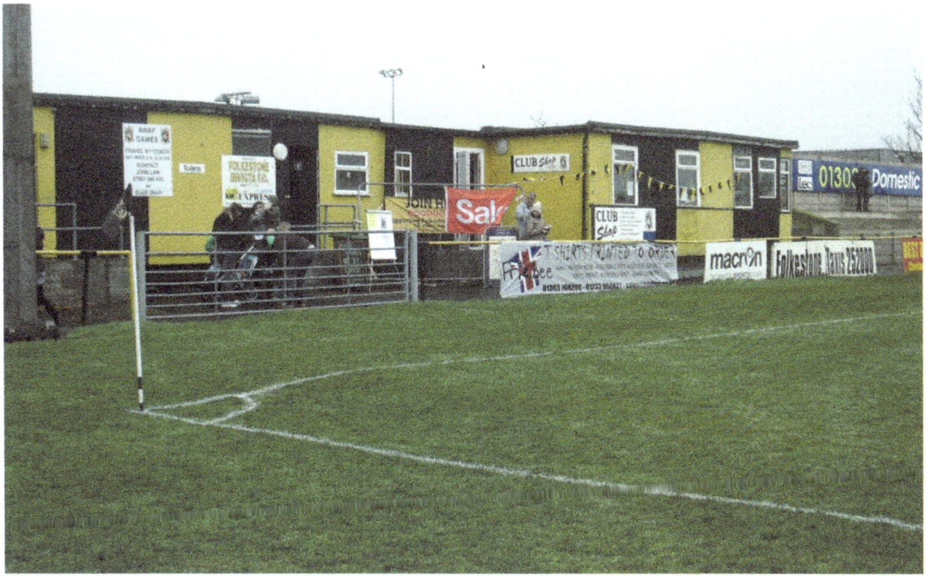

A First for Folkestone Football Club

Above: The club shop on the edge of the pitch. On Good Friday 3 April 2014 the club arranged the first family day, with free Easter eggs for the children and half-price sale of football memorabilia, to help the children to start collecting various football badges, programs and shirts etc. The aim was for the club to get children interested, as young as seven, to play football, in the hope that they might have the potential to be a good player.

Below: Inside the shop: many items to entice collectors to buy and three children that have just received their eggs.

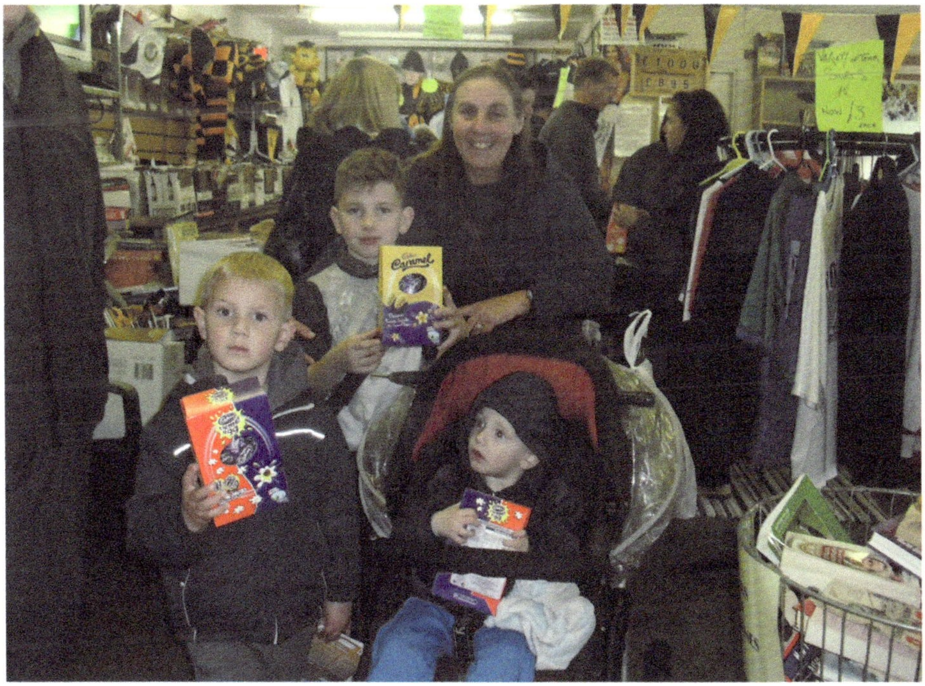

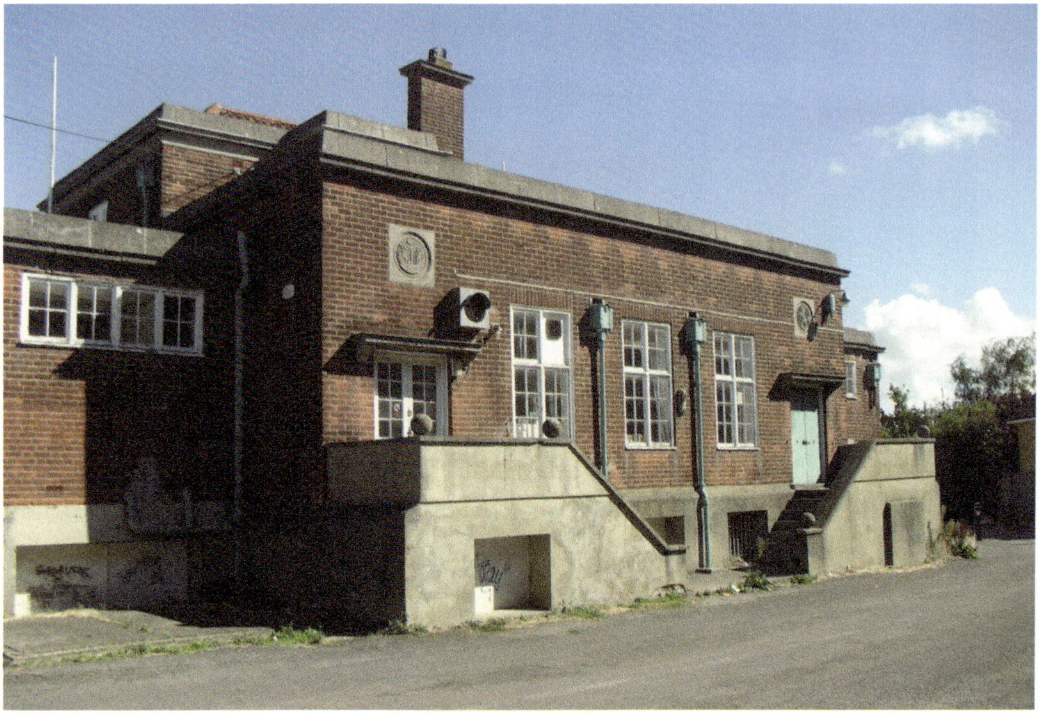

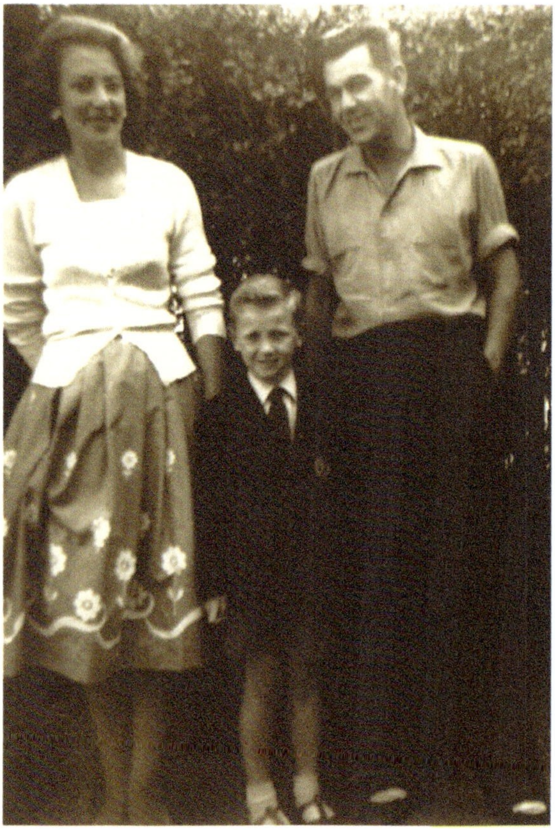

Another Building Soon to Bite the Dust

Above: This is the back of the old cricket pavilion, just off Cheriton Road, taken in 2014, just before demolition. Up the steps Peter and Margaret Davies and their son Roy lived in the flat in the 1950s. Peter worked for the council as a gardener and almost opposite the flat was the corporation greenhouses. I spent many happy hours with him and his workmates, helping out in the greenhouses. This was a place I wanted to work when I left school in 1955, but it wasn't to be as after the war no women were taken on.

Left: The Davies family in 1961, standing roughly opposite the pavilion. The hedge hides the Morrison's supermarket car park where the corporation greenhouses once stood; still a walkway for football fans as well as cricket fans to reach the pitches.

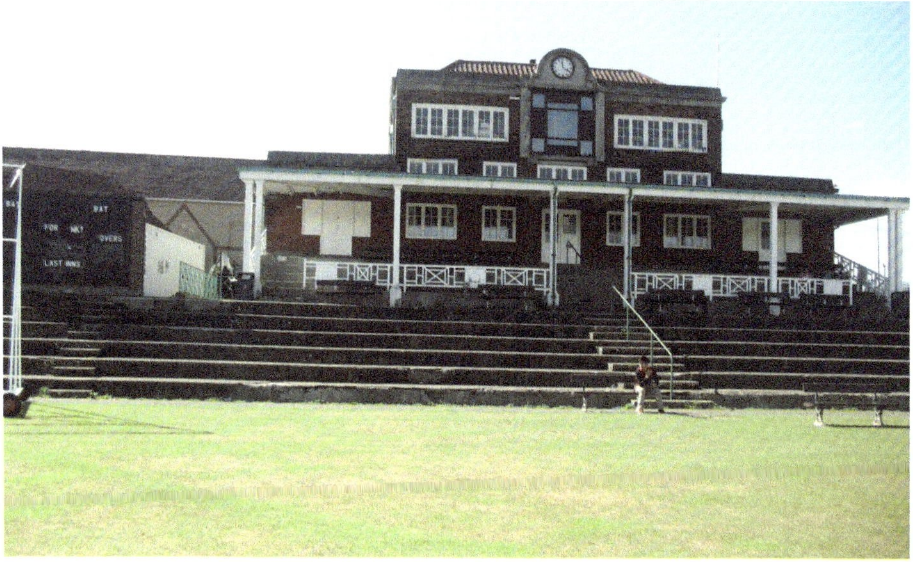

One Last Look, 19 September 2014

Above: The front of the Cricket Pavilion that has stood there since 1905, still looking a lovely place at a distance. It was financed by Lord Radnor, costing £1,000 to build and unused since 1995. In 1934 Don Bradman, the famous cricketer, played at Cheriton Road ground in an Australian *v.* England match and scored 149 not out. In 2014 Himanshu 'Himmy' Waingankar scored 921 runs; over the past nine years he has travelled from India to play for Folkestone. Last season Himmy scored his third double hundred for the club.

Below: The demolition men taking down the last remnants of the pavilion. A sad day, as I am sure many happy hours were spent there by many followers of cricket and even the ex-tenants of the cricket pavilion flat, who had a good view of the cricket games being played.

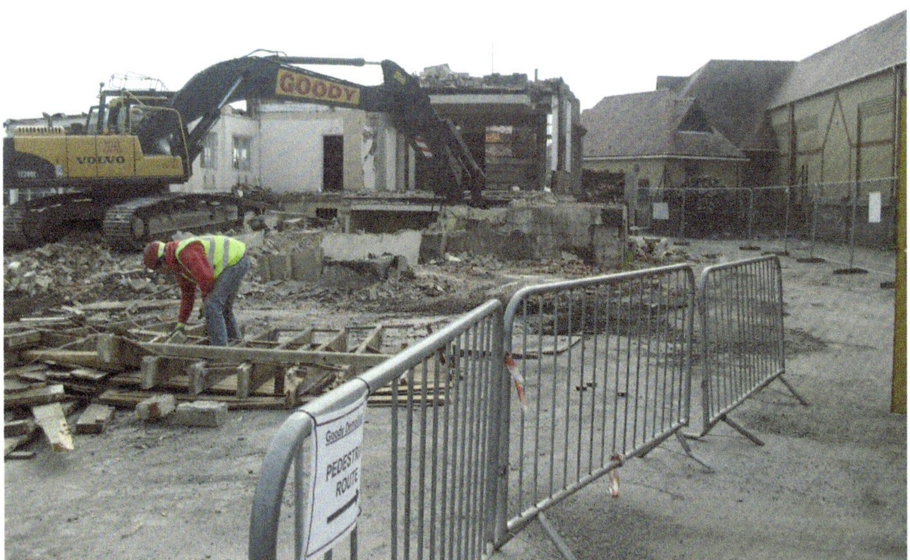

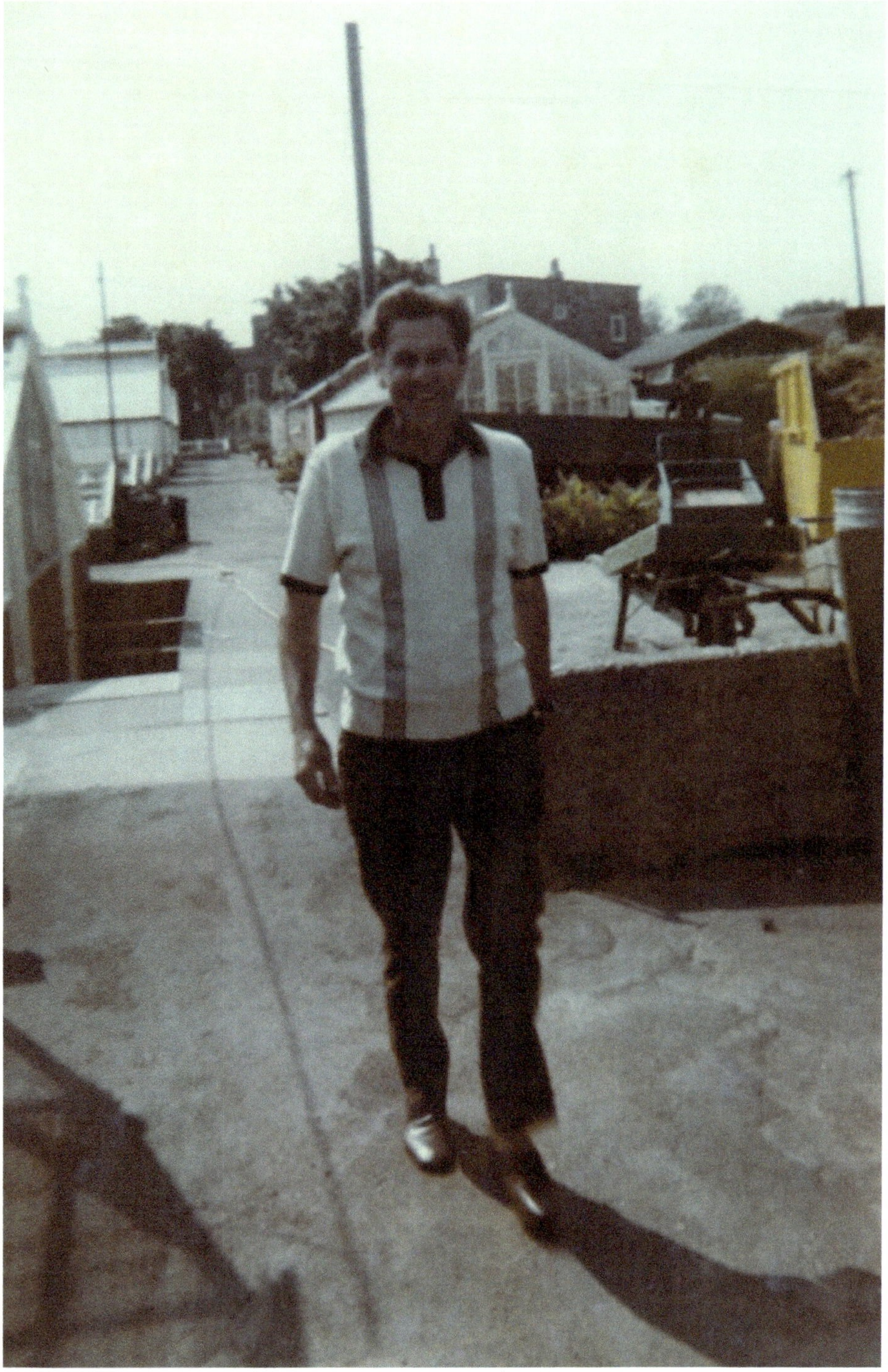

Peter Davies 1927–2014

Peter Davies in the 1970s walking through the greenhouses area. In the back right of the picture is the cricket pavilion where Peter and his family lived. How nice to have lived so close to work.

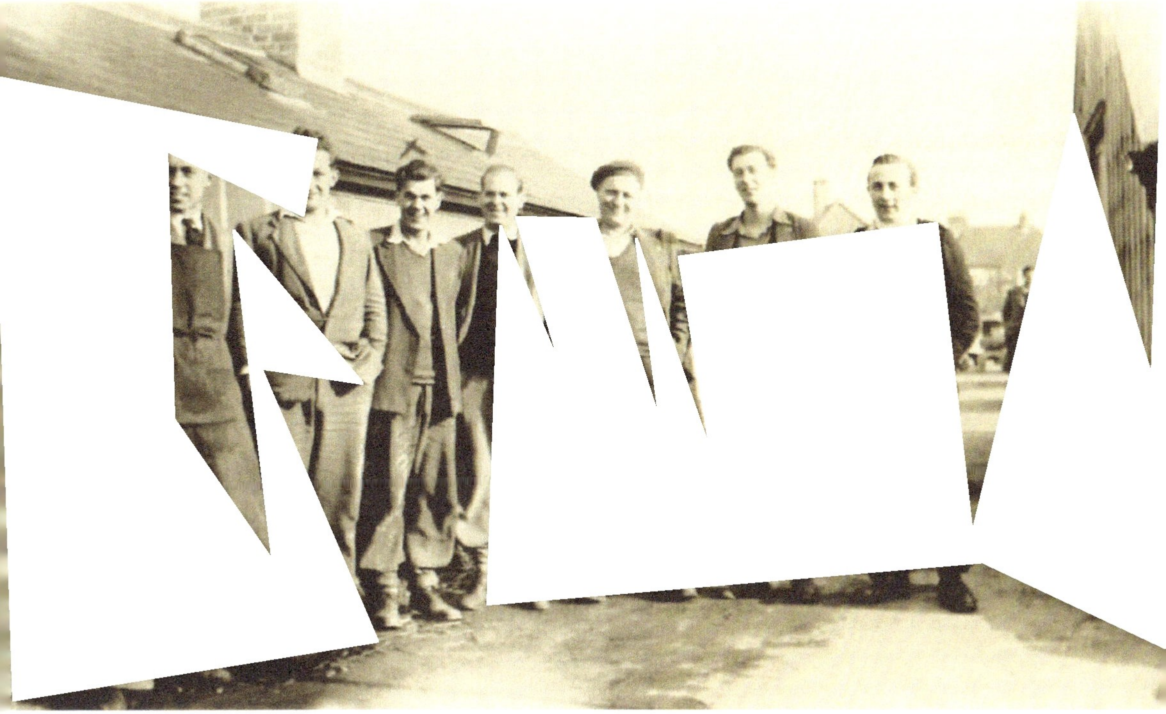

Corporation Greenhouses, Cheriton Road

Above: I call them my greenhouse gang as they were all very nice and helpful to me in the mid-1950s. *From the left:* George Priest, Kenny Vant, Pete Davies, Bill Milton, Ted Bartlett, Charlie Brazier and John Grinstead. I sometimes volunteered to help out when the men were on overtime; they gave me many tips with potting on and showed me how to arrange plants in the Leas Cliff Hall when they had special events on. It was all experience for me as I wanted to go into horticulture. Ted Bartlett, I remember, would often give me a lovely coleus plant to take home.

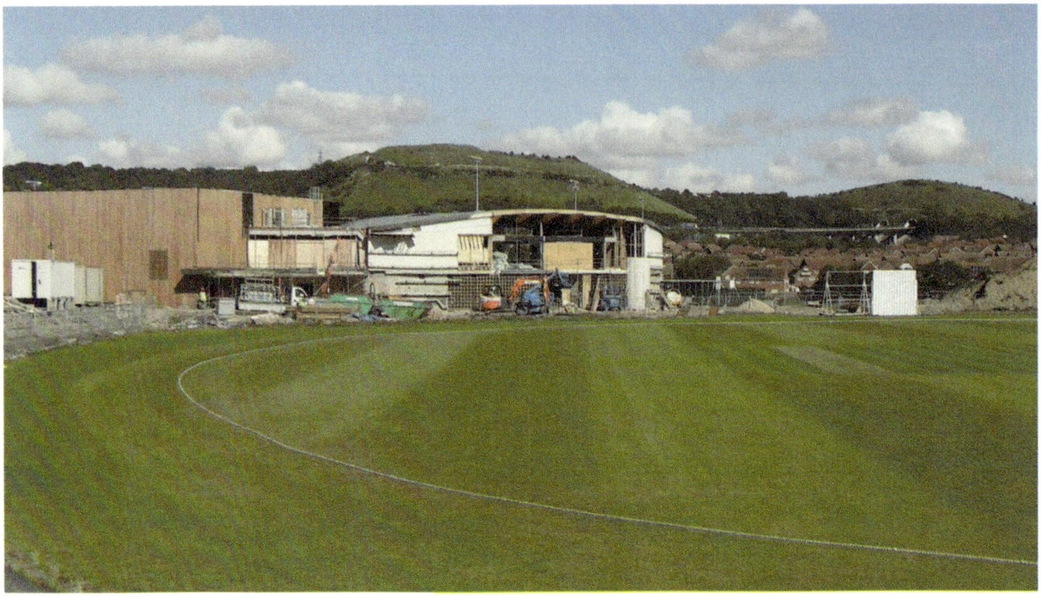

New Cricket Pavilion Named The Three Hills
Above: The new cricket pavilion in the process of being built. This picture was taken 13 September 2012.

Below: The new cricket pavilion, taken April 2013, after completion. It was named after The Three Hills with the view of the hills in the background. Well what can I say? A vast improvement and by all accounts this place is working better as it is larger and can hold various events. It has a range of artificial playing surfaces so they can accommodate cricket, hockey, netball and running. There are various halls to rent for functions, so I wish this new venture well for the town. This £7 million facility, of which backers hope will become a centre of excellence, was mainly funded by the Roger De Haan Charitable Trust.

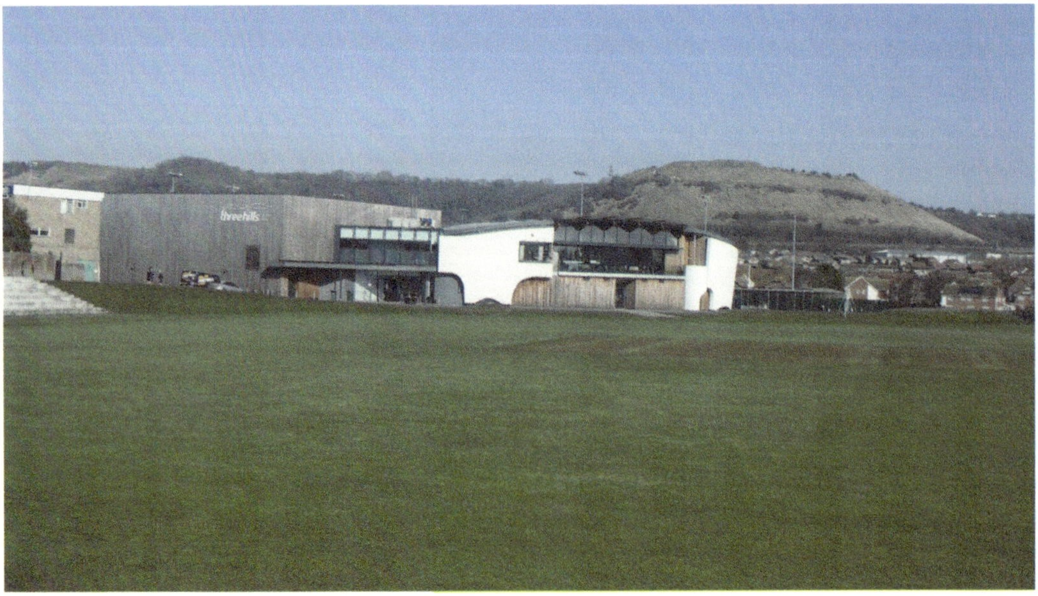

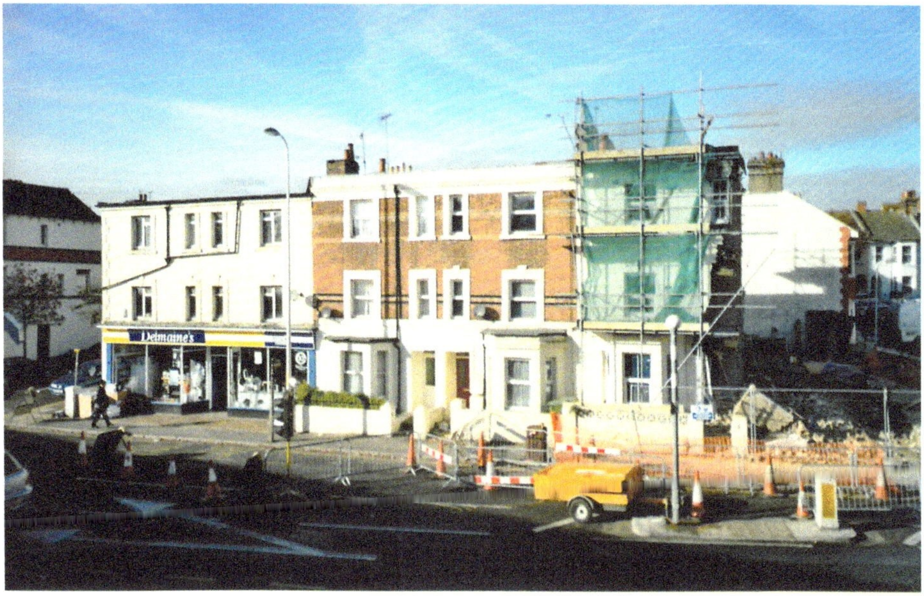

Nos 47–45 Blackbull Road is Falling down, Falling Down!
Above: This building was made safe in the hope it would be quickly rebuilt. After around six years of the site being a rubbish tip for all and sundry, up went the boards but nothing happened.

Below: In 2015, much to our delight and after months of various official graffiti pictures, what do we see two sold signs put up on the old shop and house area; hopefully in the near future we will see the site built on and that little area tidied up. Nos 37–39 Blackbull Road was Delmaines ten years ago, which sold white goods. Delmaines closed and Hambrook and Johns the undertakers relocated from Dover Road to the location. Hambrook and Johns have been trading there for the past couple of years.

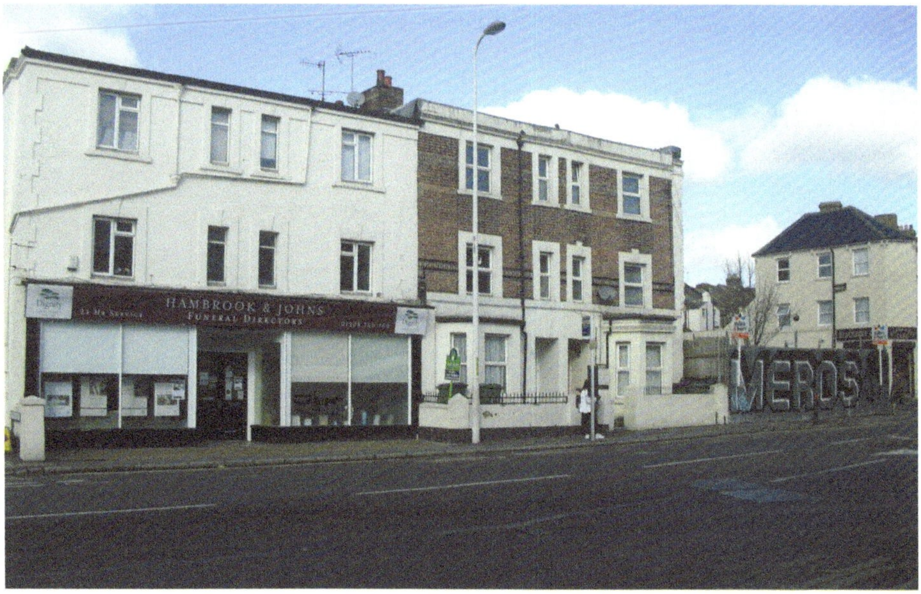

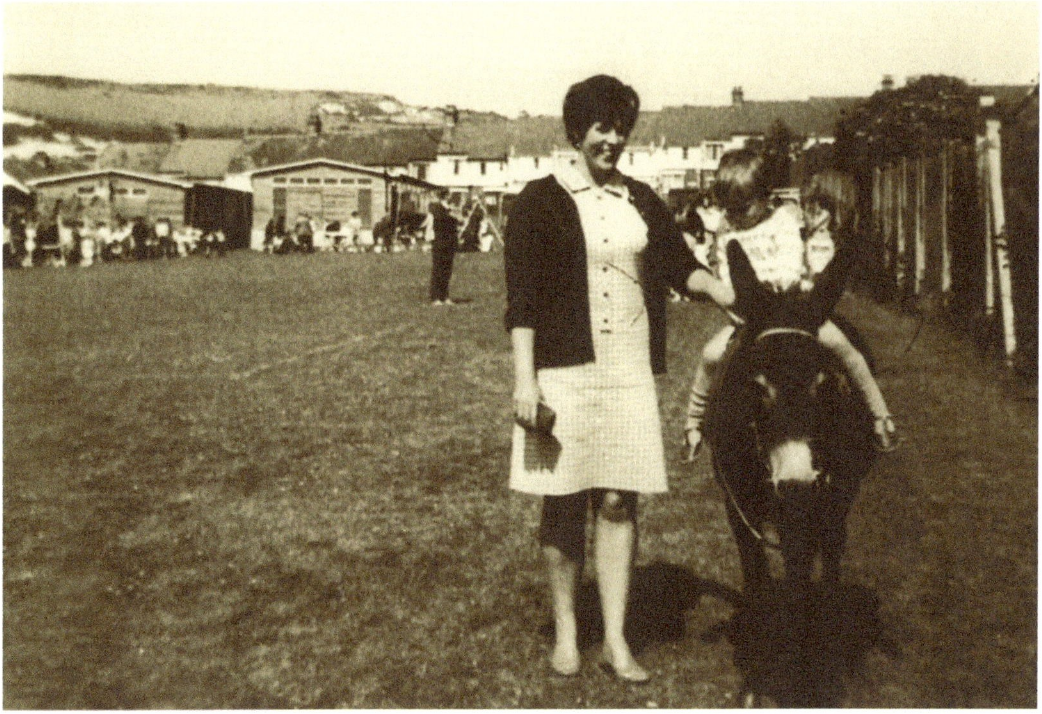

Risen from Demolition

Above: Pat Goodman standing beside her son Lee on a donkey ride in the 1960s. In the background is the Dawson Road Youth Centre. Taking place was one of the many events the local clubs and churches used, for summer fetes, boot fairs, and was once used by Mundella School for Sports.

Bottom: Completed in 2014, the new houses and flats in Walter Tull Way, built on the site of the Dawson Road Youth Club. Named after Walter Tull of Folkestone, the first black football player for Tottenham and the first black officer commissioned into the British Army and who sadly died on the Somme in 1918.

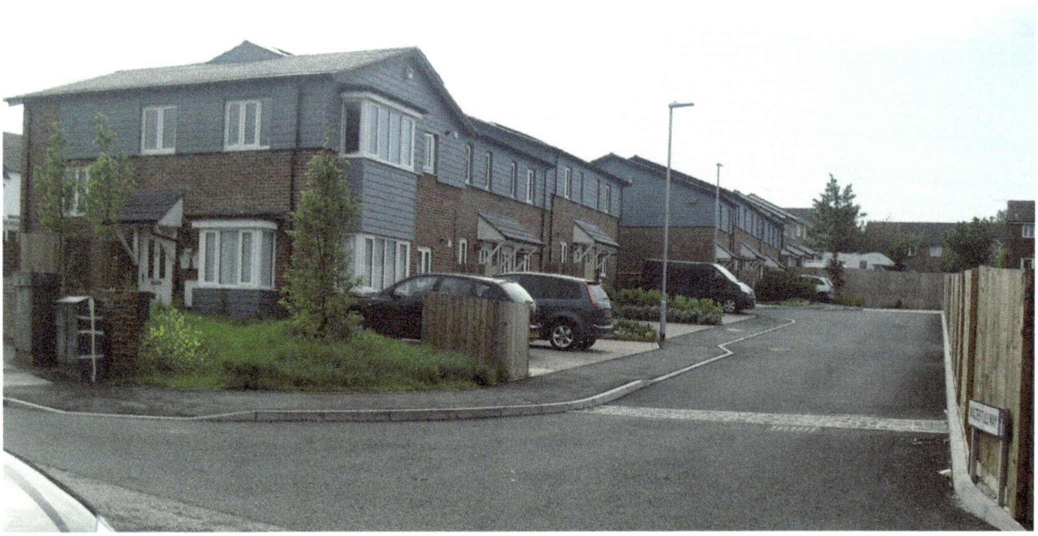

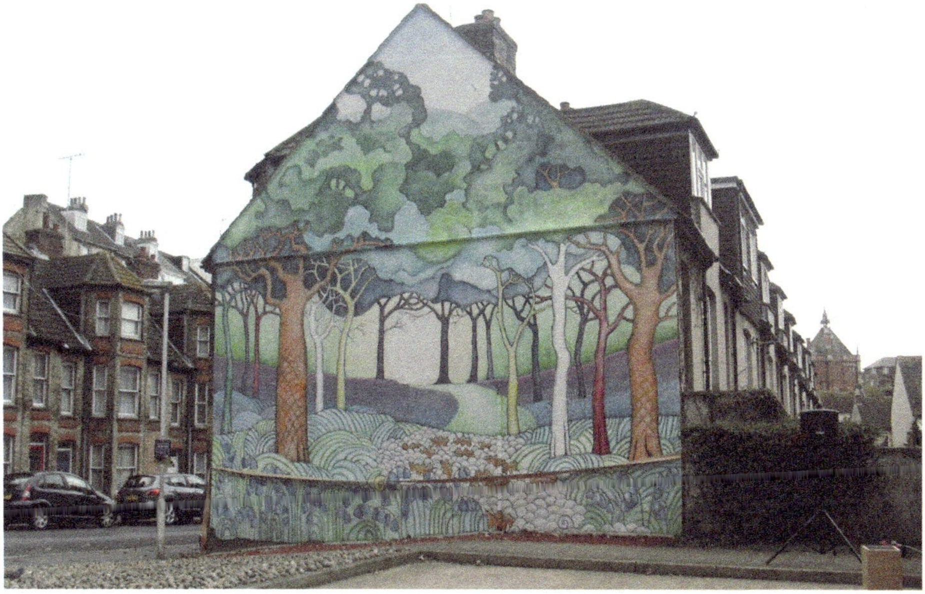

A Mural to Deter Graffiti Artists

Above: The mural on the sidewall directly opposite the viaduct in Bradstone Road. This idea was thought up by the Residents Association to help make the run-down area look better. On completion of the mural an opening day was arranged for 9 November 2012, attended by Damien Collins MP, the mayor of Folkestone, Rodica Wheeler and the person who painted the mural. Philippa Goddard of New Romney cut the tape to declare the painting finished. Philippa said the mural depicted what could have been a bluebell valley with the Pent stream running down to the sea.

Below: Willing helpers on the empty site a few yards away from the viaduct for the children to play in, nearer their homes, was being cleared in November 2011 by two volunteers of the residents association, who I saw having a bonfire. They had high hopes for this site; sadly in 2015 it still hasn't been finished.

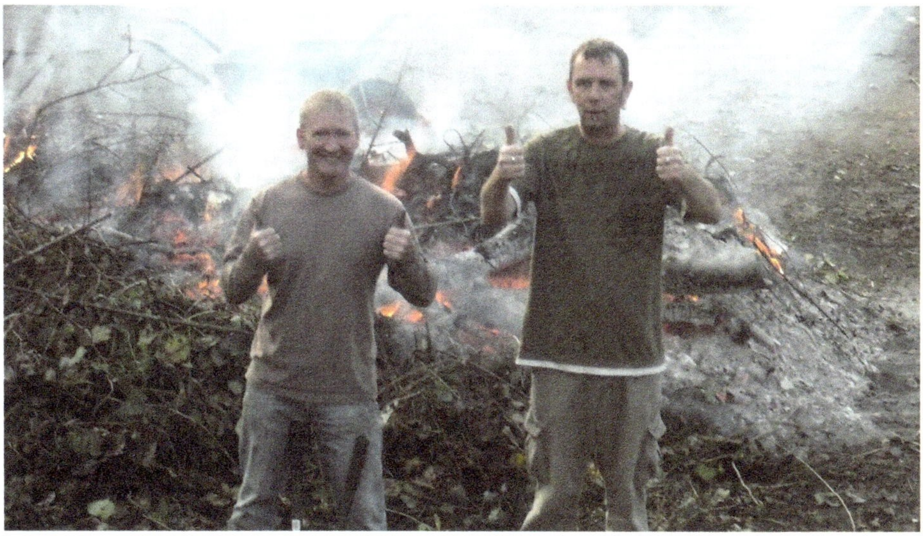

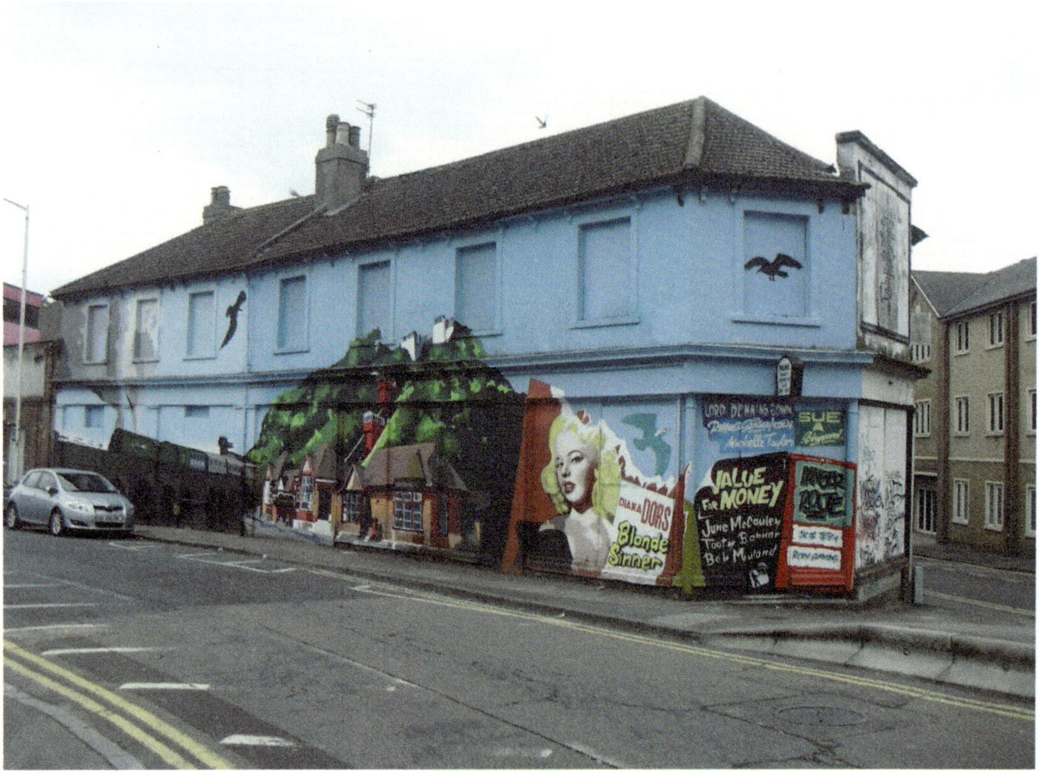

From a Co-op to a Sports Centre

Above: The building was such an eyesore that the Dover Road Residents Association raised funds to make it look smarter. This mural was commissioned and painted within six months. The area of the building with the bird on was once W. P. J. Crouch, a wallpaper shop. The rest of the building to the right and a round the corner was the Co-op, built in 1923. In the 1970s it was a bingo hall with the Sundowners nightclub next to it.

Below left: The demolition of the old Co-op building began in April 2015 and in July was completed.

Below right: A concept just released from the Roger De Haan Charitable Trust. This artist impression is a 'World First' indoor sports centre on three levels, which will contain skating, biking, a high climbing frame and other youth projects. Apparently it will be a reduced entrance price for local youths to be able to use. Spokesman Mr Trevor Minter reported that 80 per cent of the work should be completed by the end of 2016.

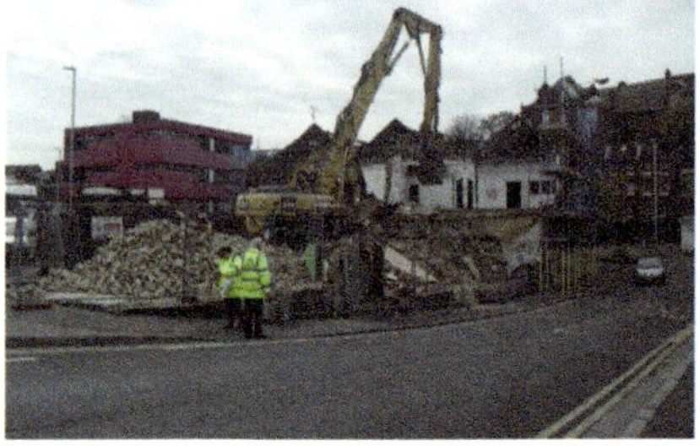

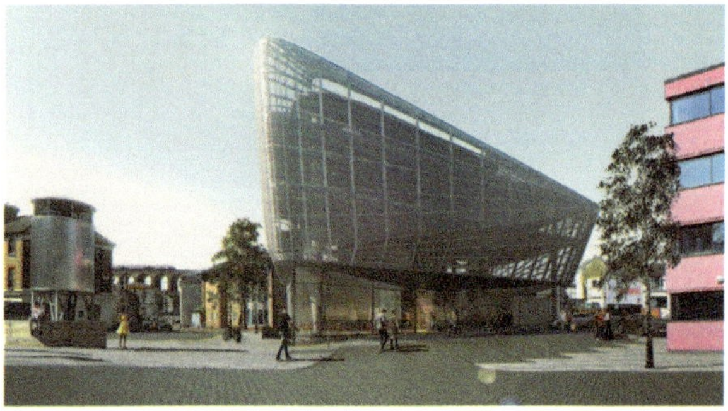

Free for All?

Right: Albert Davies standing outside his shop at No. 6 St John Street in the late 1930s. Albert's cousins from Newington ran the shop for him during the war, when Albert was in the fire brigade. The shop was badly damaged in 1941 by a bomb, at the time Albert was stationed in Folkestone and living at home in Downs Road. A policeman went round to the house in the middle of the night to inform him his stock was on the pavement. I bet the residents in the area thought their luck had changed. The shop never reopened, and shortly after Albert was posted to Ramsgate to fight fires on board ships coming up the channel. On a few visits back home while on leave, the shop was cleared of stock and sold on to a shop in Blackbull Road.

Below: The garages at the bottom of Queen Street and corner of St John Street where Albert Davies' shop stood. Albert's son Peter told me a story of how the headmaster of Dover Road School came across to the shop one day and requested that he didn't sell the children peanuts as the caretaker was fed up with the mess they made.

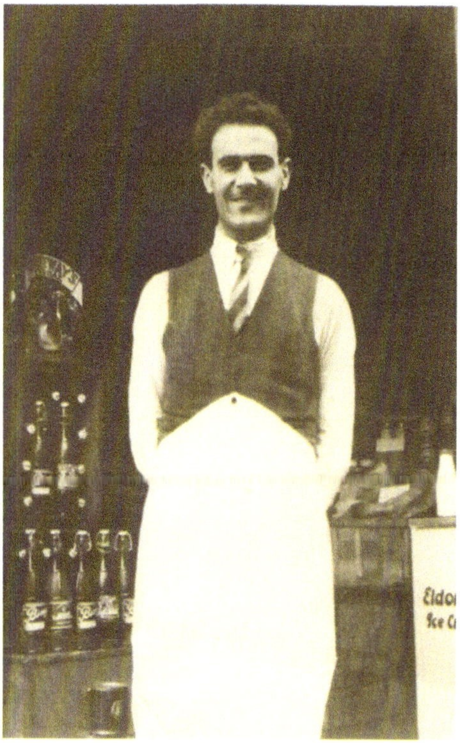

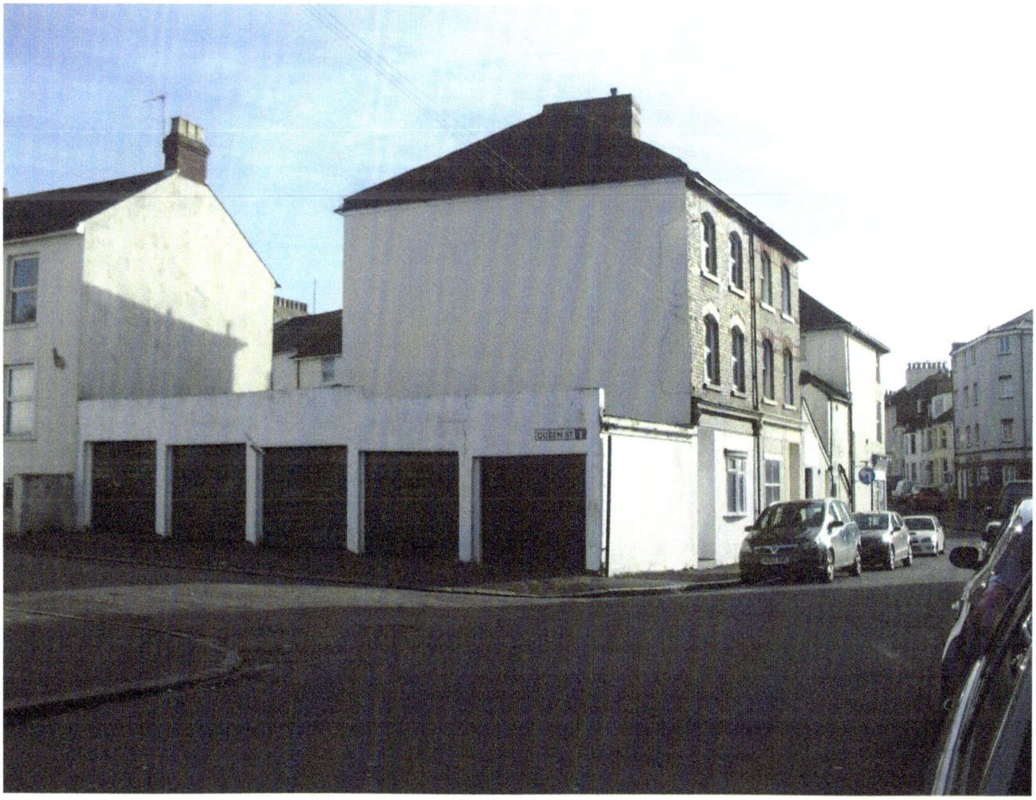

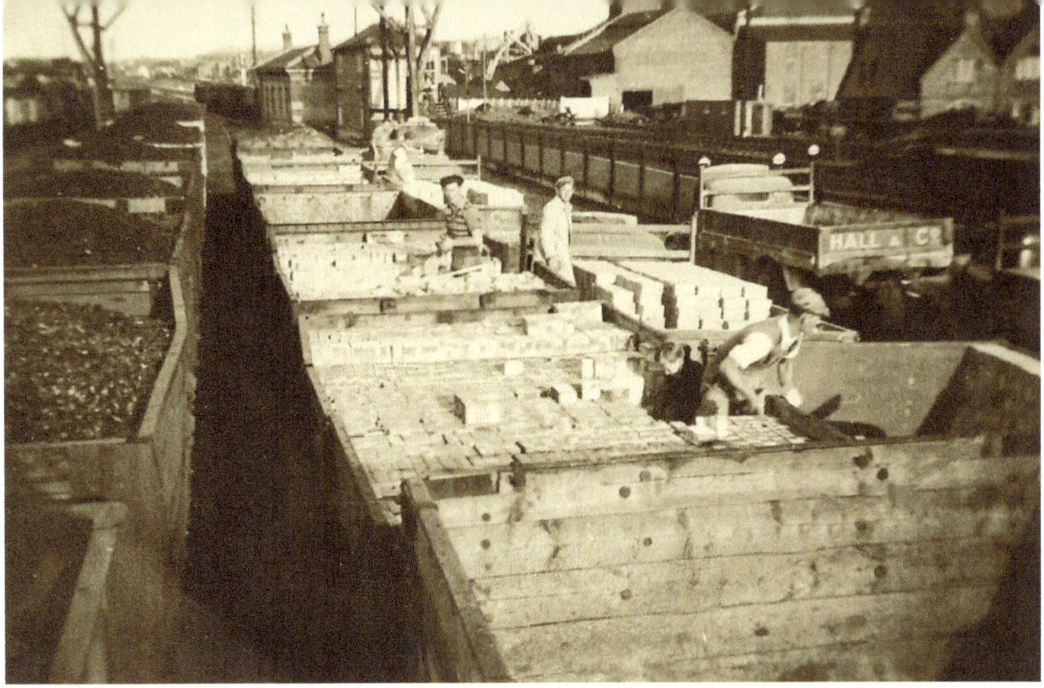

Guess Where This Is in 1950?

Above: A long time has passed since this area was used as a marshalling yard. In the centre of the picture is Ernie Gray, who at the time was working for Hall and Co. building suppliers. This marshalling yard was at Folkestone's Junction Station. The men are unloading bricks that were put into the Hall and Co. lorry, where Ernie was the driver. Murmurings in various sectors state that if only marshalling yards existed today it would save so much traffic on the roads, the goods traveling by rail.

Below: The triangle-shaped grass and shrubs to the left of the railway line is where the marshalling yards were when the Junction Station was operating. When the yard was closed, Southern Water took over the site so it could build a building with underground tunnels that went down to the sea. The treatment work buildings are the square roof shapes on the edge of the triangle land that is now up for sale.

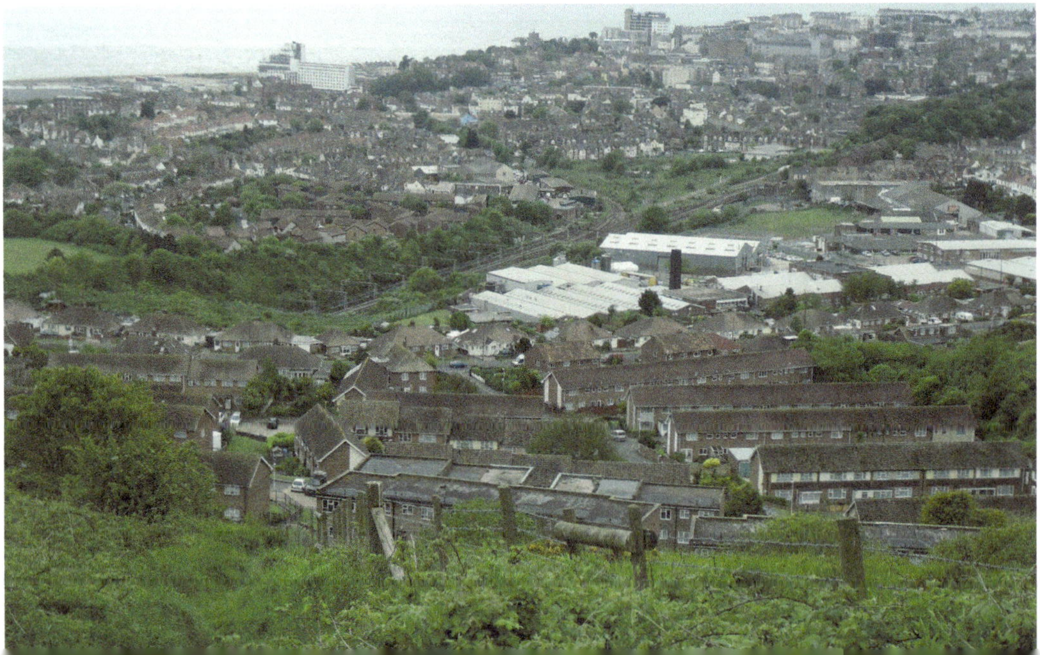

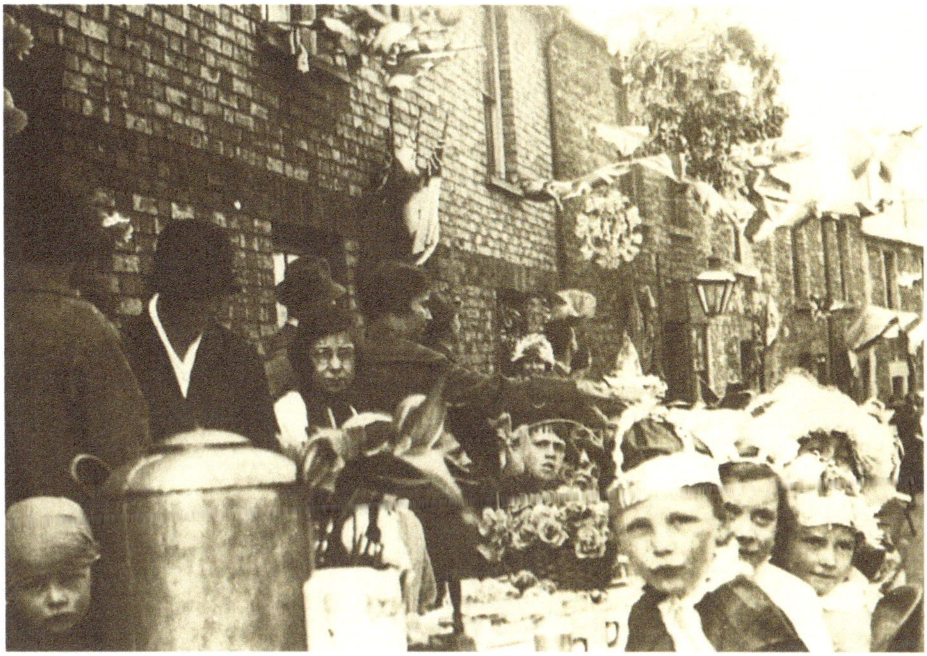

Tea Parties Again

Above: Palmeston Street, May Day 1921. Looking from the top of the street downwards. Still a very narrow street but today it has no houses in it. Some of the names of families who lived in the street: Rainer, Copping, Fagg, Marsh, Butcher, Claringbowl, Ford, Tickner, Haywood, Arnold, Cook, Andrews, Wright, Godbold, Dine and Paye.

Below: Thanet Gardens in 1937, possibly during George VI's coronation. The man with the large jug is Arthur Hall, his mother Annie Hall is the lady opposite him with the dark hat on. I wonder if anyone will recognise an aunty or grandmother in either photo.

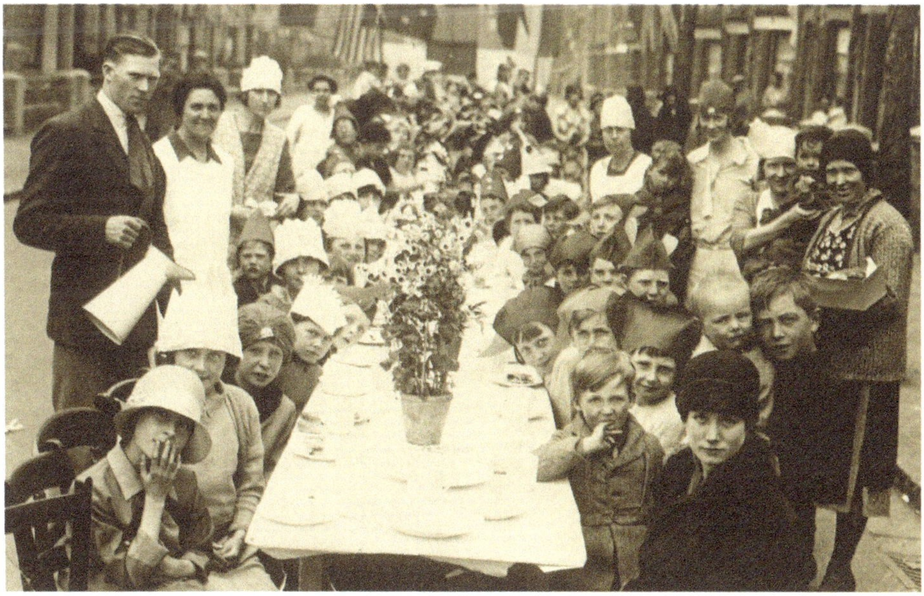

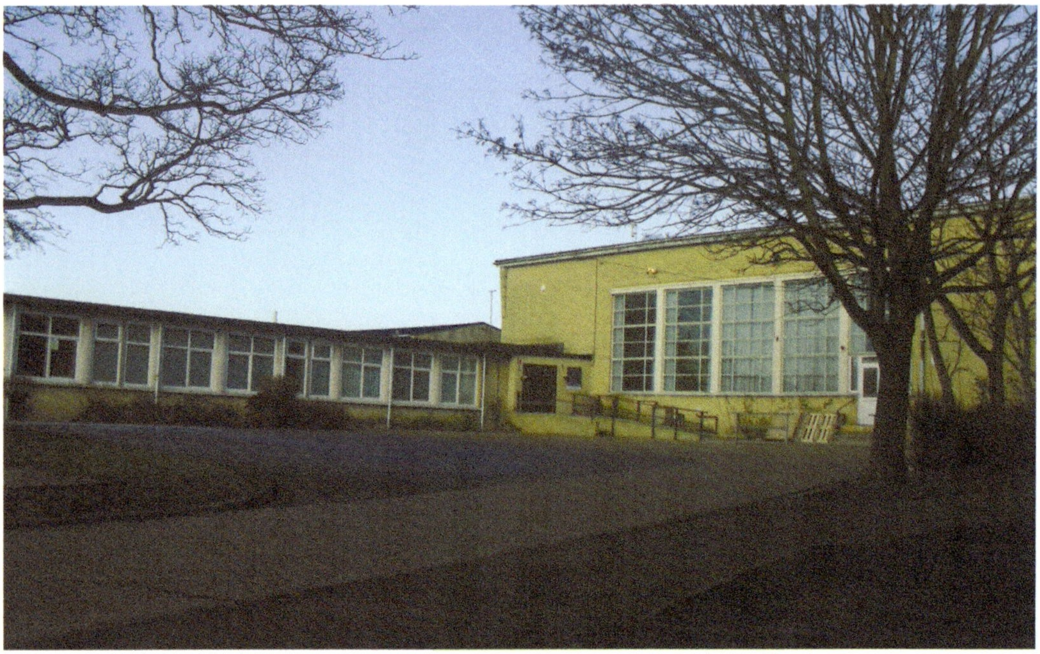

Gone Holywell School Park Farm Road, 1950–2014

Above: In my day a girls' school for those over eleven years old, now just a memory. In recent years it became a primary academy school. In 2014, the demolition of the school and its Horsa huts began for redevelopment of some eighty-four dwellings and a new school.

Below: May 2015, houses being built on the old school site and the tree. One of the site managers told me they were unable to save any of the other trees, as there were too many roots that needed to be removed so they could lay the services in. Inside the wire fence, in front of the houses, many new trees are waiting to be planted.

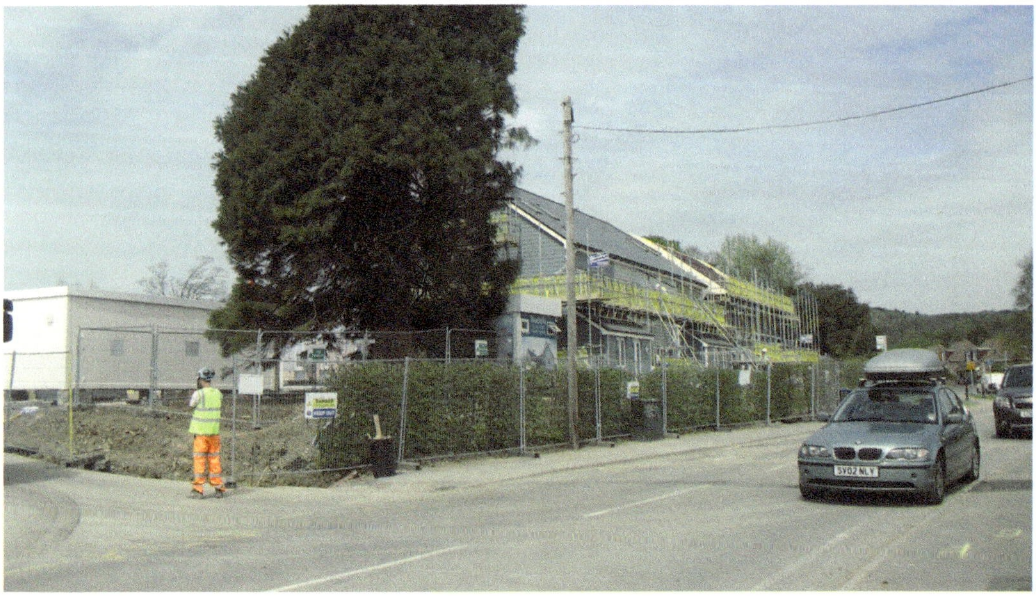

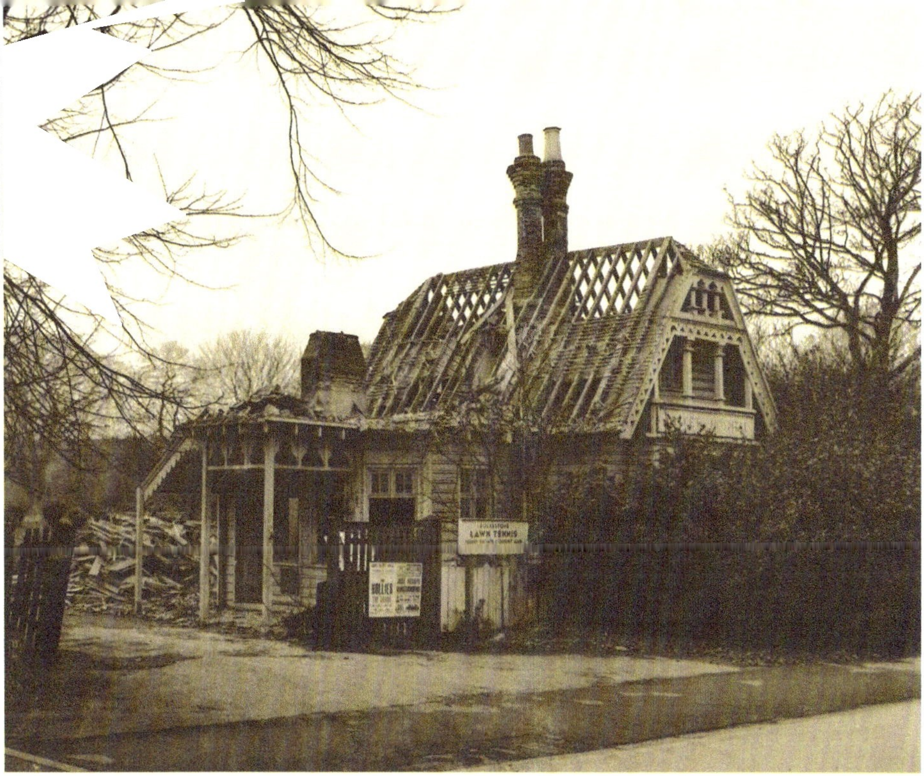

Anyone for Tennis?

Above: This old tennis club house was situated in Castle Hill Avenue, taken in around 1962, as demolition was taking place. It catered not only for tennis but for squash and croquet as well. It is believed to have stood where Court Approach is now. When demolished the land was used to build new council offices in 1967 and the magistrates' courts were completed in 1979 by local builders Jenner.

Below: Taken in 2015, the low building hiding in the background is the magistrates' court and the tall building to the right of the picture is the civic centre council offices that were built in 1967. The old tennis club building was possibly situated where the arrow is on the road.

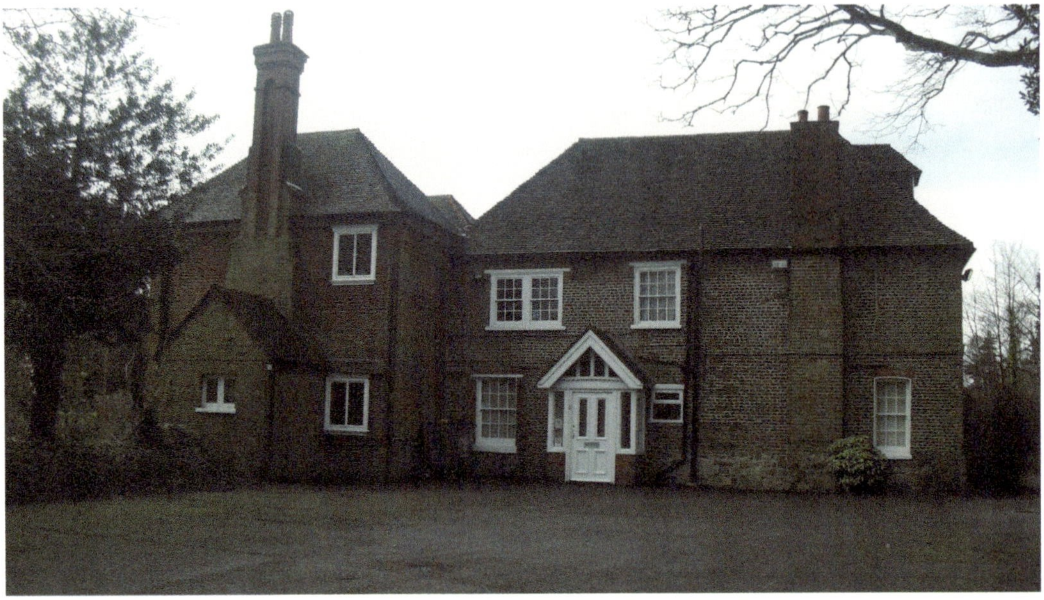

Ingles Manor, Castle Hill Avenue
Above: Situated down a long driveway is Ingles Manor, in Castle Hill Avenue, reputed to have been built in the 1700s. For many years it was used as a school and now used as offices.

Below: The manor house, in the distance and on the left is the newly finished thirteen luxury three and four bedroom houses, Castle Mews. I can remember that the manor house and the old barn behind it could be seen from Shorncliffe Road, as it was quite a large fenced-off field we called Ingles meadow, where as a child my parents would take us to feed the donkey in the field.

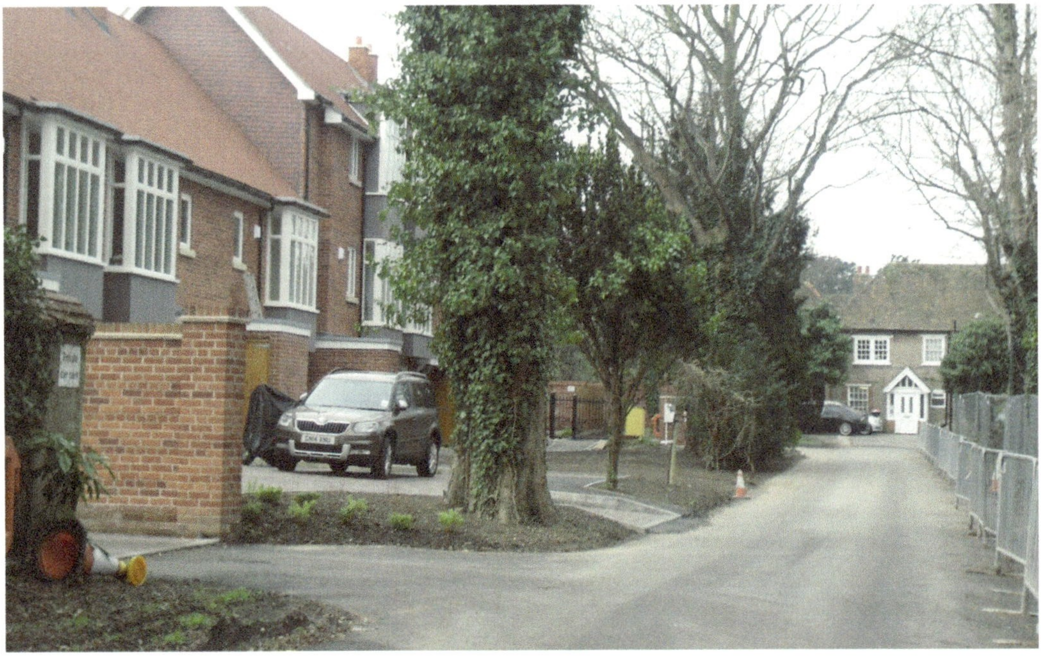

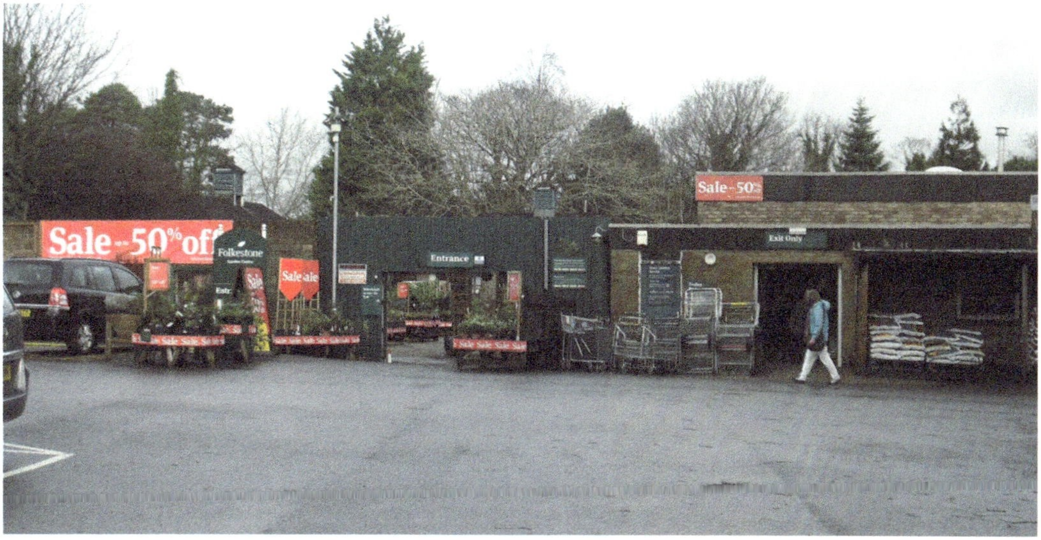

A Much-Loved Garden Centre and Café but for How Much Longer?
Above: On Ingles meadow at present is Folkestone's garden centre and café, now under threat from developers of the Castle Mews construction who plan to build on the site of the garden centre. There has been an uproar by many of the local residents who like to visit the garden centre, not only for plants but for the café as well to have a cuppa with friends.

Below: A piece of solitude where you can walk and hear the birds singing and admire the trees covered with camellias and rhododendron blooms. They are a sight to be seen in the spring among an assortment of lovely trees, a bit of heaven so near to the town centre. One of the foremen of Castle Mews site informed me that it would be a good two years before the next stage of buildings takes place and the garden centre will have a year's notice to close down. Is there a glimmer of hope for the garden centre I wonder?

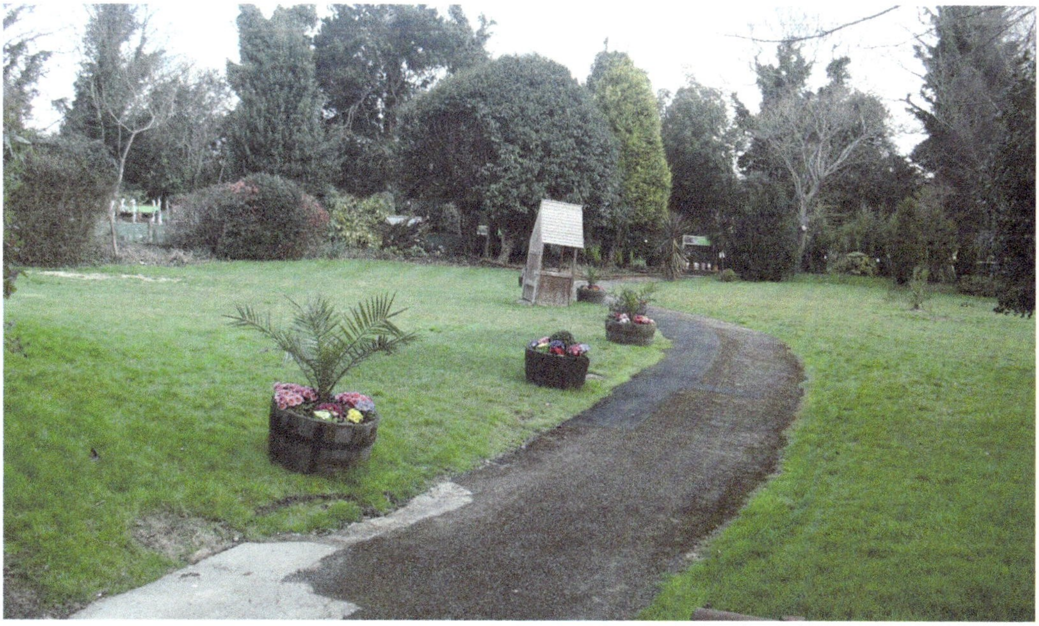

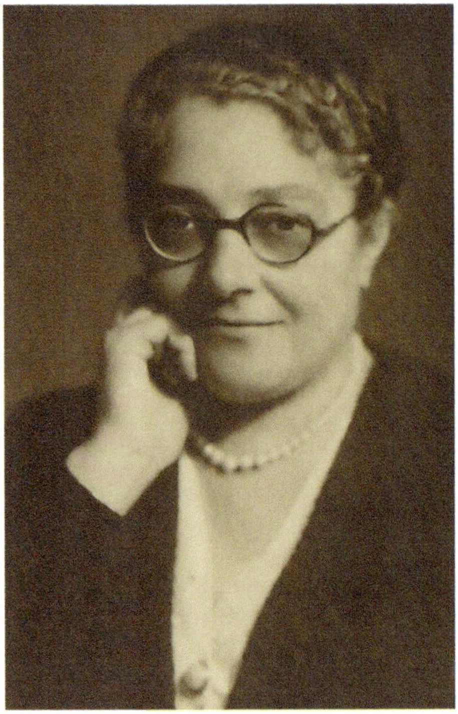

Remembering a Dedicated Matron

Philippa Hart
1885–1949
Matron of the Isolation Hospital until 1940
Daughter of DR M D Hart
practitioner in London

Below left: Taken in 2014, Philippa House was named in the memory of Philippa Hart, who for twenty-five years was assistant matron and matron of the isolation hospital, which formerly occupied this site. Sadly the hospital was closed after it was bombed in 1940 and was not rebuilt.

Below right: This is the old isolation hospital in Warren Road, built in 1878 for the Borough of Folkestone from plans by a Mr W. E. Springall who was the borough surveyor. On 6 July 1940 it was bombed during what was said to be the first alert of the Second World War. At the time only the staff were there and the patients had been moved to safety.

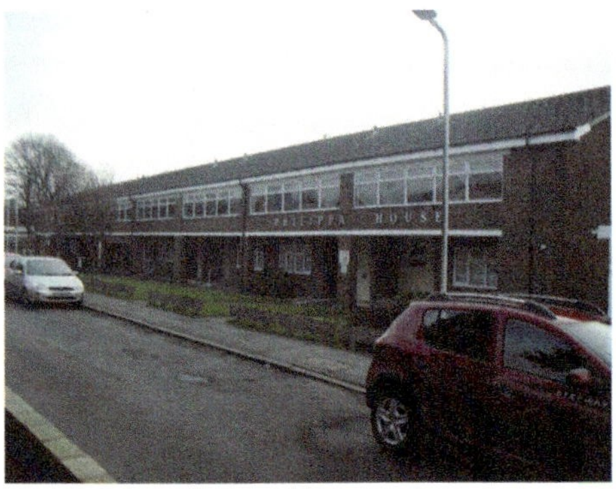

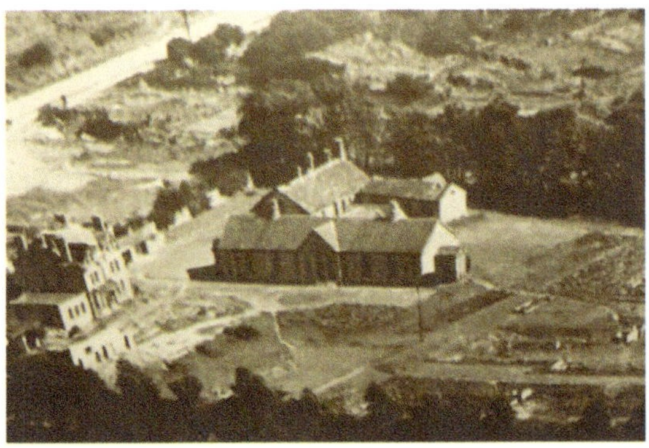

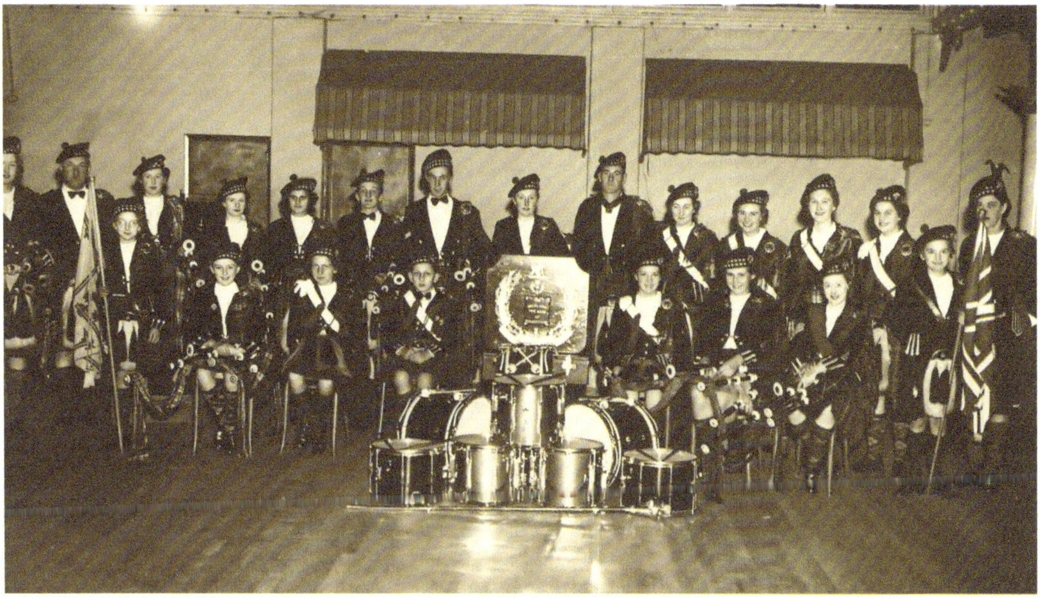

Famous Pipe and Drum Band of Folkestone

Above: A group photo of the band in 1956 in the downstairs area of the indoor swimming pool, just before the band went off to Boulogne on their four-day twinning event.

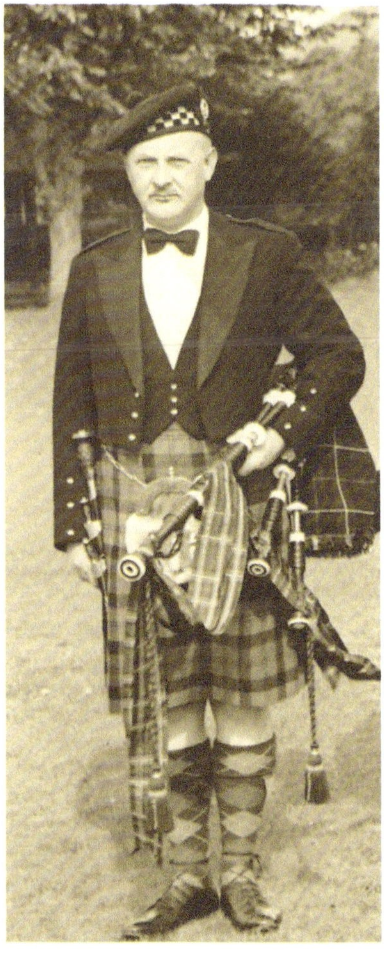

Right: Maj. Malcolm Nicolson TD was born in India in 1906 and returned to Scotland at an young age. He learnt to play the bagpipes at nine years old, his tutor being the champion piper of Scotland. He joined the Seaforth Highlanders territorial regiment while at university in Edinburgh. Joining the War Office in Shorncliff as an architect in 1937, transferring to the Royal Engineers in 1939 when he was sent to France, being one of the many escaping from Dunkirk. In 1947 he went to Tanganyika with his wife Ina on the famous 'ground nut scheme' but returned in 1949 because of Ina's health. They settled in Folkestone and Maj. Nicolson became an architect for Hythe, designing the Hythe Library and Stade Street Bridge. The Nicolson Pipe Band was formed in November 1952 for the study of bagpipe music and highland dancing. It became one of Kent's biggest ambassadors, not only in this country but on the continent where it made annual tours.

Malcolm died very suddenly aged seventy-one in 1977 and a committee was set up, which included Mrs Nicolson, and Terry Rivers became President. Terry along with his wife Pat and a few other volunteers kept the band going, but sadly disbanding eight years later after entertaining the public for thirty-five years. A sad loss to the town and Europe where they made so many friends with their displays.

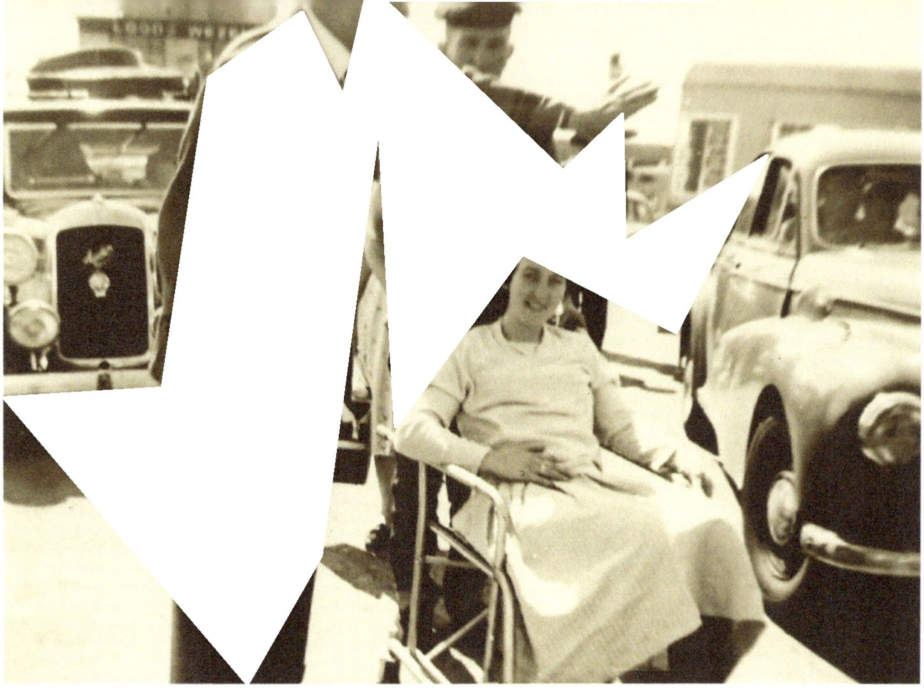

Corporal Mary Castle's Collapse in Luxemburg, 1959

Above: Trust Mary, she would never do anything by halves she would say. She told me this story after returning home: she had collapsed and was taken to hospital with appendicitis, and said she had a fright when she came round from the anaesthetic – she saw ladies around her dressed in white nun outfits looking down at her. She thought she was in Heaven; we have often laughed at this story over the years. She travelled with the band on the coach, laying on the back seat as in those days they couldn't afford to send her home.

Below: On the Leas, Folkestone in 1960. The mayor of Boulogne presenting the five-year medals to Valerie Dalton, Mary Castle and David Rivers. Maj. Nicolson is standing next to the mayor.

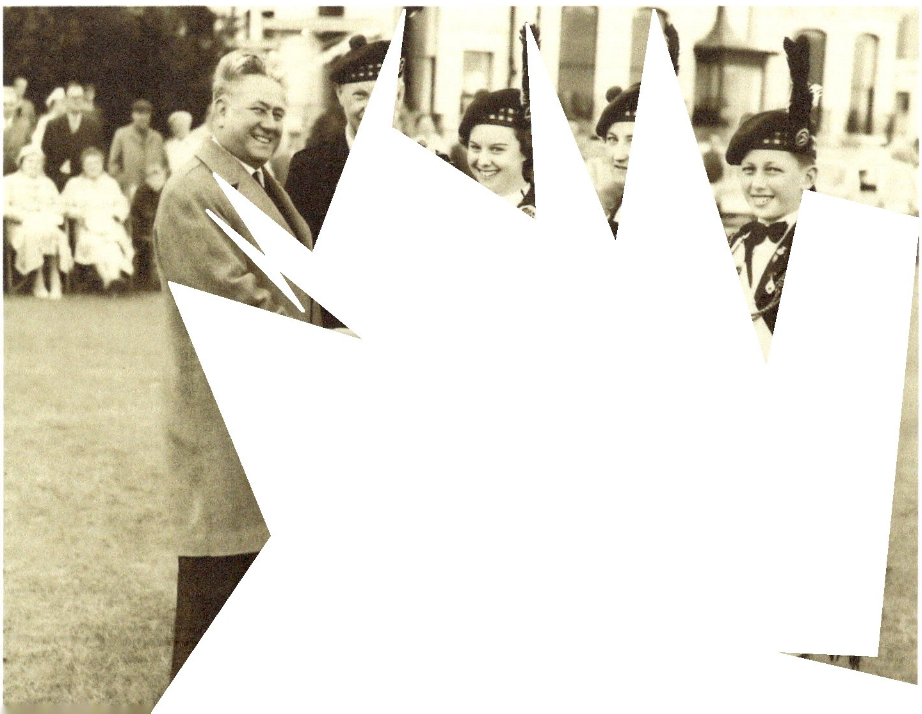

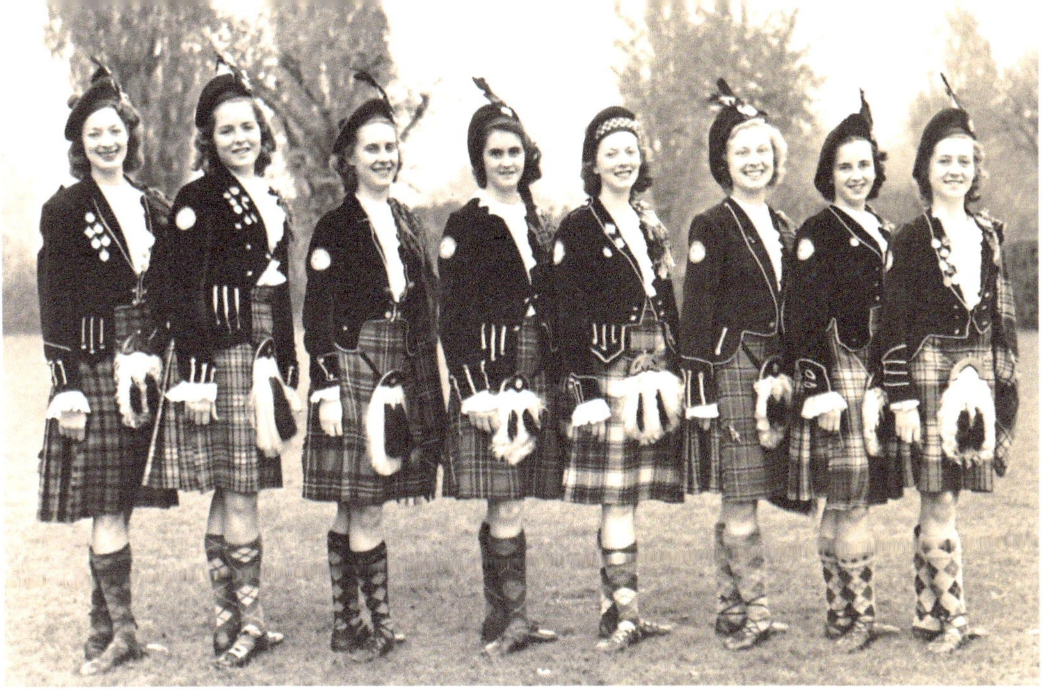

Trude Noon's Highland Dancers, 1950

Above: The dancers with Trude Noon in the centre right. Trudy also taught tap dancing at the Priory Hall School of Dancing at No. 19 The Bayle, known today as the Dance Easy. Trude was known for her troop performing in pantomimes at the Pleasure Gardens Theatre in Bouverie Road West. The police station is situated on that site today. Maj. Nicolson often played for Trude's troop but decided he wanted his own group, so in 1950 he set out to form a pipe band with drums and highland dancing, which became a great success.

Below: The Dance Easy building at No. 19 The Bayle, taken in 2015.

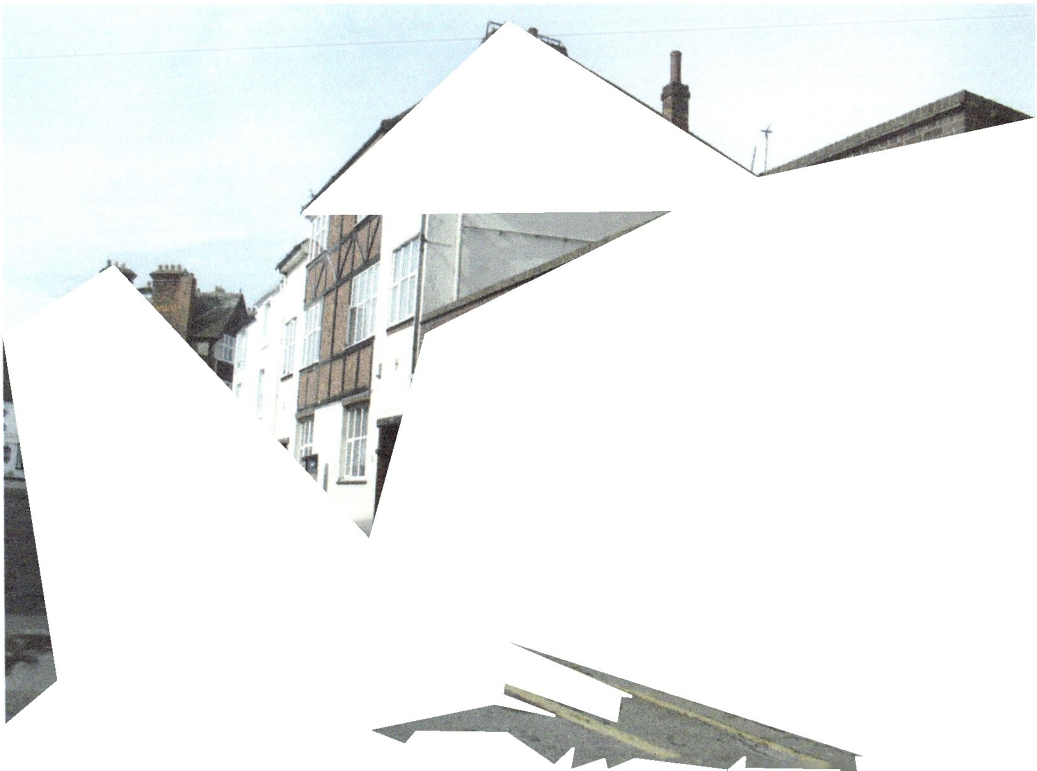

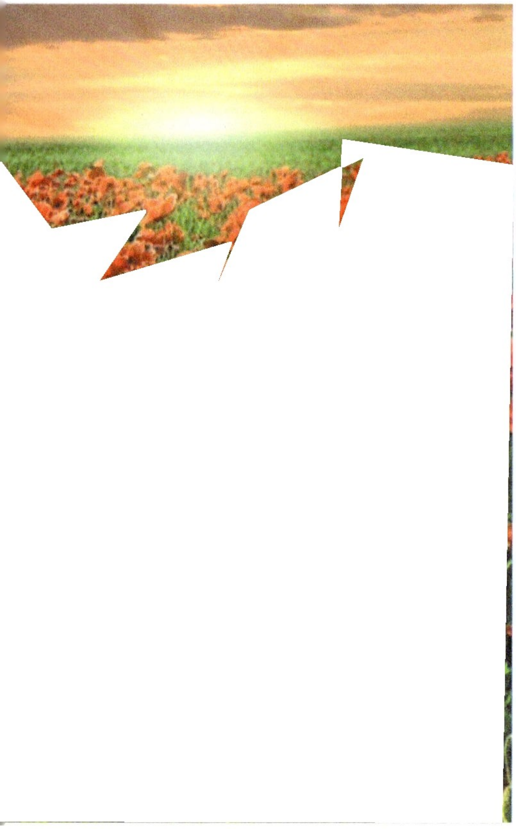

With the Going Down of the Sun and in the Morning, We Will Remember Them

These last few pages are dedicated to the preparation, events and the memorial services that took place from January 2014 to March 2015. As this period marked significant dates for several First World War and Second World War anniversaries, I felt to record these events as information for generations to come. I also felt it fitting to write about a few of Folkestone's servicemen who gallantly served their country; some who came home, some who were unlucky to perish away from their homeland, and some who served their country at home.

Knitted poppies were made in January 2014, by local women and fixed to the railings on the road of remembrance to mark the troops that marched down to the harbour to board ships taking them to France in the First World War.

Shortly after saw the start of the clearing in the Road of Remembrance area in preparation for Prince Harry's visit in August 2014. A rosemary garden and commemorative plaque was founded. Once cleared new rosemary shrubs were planted, the plaque was cleaned and replaced on the wall along with other plaques that collectively reads a memorial poem. Also found in this extensive clearing of the area was an old Victorian Latrine. A local poet wrote a poem called 'Light Relief', which referred to the latrine in Slope Road (renamed after the war as the 'Road of Remembrance').

Further down the Road of Remembrance a Second World War bunker was found built into the cliff, which was requisitioned by the Royal Navy for the use of radio equipment away from the main naval communication facility, which is now the Grand Burstin Hotel.

On the 6 June 2014, the Folkestone Normandy veterans attended the seventieth anniversary memorial service of the D-Day landings at the Garden of Remembrance Tower. Many of the veterans were in their eighties and nineties. Another memorial service took place also at the Garden of Remembrance, but on 27 January 2015. This was to mark the seventieth anniversary of the Holocaust and the liberation of the notorious Nazi extermination camp Auschwitz-Birkenau. July 2014, saw the revealing of the Folkestone Leas flower bed display, which marked the 100th anniversary of the beginning of the First World War. A local schoolgirl won a competition for her flower bed design, which was then replicated in real life.

On 4 August 2014, Prince Harry unveiled the plaque on the Step Short arch, which was Folkestone's latest memorial to commemorate the centenary of the beginning of the First World War. This memorial was called the *Step Short Arch* to commemorate the troops that walked down this road to the command of 'Step Short' – a shortened step so the men could keep marching without treading on the backs of the heels of the soldiers in front of them. The opening of the educational wing on 28 March 2015 at the Battle of Britain memorial site in Capel Le Ferne pays homage to all the airmen who lost their lives defending our country. Elizabeth II opened the spitfire shaped wing in preparation for the seventy-fifth anniversary of the Battle of Britain that took place on 12 July 2015.

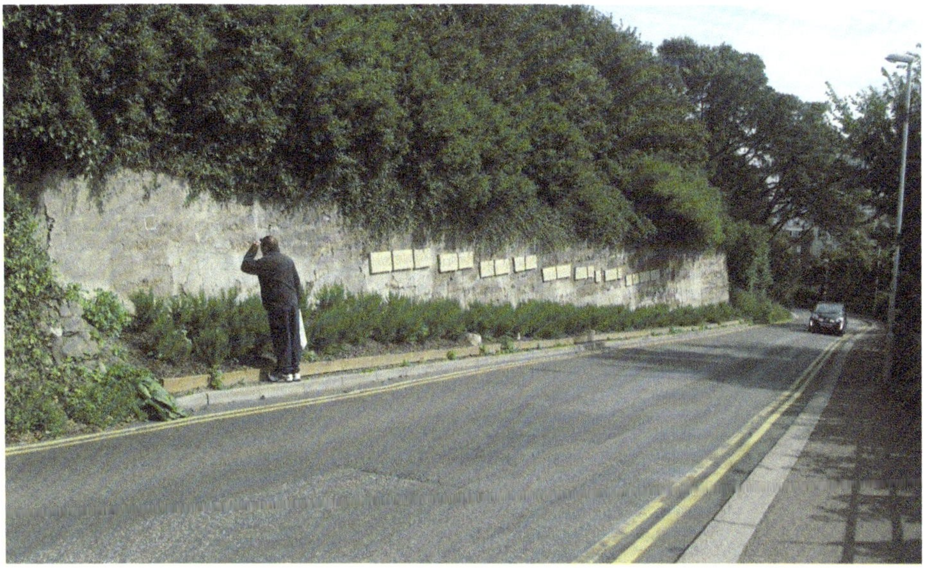

Plaques in Place

Above: The Road of Remembrance's newly refurbished rosemary garden and the plaques in position ready for Prince Harry's visit. Part of the poem 'An Unseen', written by poet laureate Carol Ann Duffy, on each plaque, reads:

Down the quiet road, away, away, towards
the dying time,
love went, brave soldier, the song dwindling;
walked to the edge of absence; all moments going,
gone; bells through rain
to fall on the carved names of the lost.

Below: A small section showing the last four plaques, close-up.

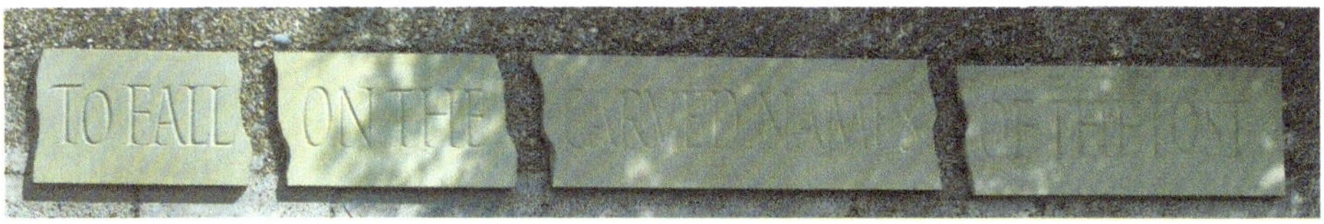

Below: This plaque is positioned on the wall above where the gentleman is reading it in the above image. It was refurbished and replaced by the Soroptimists.

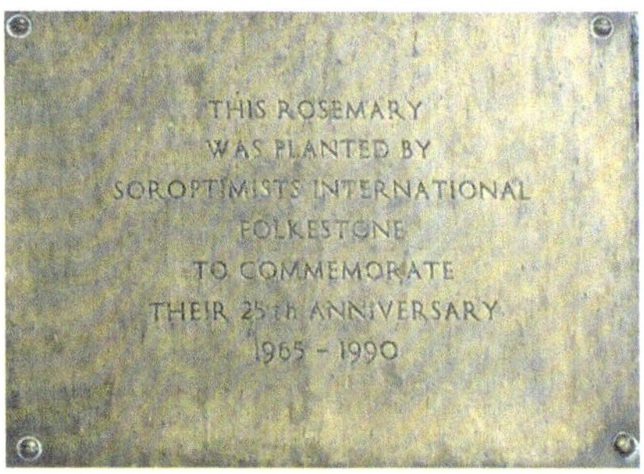

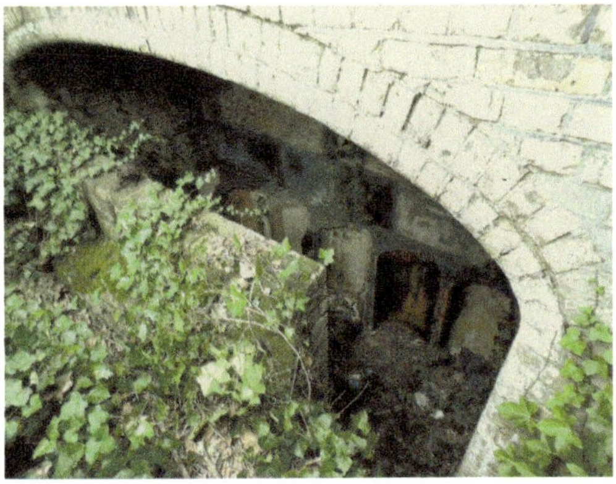

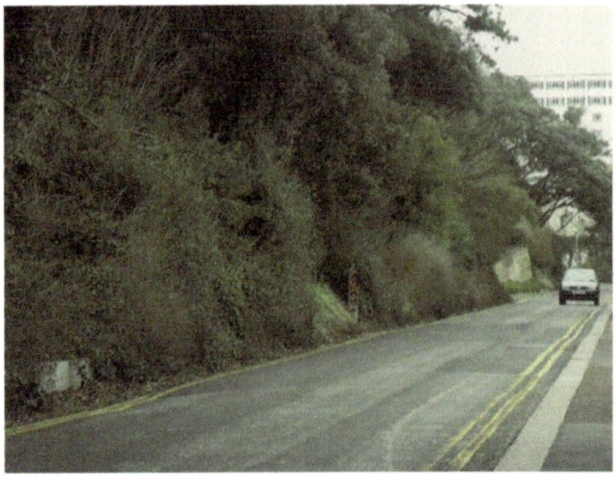

What Have We Got Hiding Here?

Slope Road was built in 1824 by a man named Potland and renamed the Road of Remembrance sometime after the First World War.

Above left: This is a picture of an old Victorian latrine which is situated down the Road of Remembrance. There appears to be no information of when it was built, it is not found on the 1881 Ordnance Survey map but is on the 1898 one.

Above right: The picture shows how hidden the latrine is. About halfway down this road are steps up to the parish church. The concrete slab in the bottom left of the picture, hidden in the undergrowth, are the latrines. 'Light Relief' *(below)* refers to the latrines.

It's a long way to the war lads,
It's a long way to go,
And often on a journey,
It's to a loo you know.

And to the loo that's nearest,
The Sergeant turned an eye,
For down Slope Road we wander,
When nature calls us nigh,

When nature calls us nigh lads,
On our way to board the boats,
Its fingers, thumbs and trousers down,
Around our machine boots.

It's a long way to the war lads,
It's a long way to go,
And often when you're bursting,
It's to the nearest loo you know.

Maxwell Dunlop

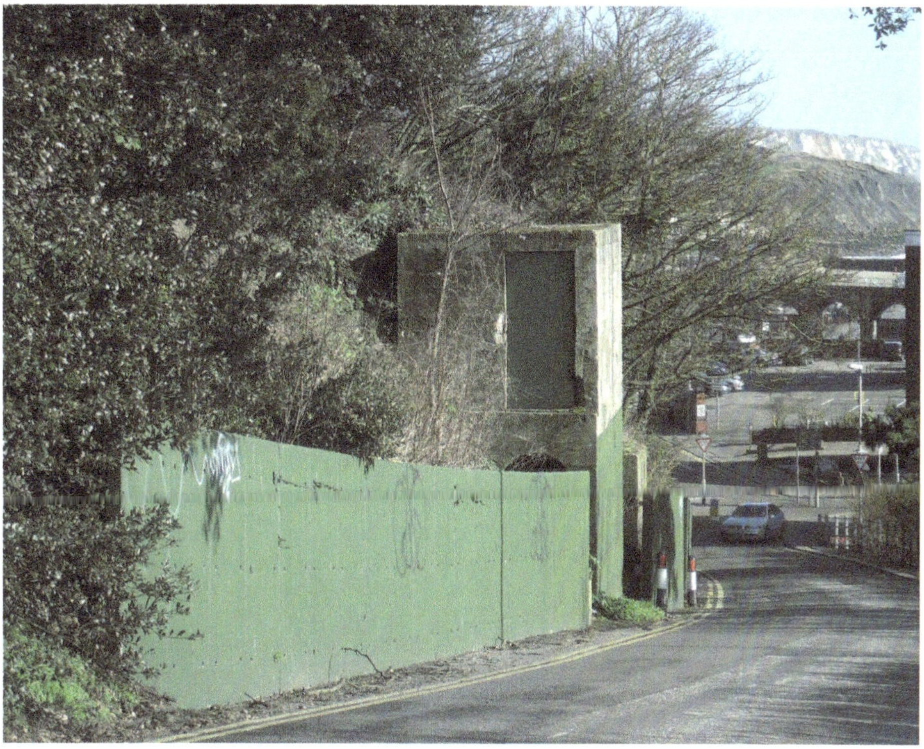

HMS Allenby Would You Believe? Down the Road of Remembrance

Above: This Second World War bunker was a naval communications facility built in 1942. The Royal Pavilion Hotel was used by combined operations 1943–45 named HMS *Allenby* and is believed to have changed its name to HMS *Bluebird* in November 1945. It also had its air conditioning placed on top of the bunker inside the green door.

Below left: The old rusty looking door with the arch space above. My husband managed to get a photo of what lays behind the door!

Below right: Inside the door is a toilet and a corridor leading to the left. In recent times a few ideas have floated around as to a use for the building, the last one being a disco! Of course this is not possible as the road is so dangerous with the traffic and there is no pathway. It would be an accident waiting to happen if people were exiting the building.

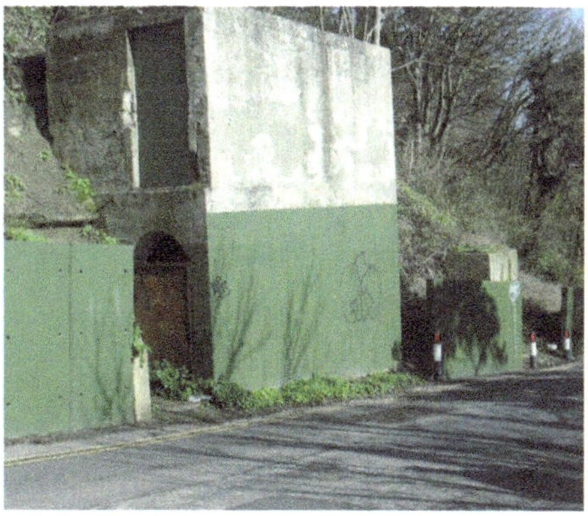

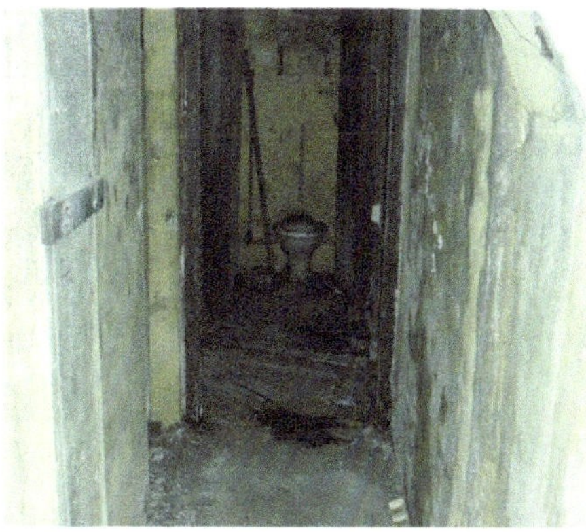

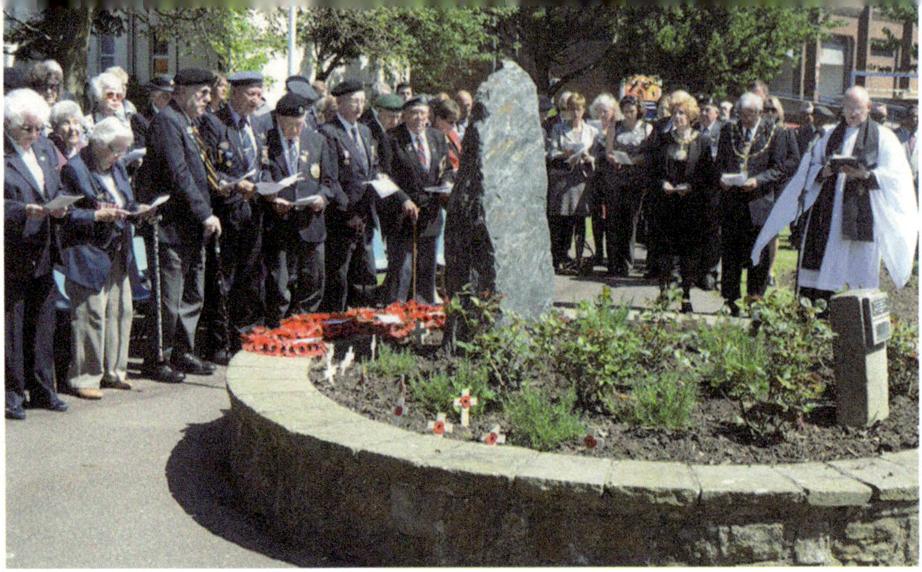

The Last Folkestone Normandy Veterans' Association Service
The service held at the Garden of Remembrance in Sandgate Road on 6 June 2014. The seventieth Anniversary of D-Day Normandy landings. Officiating was Revd Peter Ashman, son of a D-Day veteran, with civic officers from the Shepway District Council, and the chairman of Folkestone Council.

Holocaust Memorial Day Seventieth Year
The gathering (*below*) took place at the Garden of Remembrance, Christchurch Tower, on 27 January 2015 for the Holocaust Memorial Day. The event was attended by Mayor Alan North and his dignitaries. The Royal British Legion displayed their flags and the service was conducted by the Revd Mrs Rosemary Sibert, and there were short readings from five schools and colleges. I was very moved by one lady who came and stood by me just before the service started; she asked if I was Jewish. I said no but she went on to tell me her father was Polish and was shipped to Scotland from Belgium. He helped to organise and went over to help liberate the camp. She said she was very proud of him as the sights he saw lived with him forever.

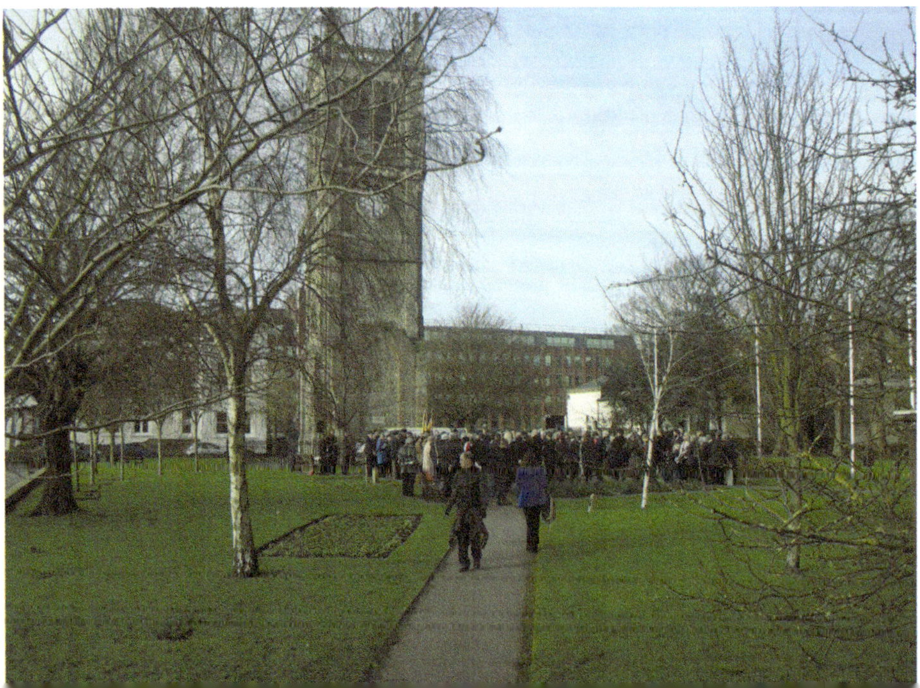

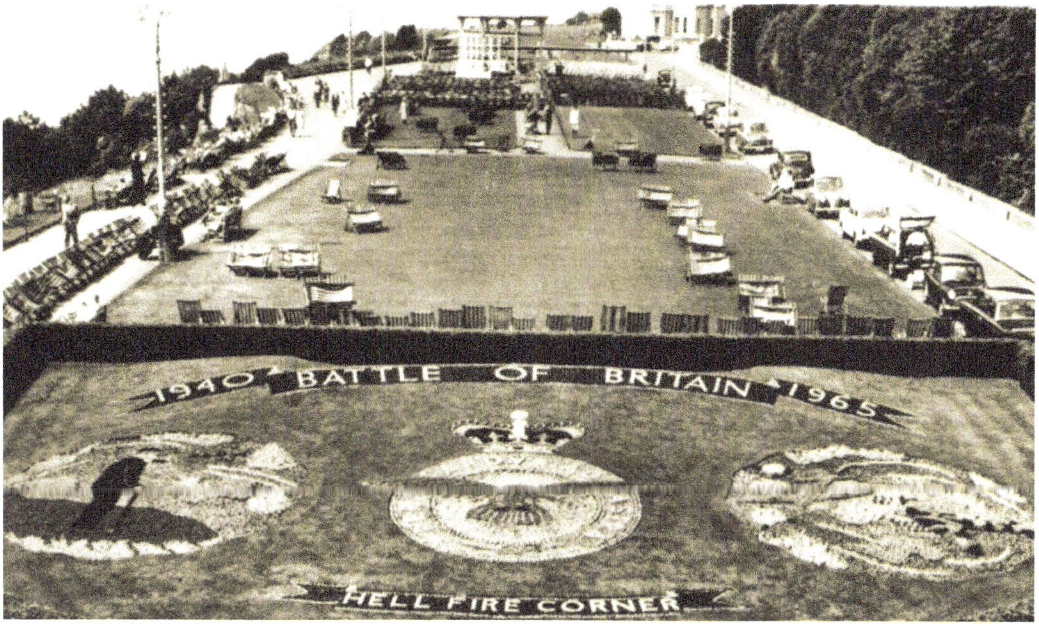

The Leas Annual Flower Display

Above: A flower display commemorating the twenty-fifth anniversary of the Battle of Britain in 1965.

Below left: The floral display in 2014 was designed by Viktoria, aged seven, from Christchurch Primary Academy. Viktoria's design was chosen out of 150 other entrants from schools in the Shepway area. Either side of Viktoria is Ann Berry, vice-chairman for the First World War commemoration charity Step Short, and Cllr Malcolm Dearden Shepway, cabinet member for grounds maintenance. What a proud day for the academy and Viktoria's family to have her design for all to see on the Folkestone Leas.

Below right: A photo of Viktoria's flowerbed design.

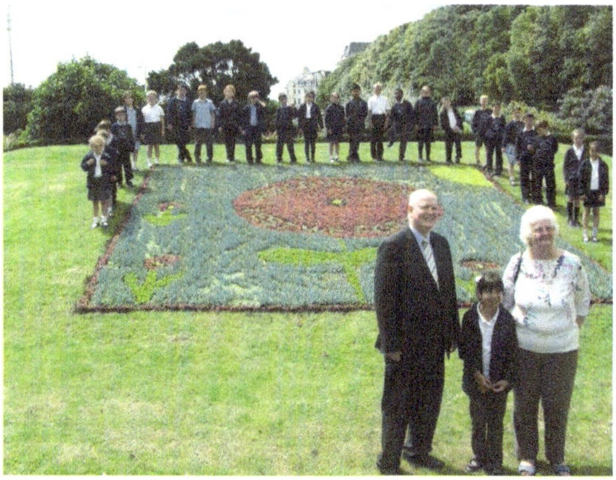

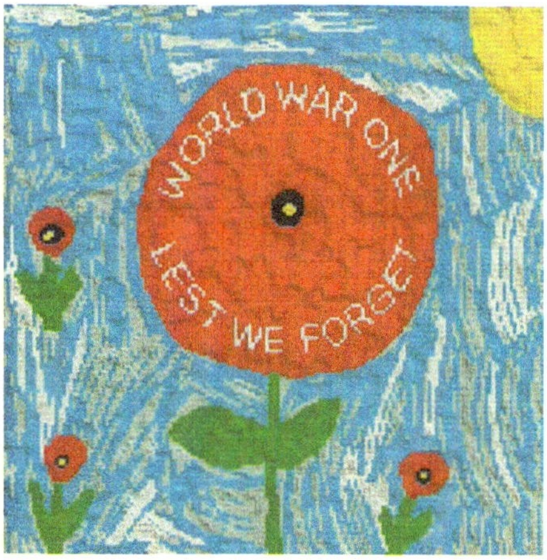

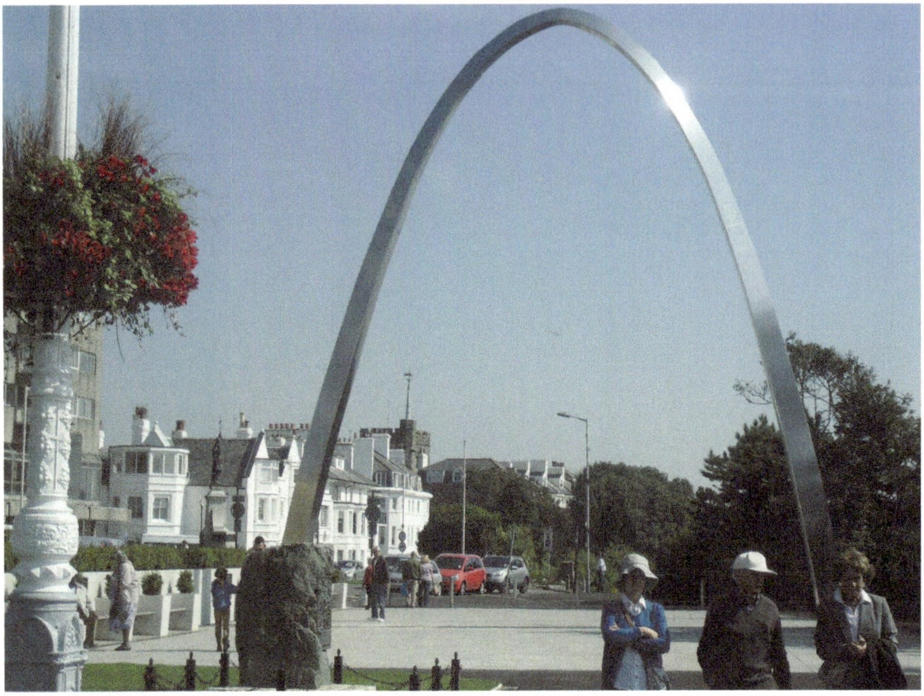

A Memorable Day For Everyone

Above: Step Short's stainless-steel arch was unveiled on 4 August 2014 by Prince Harry. If you look carefully at the picture you can see the other three memorials: one that looks like a rock by the arch, one near the lamp post in the distance at the top of the Road of Remembrance. The top of the third can be seen to the left of the arch as if it is on the roof.

Below: Prince Harry unveiling the plaque of Step Short's Memorial Arch, with Cllr Damian Collins looking on.

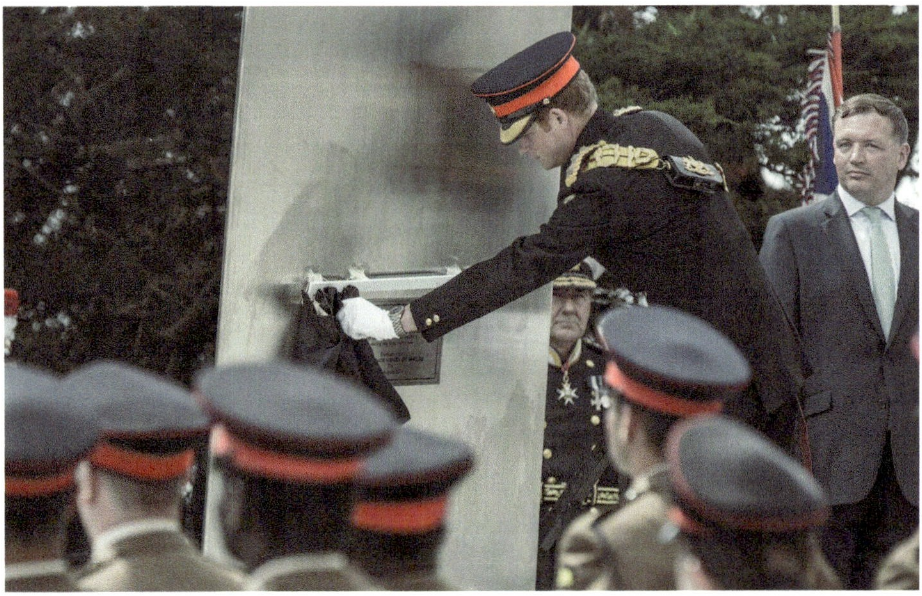

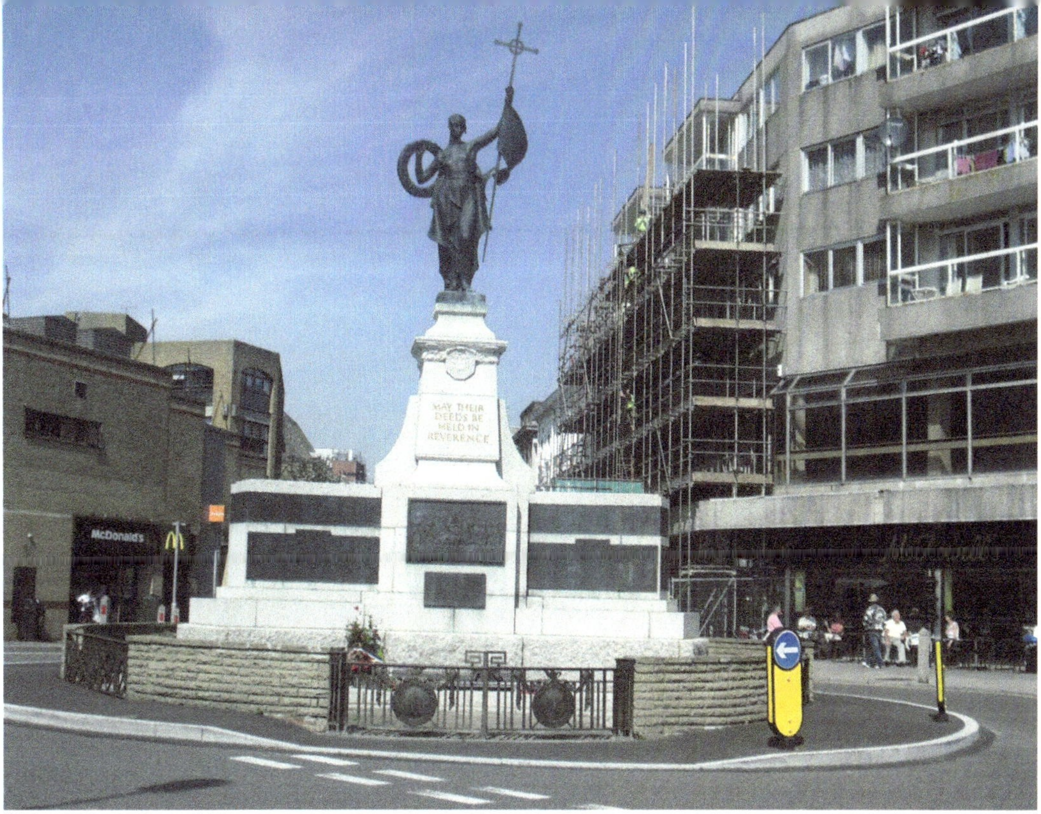

These are the three memorials described on the previous page. It was felt that a new memorial for the centenary of the First World War would be fitting to honour the men and women who served their country and millions who left Folkestone that did not return.

Above: The Statue of Victory memorial directly faces France on the top of the Road of Remembrance. Mr Blundstone, the sculptor, accepted the commission in October 1921 and the memorial was unveiled at a dedication service on the 2 December 1922.

Below left: Here stands the Road of Remembrance Memorial to the tens of thousands of soldiers that passed this way to and from the battlefields of Europe during the First and Second World Wars.

Below right: The plaque here states that the memorial is 'To Commemorate The Airmen and Women Who Served in Two World Wars In Defence of an Ideal'.

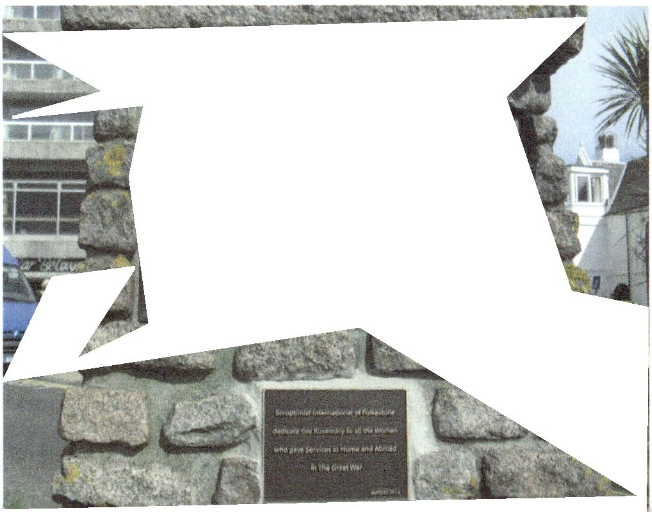

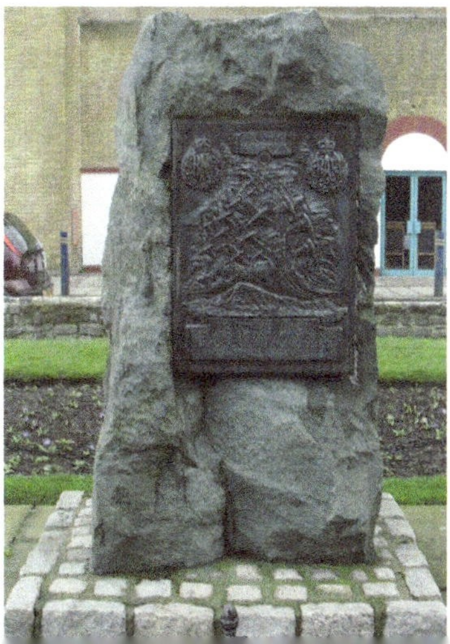

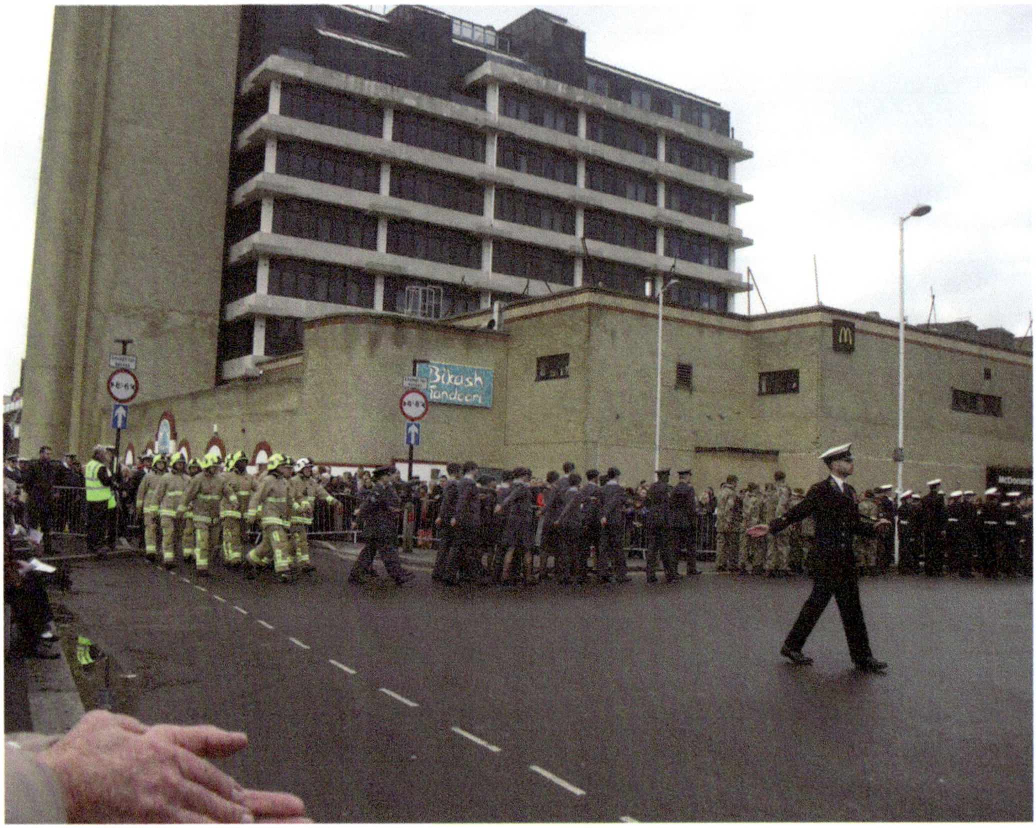

Remembrance and Armistice Day Services

Above: Taken Sunday 9 November 2014 with the services marching to the memorial that has the names of the Folkestone casualties in the two wars. Every year a Remembrance Sunday service is held at this memorial with the mayor, his dignitaries and service men placing wreaths.

Below: Taken on Tuesday 11 November to commemorate Armistice Day. This was a more informal affair with not so many people in attendance, but the service was still very moving and meaningful.

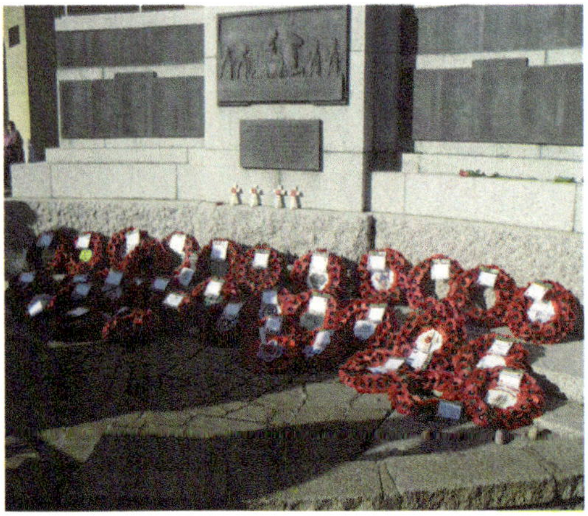

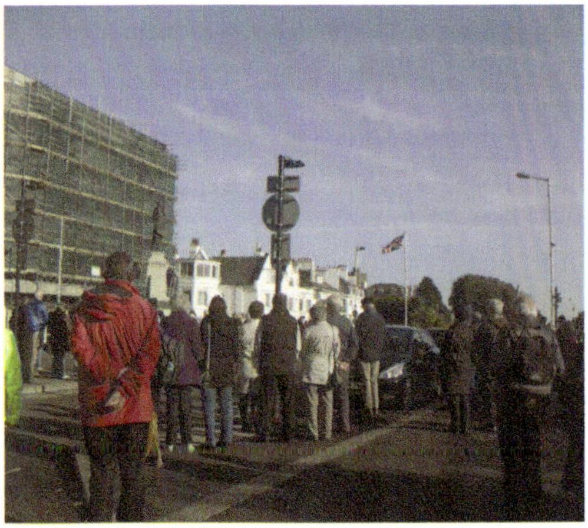

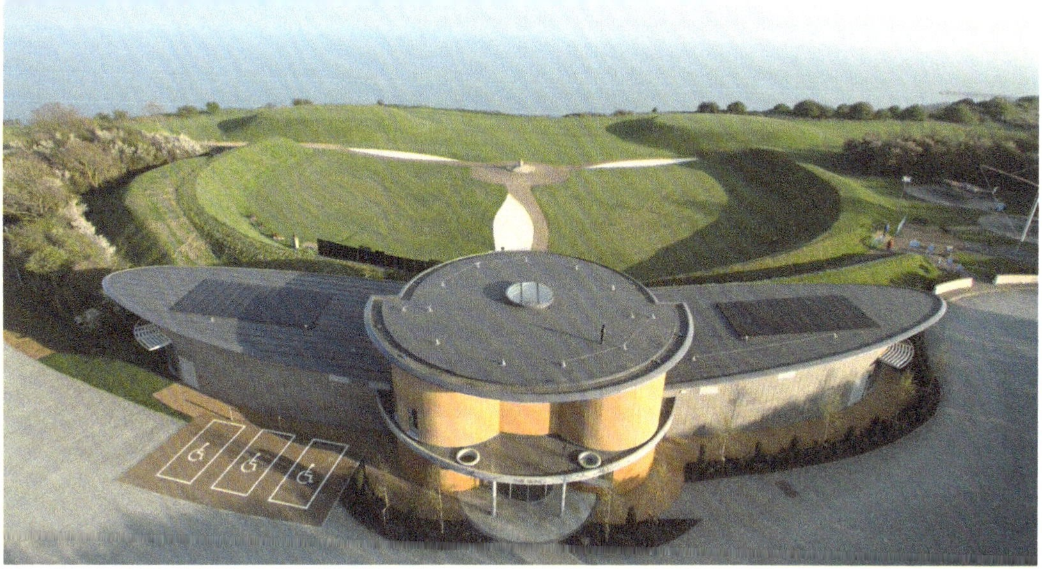

The New Wing Experience at Capel-Le-Ferne, Kent

Above: The idea for a Battle of Britain memorial site was conceived by Wing Cdr Geoffrey Page, who was founding member of the Guinea Pig Club – plastic surgery patients like himself. With no designated site for the airmen, Geoffrey started to create one here at Capel Le Ferne. The memorial (the small dot in the centre of the propeller in the grass area) depicts a figure of a young airman staring out to sea, thinking of his fellow men facing dangerous conditions, fighting the enemy, and praying for their safe return. The Battle of Britain Trust concept is to remember some 3,000 airmen who defended our country in the skies over the channel above these cliffs.

Below: Elizabeth II following in her mother's footsteps, as the Queen Mother opened this Battle of Britain site in 1993. The queen opened the new wing on 26 March 2015. It has educational functions such as the Scramble Experience, a classroom, and hands on activities. Here the Queen is being introduced to the trust's volunteers by Maj. (Retd) Jules Gomez inside the wing. The trust stressed that the site will remain free apart from a small charge for the Scramble Experience. An interesting, beautifully maintained site I am sure will be of interest to future generations for many years to come.

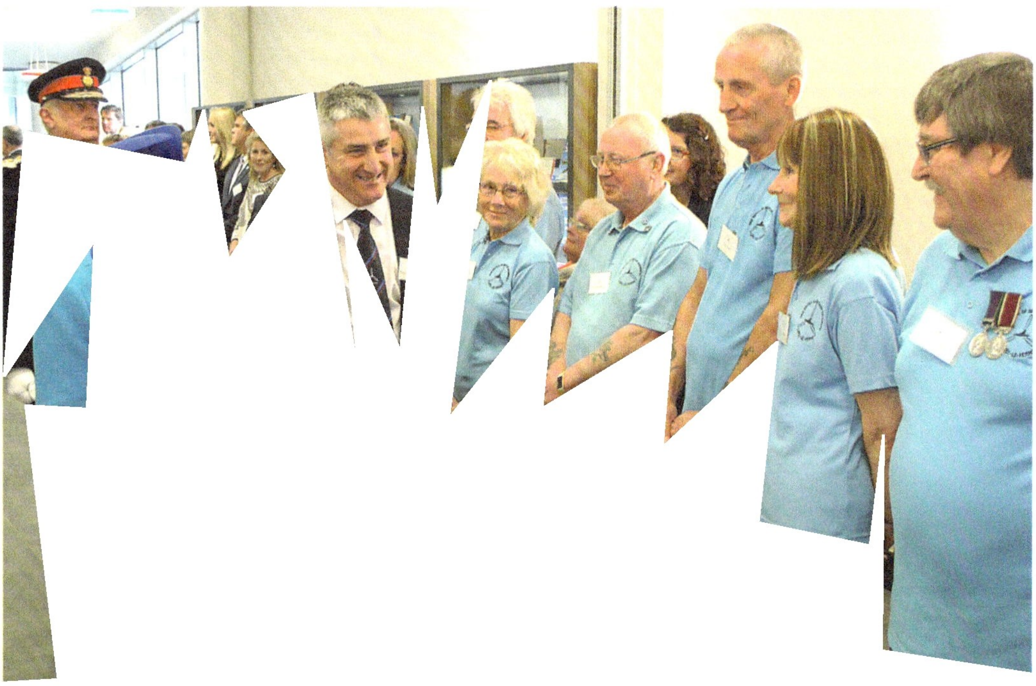

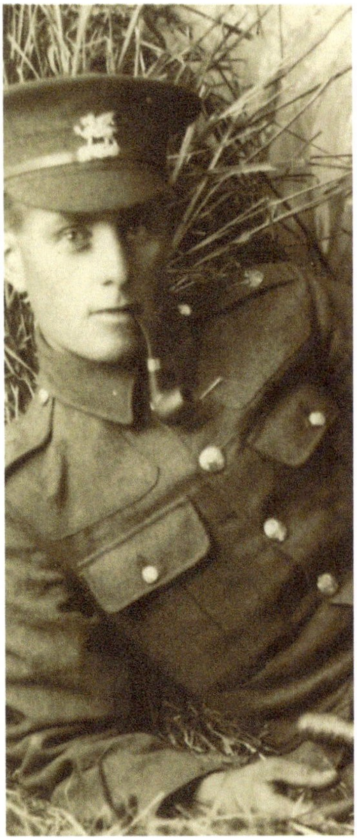

Two Cousins Went to War and Only One Came Back

Left: Herbert Henry Milton (1889–1975), son of Edgar and Martha Milton, was from an old fishing family. Herbert didn't want to be a fisherman as he said it was hard work and unreliable pay, so he became a postman until he retired.

Below: Herbert sent a postcard to his wife from Mhow in India while he was stationed there. Herbert was a postman and in the Territorial Army when he volunteered for the army. When he was in the desert he was in the camel corps and one night an Arab sneaked into the camp and, amazingly, they discovered it was Lawrence of Arabia.

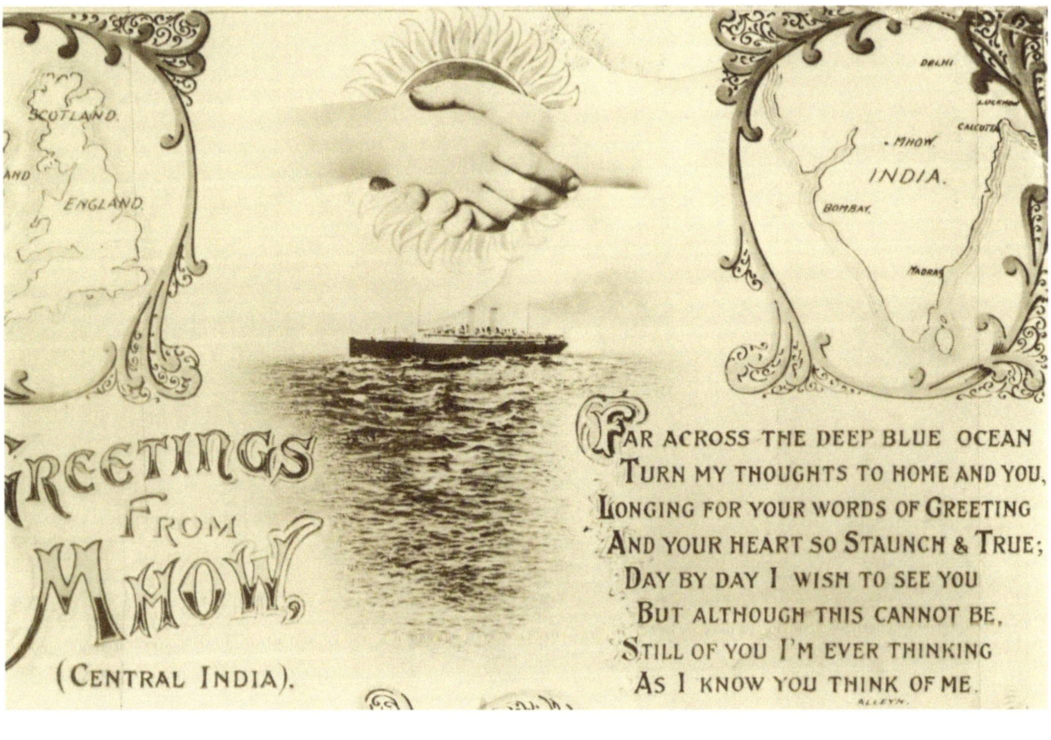

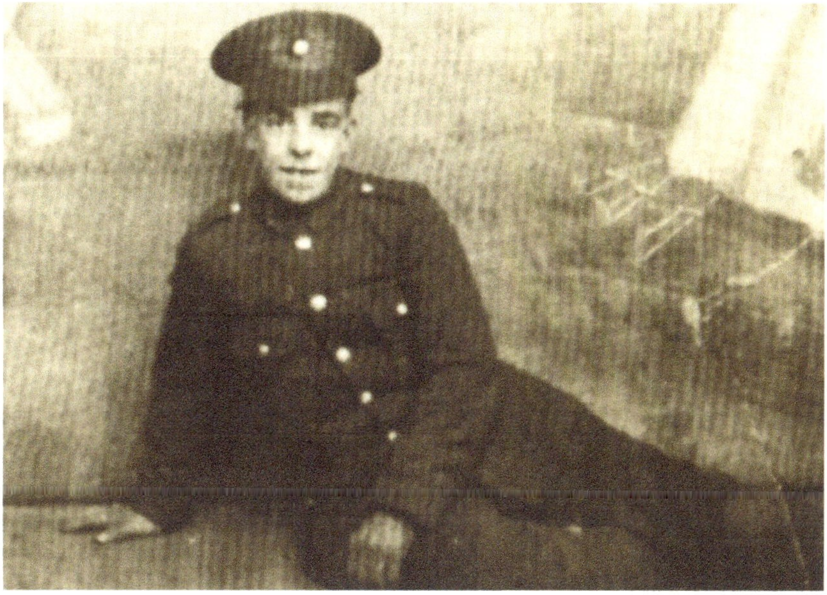

Above: Frederick John Milton (1898–1917) was the last child of William and Elizabeth Milton. He was a fisherman from an old Folkestone fishing family from Bates Alley. Frederick lost his life on 12 September at Ypres, aged just nineteen. He was a private in the 8th Battalion, The Buffs (East Kent Regiment). Sadly his body was never found and he is remembered on the Tyne Cot memorial, Zonnebeke, West-Vlaanderen, Belgium.

Below: A picture of the bronze Memorial Plaque, also known as a Dead Man's Penny, sent to Frederick's family. These were issued after the First World War to the next-of-kin of British and Empire military service personnel who were killed during the war.

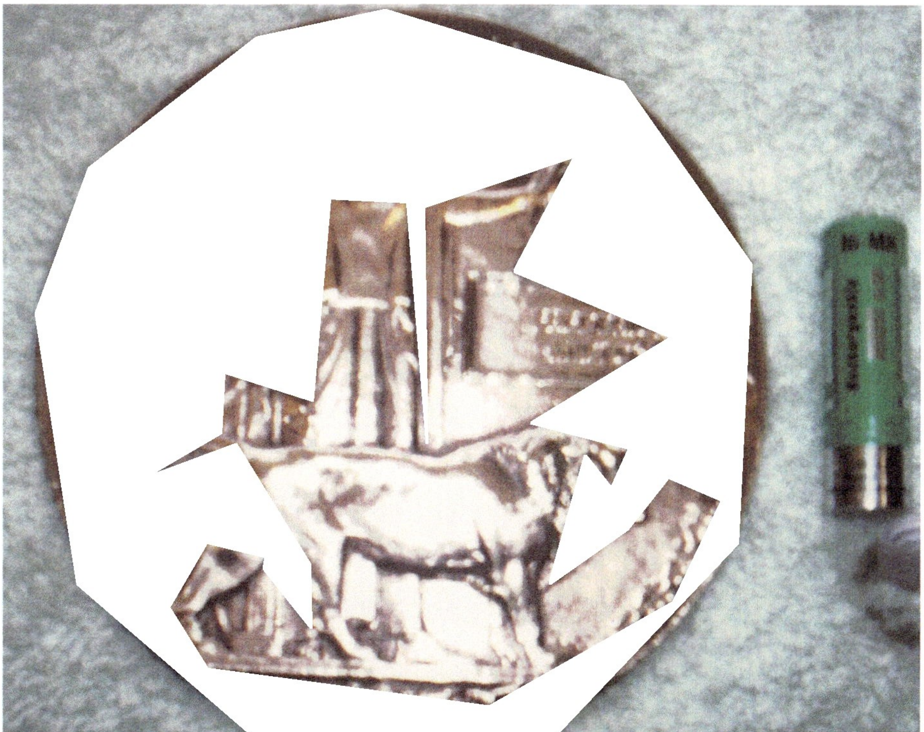

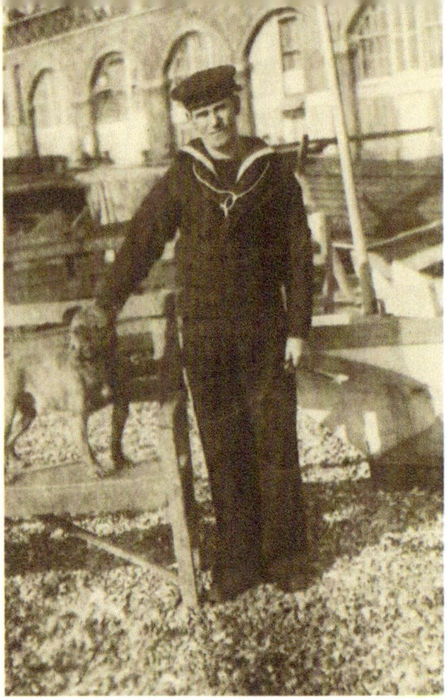

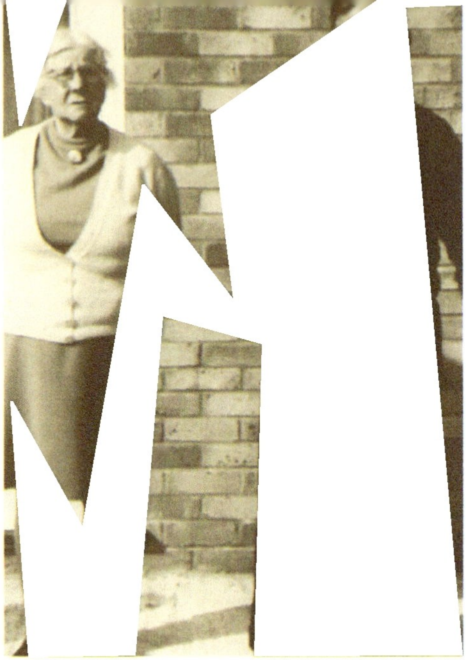

Above left: Thomas James Allen, son of Thomas and Eliza Allen, was born in Oxford but moved to Folkestone. He signed up as a Royal Naval volunteer in 1904 at Eastbourne, and went on board the *Ramsey* as a stoker. On 8 August 1915 Thomas lost his life in aiding a supposed ship in distress, which turned out to be a German ship. They torpedoed Thomas's ship and then picked up 147 survivors.

The German captain looked after the men very well as he was upset at having to kill others. Eventually his ship was captured and as he was the last person left on board, he detonated and blew it up. The Deadman's Penny medallion sent to his parents is now on display in the Folkestone Museum.

Above right: William Harris (1892–1973) came from a long line of fishermen but became a dock gateman at the harbour. In 1940, a mine drifted into the harbour and William, along with three others, secured the mine between The Hawk and a buoy until the tide was right for the Naval mine clearance to get to it and was then blown up. For their bravery the railway company invited them to receive a medal and a meal at the Waterloo railway station offices in London. Looking forward to some nice food, they were about to eat when the siren went off and unfortunately they had to leave the buildings. On the way out they were hurriedly given their medals and a £5 note while making their way to a bomb shelter.

Below: The wooden structure was where the mine rested.

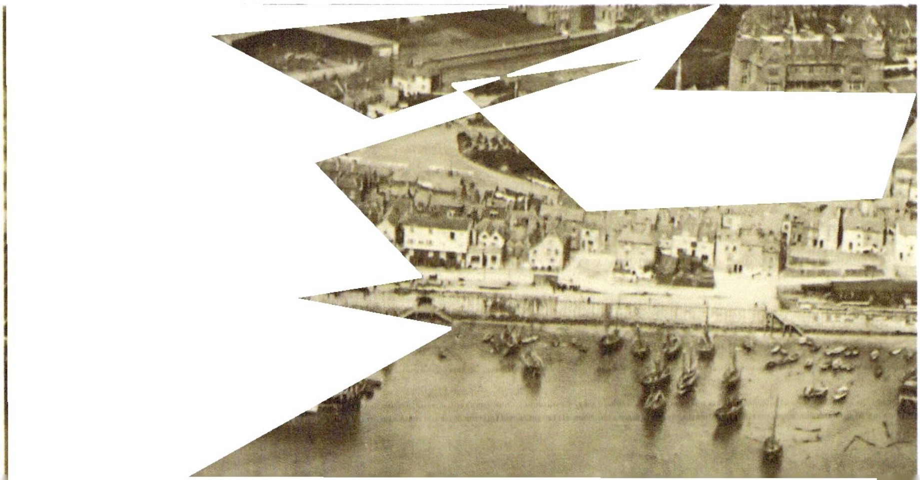

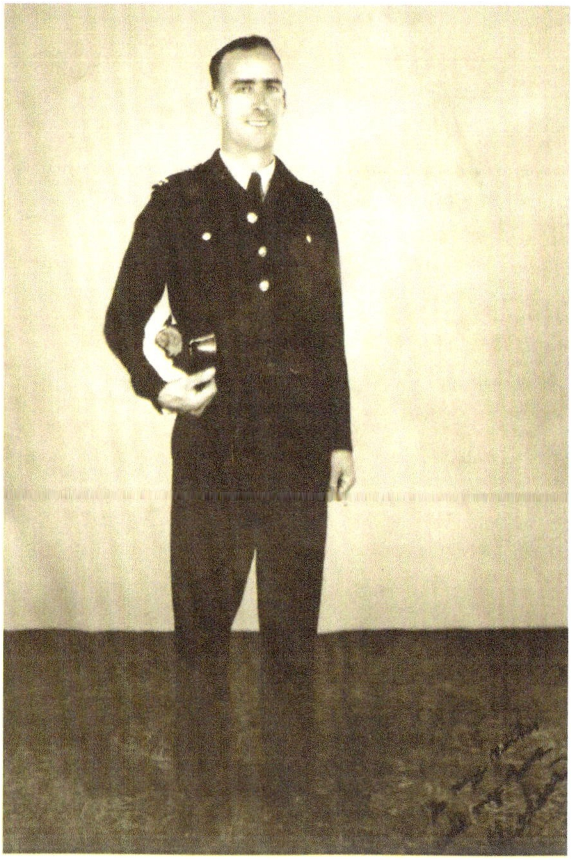

Robert Frederick William Harris, eldest son of Frederick and Daisy Harris, born in 1911. He was always a fisherman at heart but joined the TA in 1928, and when the war broke out he went into the Royal Naval Reserve. He joined the Merchant Navy as an engineer in 1945, on the fast motor torpedo boats which were around 15 tonnes. In 1952 he left the service so he could be on shore with his wife and daughters.

Below: The bombed remains of the Salvation Army Citadel in Dover High Street.

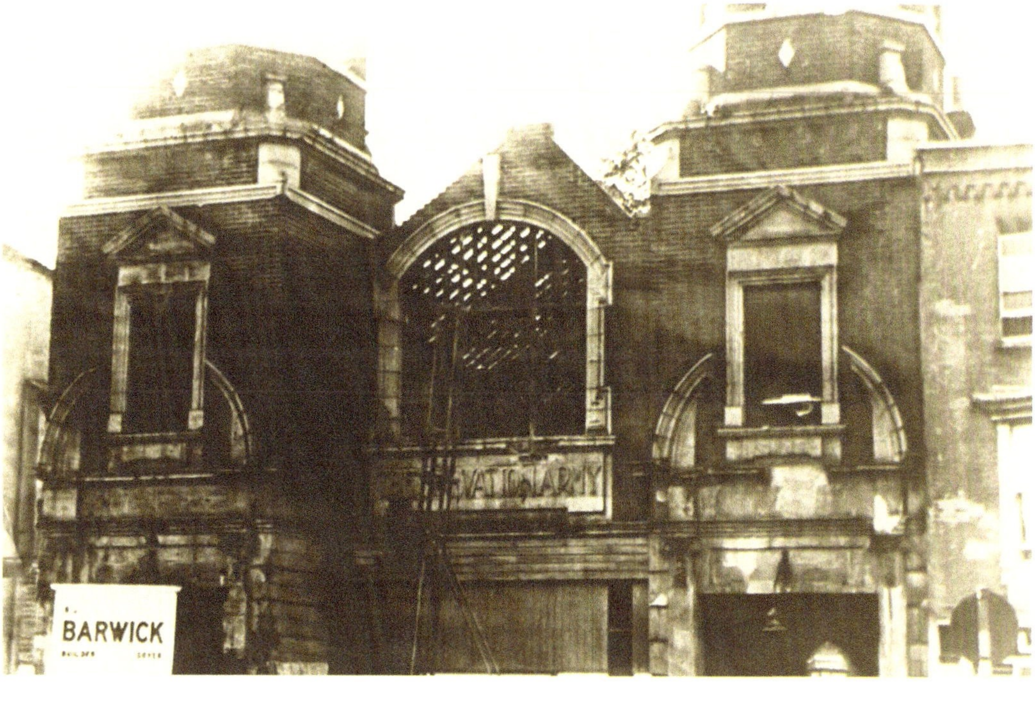

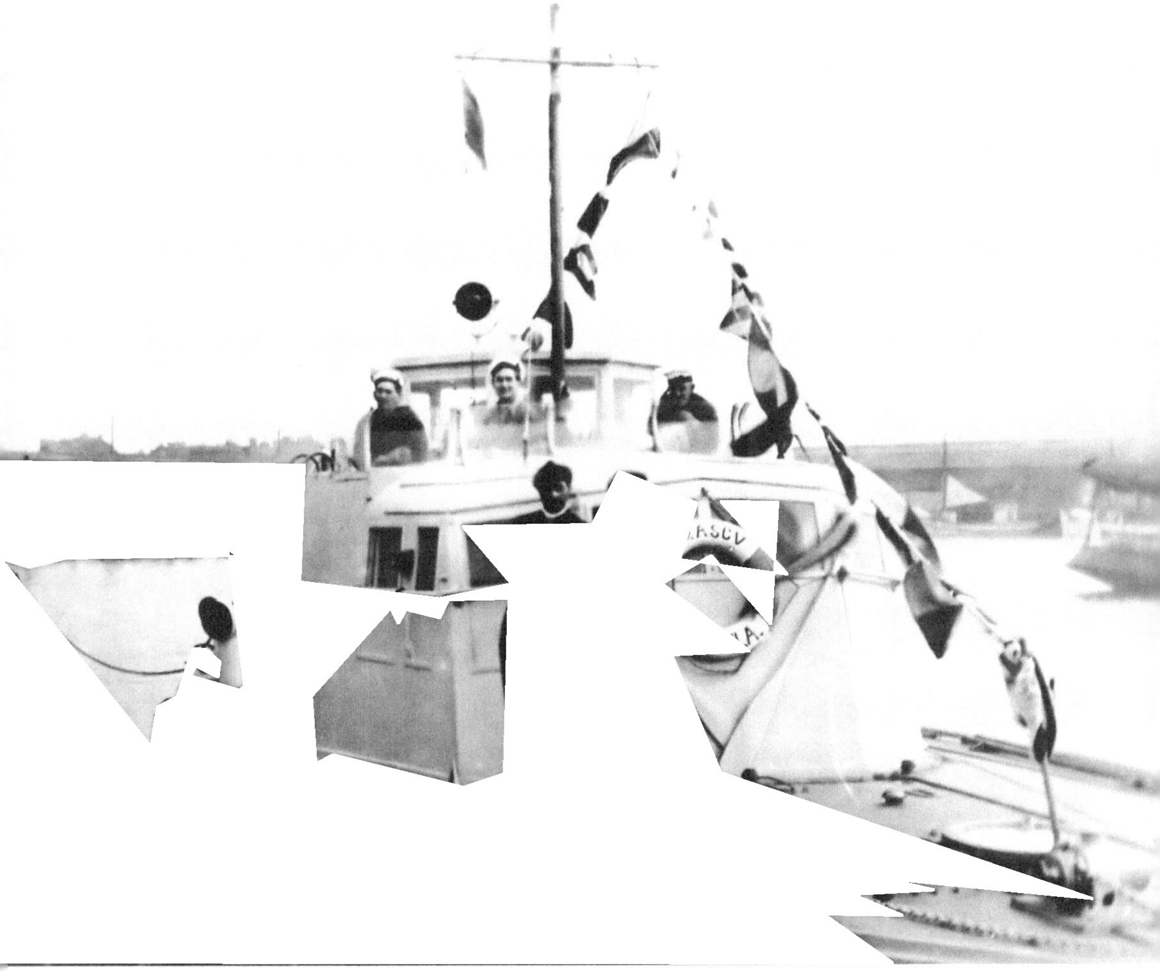

How Lucky I Was to Survive

Robert was stationed in Dover docks during the war and was on the flare drifter *Shipmates*, a fishing vessel built in 1911 commandeered by the navy for war work. They were equipped with a one million candle power, the Dover Flare, which lit the area up like daylight so they could see the German submarines and ships in the channel. *Shipmates* helped evacuate 130 British civilians from Calais in May 1940 and also helped with the evacuation at Dunkirk. On 14 November 1940 Robert left his ship to go to the Salvation Army Citadel in Dover High Street. While in between the two a flight of Junkers Ju87, also known as Stuka, dive bombers attacked Dover harbour, causing much damage. The only ship that sunk that day was *Shipmates*. On arriving at the Salvation Army Citadel Robert found it in ruins; he remarked, 'The Lord was certainly looking after me that day.'

Above: Robert in the Merchant Navy, standing on the right on the MTB *Suvla*, stationed at Cowes in the Isle of Wight in around 1948.

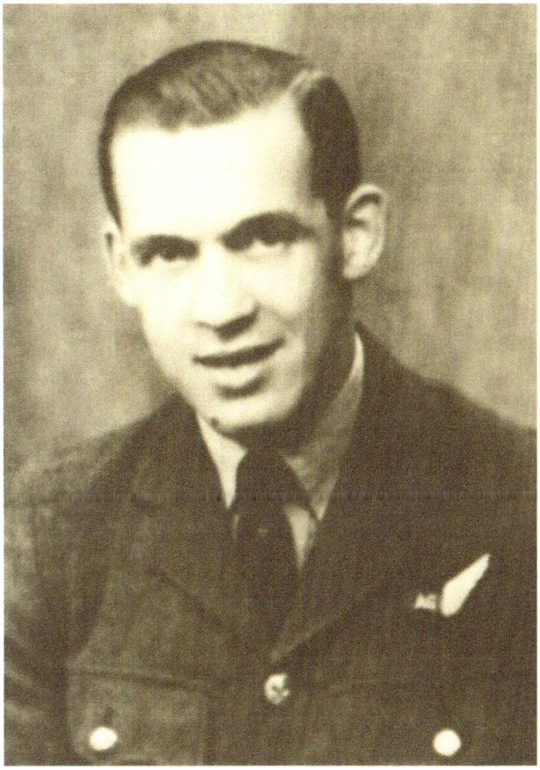

Above: Eric Douglas Huntley (1924–43), son of Joseph and Emmeline Huntley. Eric served in the RAF voluntary reserve as a sergeant (WOP/Air Gunner). On the night he died, along with the other two men in the crew, they were flying a Wellington IC serial number HX 367. That fateful night they set off from Hamstead, for dusk solo circuits and landings. They crashed at 8.45 p.m. a little fewer than two miles south east of Pangbourne, Reading. Coincidentally Eric is the brother of Elsie on page 22. I had two different contacts, unknown to each other when they told me the story.

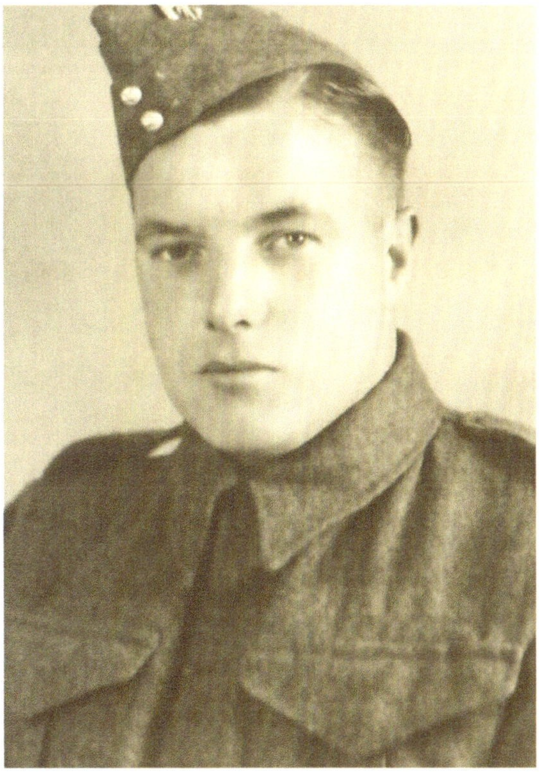

Below: Thomas Sutton (1913–78). Thomas was called up for the army in June 1940 and transferred from the Oxford and Buckinghamshire Regiment to the Yorkshire and Lancashire Regiment from June 1942 to June 1945. He was demobbed ten days before his thirty-third birthday, having served in Africa and Burma until the end of the war. In civilian life Thomas worked for John Lukey, the wine merchants in Sandgate Road, and he continued to for forty-eight years.

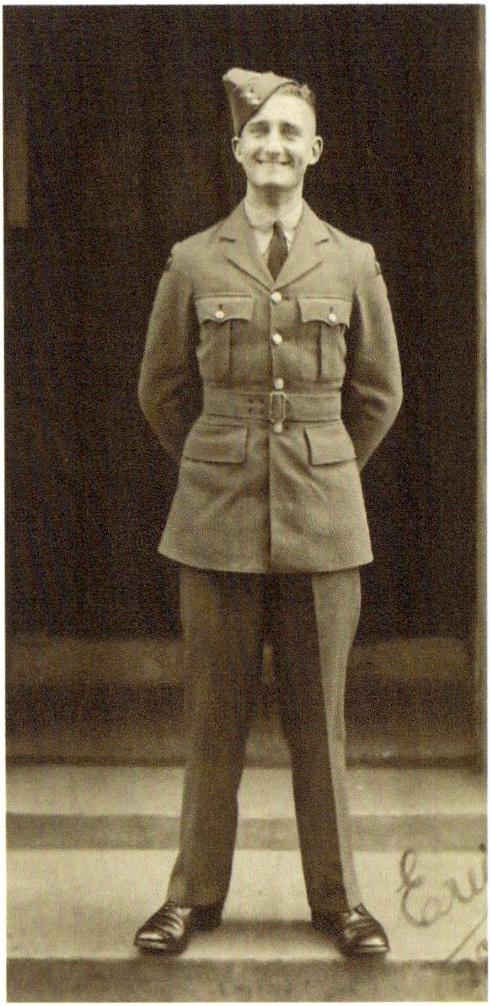

Left: Sergeant Eric L Scott who lived in Archer Road. During the war Sergeant Eric L. Scott, No. 538392, was stationed at Grange-Over-Sand, Cumbria. Eric had hoped to become a pilot but his dream was dashed when a medical examination revealed that he had perforated eardrums rendering him unfit to fly, so he became an instructor for rifle and survival skills. He was posted to Worli Malaya late in 1944 to help remove the last of the Japanese snipers from the jungle. As you can imagine with his ears perforated flying was stressful but he was fitted with special earplugs to help him with the altitude.

In 1958, he was flown to Christmas Island with the same special earplugs and was there in 1958 when the atom bomb went off. The men were told to turn their backs when the bomb went off, after he took the picture of the fall-out. On asking family if he was affected by the radiation, I was informed they believed the cancer he died of in 1974, aged sixty years old, was the result of that time in 1958.

Bottom left: This amazing picture was taken by Sgt Eric Scott on Christmas Island 1958 when it was supposed to be safe to look at the fall-out.

Bottom right: Sergeant Eric L. Scott outside the Station Warrant Officers' tent on Christmas Island in 1958.

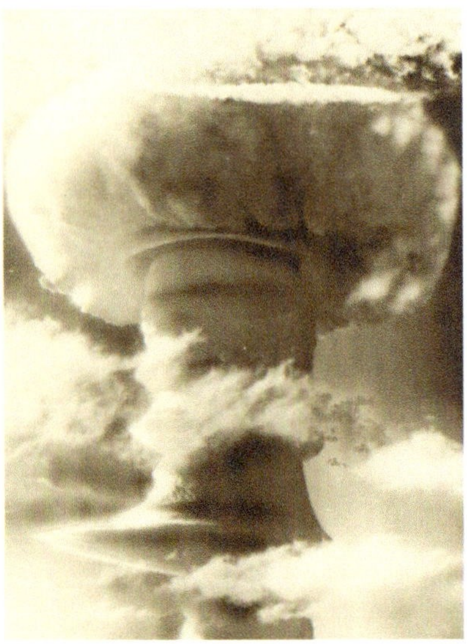

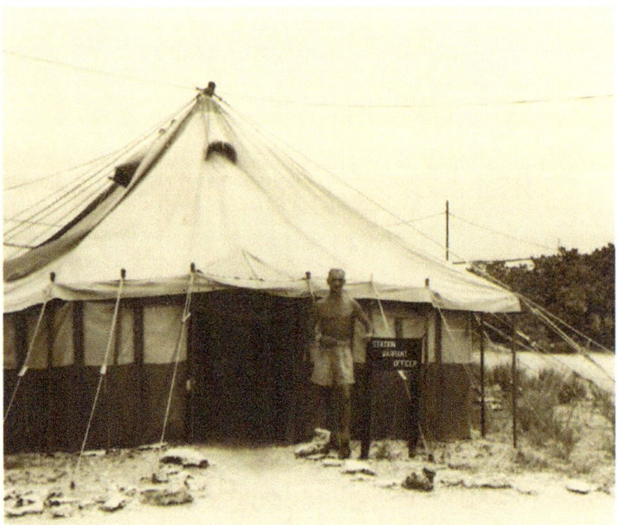

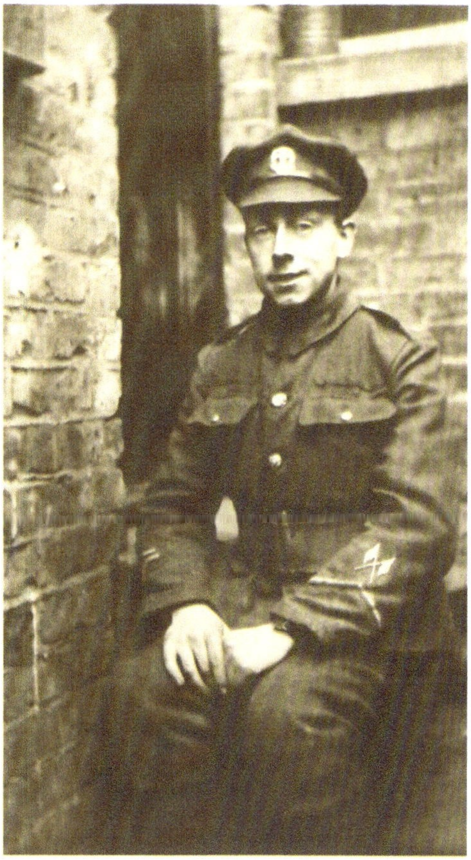

Right: Private Hubert Worsley (1890–1990). Taken in 1915, the picture shows Hubert proudly displaying his Signals Regimental badge on his left sleeve with a good conduct stripe below the Signals badge. On his right sleeve are two overseas service stripes, each earned for one complete year of service abroad. This remarkable talented man worked at the Co-op in Folkestone. He loved photography; many of his photos have been used in local history books, and some of his glass-plate photos have been donated to the Folkestone heritage room. Hubert was also in Scarlet Follies, a charity musical group, between 1920 and 1930. They raised thousands of pounds for charity. Hubert sang and played the piano, violin and organ.

Below: Hubert's photo, taken on a glass plate, of the German sailing ship *Preussen*, wrecked off the South Foreland in 1910. Apparently, Hubert almost fell off the cliff trying to get a closer view of the ship.

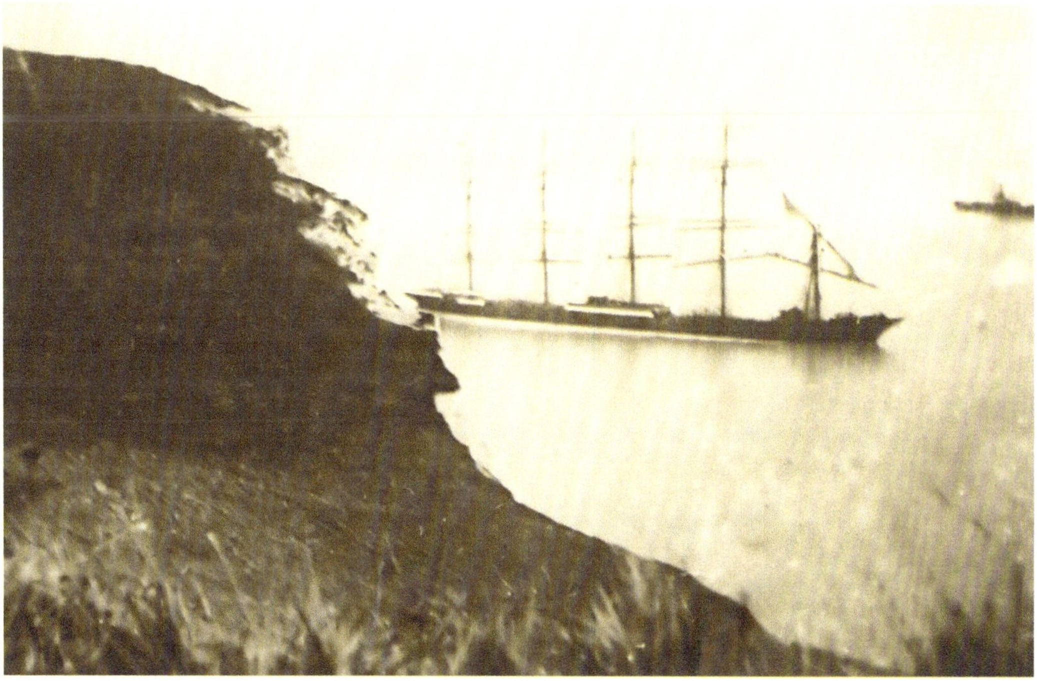

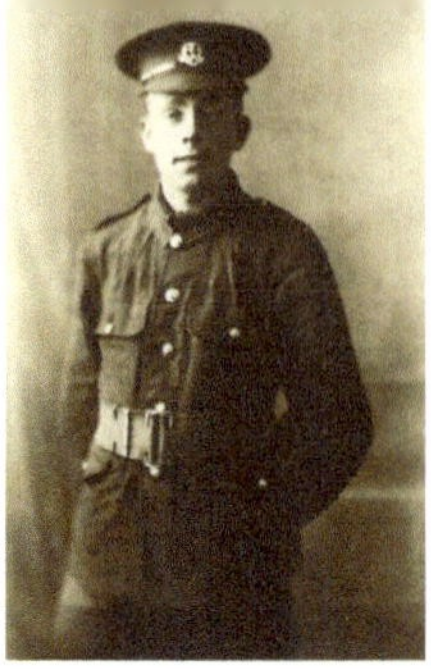

The Road to Remembrance

There's a town overlooking the Channel,
There's a road leading down to the sea
They call it the Road of Remembrance
And it's planted with Rosemary,
Let us pass down the road in silence, and
Think of them once more,
Them who marched down here with us
our comrades of the war,
For this is the Road of Remembrance,
Where many a mother's son,
Passed here he made the sacrifice, that
Victory might be won.

There was Bobby who came from Birmingham,
And Wally who came from York,
There was Jock who came frae Glasgow Toon,
And Paddy who came from Cork,
There was 'Arry who came from 'Oxton way,
And many a comrade more
Who marched with us down the steep cliff road,
When we sailed away to war,
And there were men from Australia too;
The Canadian's and the 'Yanks',
Infantrymen, artillerymen, the men who
Manned the tanks;
An endless army, all Khaki-clad marching
Away to war
Marching down the steep cliff road to
Sail from old England's shore.

And some wore a smile, or joked a while,
And some sang snatches of songs:
But some were silent and thoughtful as
They proudly marched along:

For this was farewell to the homeland
Many a man would see no more,
As they marched away down the steep cliff Road
To sail from old England's shore.
And side by side by side we fought with them till
We missed them one by one,
And we left them over yonder when the
Victory had been won,
So we pass down the road in silence, and
Think of them once more
As they marched down this self-same road with
us,
As we sailed away to war.

Oh, where is Bobby from Birmingham, and
Wally who came from York?
And where is Jack frae Glasgow Toon,
And Paddy who came from Cork?
And where is 'Arry from Oxton Way,
And many a comrade more
Who marched with us down the steep cliff road
When we sailed away to war?

Poor Bobby he sleeps at Havincourt
And Wally out Ypres way,
And Paddy I missed at Bourlon Wood,
He fell in the fight they say;
And Jock and Harry are sleeping too
With others I used to know,
'Neath their little wooden crosses where
The Flanders poppies grow.

And so we pass from days of war to days
Of peace instead,
And we build our glorious monuments in
Memory of our dead-
To remind us of our comrades, when many
A year has flown,
Who passed down the Road of Remembrance,
And into the great unknown;
And here in this town by the Channel,
The road leading down to the sea
Is the nation's Road of Remembrance
All planted with rosemary.

Private Hubert Worsley, 1923